Good luck ♡ W9-CHC-551

Leading & Coaching,

Kelly

PRAISE FOR *LEADERS' PLAYBOOK*

"I read *Leaders' Playbook* and I was quite impressed. You did a great job presenting the material in a straightforward, credible way; more important, your process for building the EI competencies is both very practical and sensible. Nice job."

Bill Tredwell, Vice President
Hay Group, Inc.

"Relly Nadler, one of the world's foremost executive coaches, provides the reader with detailed and easy-to-use practices to make you and your leaders superstars. One of the most valuable leadership books available!"

Jeffrey E. Auerbach, Ph.D., President
College of Executive Coaching
Author of Personal and Executive Coaching

"Dr. Relly Nadler is continually on the cutting edge when it comes to Leadership Development. His innovative ideas and tools in the *Leaders' Playbook* are the reason our localized Leadership Development efforts have been so successful year after year."

Lynda Hollens, Director of Employee Development
Wholesale Operations, Anheuser-Busch, Inc.

"One of the most practical and useful books on the topic that I've seen. The user-friendly layout makes it easy to find useful tips and ideas. The book is full of vivid examples that bring the issues to life."

David B. Peterson, Ph.D., Senior Vice President
Personnel Decisions International
Author of Leader as Coach *and* Development FIRST

"The EI Star Profile and Derailer Detector in the *Leaders' Playbook* have provided great insights for my clients. These tools give leaders an opportunity to improve their understanding of Emotional Intelligence competencies and gain insight into their own Emotional Intelligence strengths and weaknesses."

Guy Summers, President
Farrell Group, LLC

"Nadler's *Leaders' Playbook* is a great way for both leaders and coaches to learn and grow. EI is powerful. It is an essential element for both business and coaching, and when integrated with wellness is a strong formula for success. Read this book, apply it, and the positive effects for you and your firm will be the reward."

Cathy L. Greenberg, Ph.D., Co-author of What Happy Companies Know, *Managing Partner, h2c, LLC, Happy Companies, Healthy People*

"Dr. Reldan Nadler has provided a useful tool for women seeking to advance their careers and themselves. Few women are lucky enough to have a personal coach, but the content of this book is going to be very helpful, particularly the worksheets, inventories, and templates. *Leaders' Playbook* can only encourage women to have confidence in these skills and motivate women to stretch themselves in new directions—including reaching for top executive leadership positions."

Lois Phillips, Ph.D., Co-author of Women Seen and Heard: Lessons Learned from Successful Speakers

"Relly Nadler's *Leaders' Playbook* provides the kind of real-world guidance that is so often missing from leadership books. The tools and techniques are immediately applicable, and it has become the primary text I use for my training and coaching work."

Nick Rothenberg, OD Consultant and Owner, 2Be, LLC

"I was able to apply how the stages of a team's development can be used for building trust and cohesion even in the midst of conflict. The strategies for developing others outlined in the book are full of practical take-aways and valuable for any leader's coaching toolbox."

Steve Romano
Director of Organizational Development and Training
The Kleinfelder Group

"All coaches know that a practical, hands-on guide to how you actually improve EI is critical to building this competency. This is the 'field guide' we needed."

Diane Foster, Certified Master Coach
M.A. Career Development
Principal, Diane Foster & Associates

"*Leaders' Playbook* and the *Leadership Keys* are not for 'short-ball-hitter' leaders. They are practical and insightful tools for leaders who know that blind spots and things that go bump in the night are what cause failure. These tools bring insight and therefore awareness that can support overall success."

T.H. Stevenson, President/CEO
Cleveland Consulting Group, Inc.

"Relly Nadler's *Leaders' Playbook* represents a very rich starter toolkit for new coaches and a great reference for the experienced coach. I was impressed by the strategies' simplicity and how quickly I was able to integrate them into my coaching practice."

Brigadier-General (Retired) Charles Lemieux
OMM, MSC, CHRP, MPEC
President, CNSL Consultants, Inc.

"Relly Nadler, in the *Leaders' Playbook*, shares 100+ strategies for leaders to turn 'just-another-player' employees into Star Performers. With the *Leaders' Playbook*, you're never at a loss for ideas. Pick up the *Playbook*, open to any page, and you will find a key lesson in leadership."

Sylva K. Leduc, M.Ed., MPEC
Leadership Specialist

"Emotional Intelligence behaviours can be learned, and *Leaders' Playbook* combines practical techniques for improvement with real-life experiences of leaders in business and politics. This is an essential resource for everyone interested in how leaders can improve their relationships with others, and ultimately achieve greater business results."

Anna Hinder, Searl Street Consulting, Australia

LEADERS'
PLAYBOOK

LEADERS'
PLAYBOOK

How to Apply Emotional Intelligence-
Keys to Great Leadership

by

Reldan S. Nadler, Psy.D.

PSYCCESS PRESS

Santa Barbara, CA

PSYCCESS PRESS

A Division of True North Leadership, Inc.
1170 Camino Meleno
Santa Barbara, CA 93111
805/683-1066   FAX 805/692-6738
www.truenorthleadership.com

Publisher's Cataloging-In-Publication
Nadler, Reldan S., 1951-
        Leaders' playbook : how to apply emotional intelligence—keys to
        great leadership / Reldan S. Nadler — 1st ed. — Santa Barbara, CA :
        Psyccess Press, 2006.

        p. ; cm.
        ISBN-13: 978-0-9759477-4-6
        ISBN-10: 0-9759477-4-5
        Includes bibliographical references and index.
        1. Leadership. 2. Emotional intelligence. 3. Personnel
management. 4. Motivation (Psychology) 5. Self-confidence.
        I. Title.

HD57.7 .N33 2006
658.4/092—dc22   0610   2006907038

Cover and Book Design: Patricia Bacall
Editor: Ilene Segalove
Copyeditor: Brookes Nohlgren
Proofreader: Julie Simpson
Book Consultant: Ellen Reid
Author Photograph: Juli Hayes

Printed in Canada

*This book is dedicated to Martin S.
and Patricia S. for their inspiration, years of teamwork,
and love of the written word.*

*Also in memory of Ann Nadler, L.O.M.,
for her teachings on love, nurturance, fun, and
the art of giving and relationship-building.*

CONTENTS

ACKNOWLEDGEMENTS xxi

PREFACE xxiii

INTRODUCTION: WHY EMOTIONAL INTELLIGENCE? 1

EI vs. IQ 2
Star Performers Shine and So Can You 3
Who Is This Book For? 5
What You'll Learn to Do 5
Getting Started: The Ideal Plan 6

CHAPTER ONE: ARE YOU A STAR PERFORMER OR JUST AVERAGE? 9

EQ, IQ, or Technical Expertise? 11
How to Be a Star Performer—New Rules for Success 13
The Four Areas of Emotional Intelligence 14
The 20 Competencies of Emotional Intelligence 15
Profiles of Star Performers 16
• Rudy Giuliani 17
• Carly Fiorina 20
• Jeffrey Immelt 23
• Sergey Brin 26
• Pete Carroll 30
• Meg Whitman 33
• Bill Clinton 36
• Howard Dean 38
• Condoleeza Rice 41
Lack of Self-Control and the Inability to Delay Gratification 45
Stretching Strengths: Going from Good to Great Leadership 47
Micro-Initiatives: D.O.D. of Great Leadership 50
Taking the EI Star Profile Assessment 54
Are You or Your Boss Debilitating? 58

The Derailer Detector   62

Strategic Use of Strengths   64

Star Performer Action Plan   67

CHAPTER TWO: SELF-CONFIDENCE TOOLS AND STRATEGIES   69

What Is the Self-Confidence Competency?   69

Emotional Intelligence Research Examples   70

Are You a Star Performer in Self-Confidence or Just Average?   70

Star Profile: Henrik Fisker, CEO, Fisker Coachbuild, LLC   71

10 Secrets & Current Practices of Henrik Fisker—
Star Performer   72

   1. Take Private Time   73

   2. Get Third Opinions   73

   3. Evaluate Capacities   73

   4. Shoot from the Hip   73

   5. Go with That Gut Feeling   74

   6. Take Initiative   74

   7. Identify Strengths and Weaknesses   74

   8. Take Responsibility for Your Mistakes   75

   9. Reinforce People   75

   10. Be Willing to Make Decisions That Are Exceptions
to the Rule   75

The Coach's Corner: 10 Strategies for Self-Confidence   76

   1. Being on Your Case vs. Being on Your Side   77

   2. Reflections on Thinking   82

   3. Busting Perfection: Creating Realistic Expectations   84

   4. Success Rules: Who Is Running You?   89

   5. Success Log   91

   6. Current Success Log   92

   7. The Five Pivotal People in Your Life   93

   8. Visualization   93

   9. Decisiveness   94

   10. Thin-Slicing   95

Star Performer Action Plan   96

CHAPTER THREE: TEAMWORK AND COLLABORATION TOOLS AND STRATEGIES   99

What Is the Teamwork and Collaboration Competency?   99
Emotional Intelligence Research Examples   100
Are You a Star Performer in Teamwork and Collaboration
    or Just Average?   100
Star Profile: Paulette Jones, Director of Technical and Strategic
    Business Development, NMB Technologies Corporation   101
10 Secrets & Current Practices of Paulette Jones—
    Star Performer   102
    1. Start the Day with "An Attitude of Gratitude"   102
    2. Focused Greeting of People   103
    3. Communication   103
    4. Red Flag Meetings   103
    5. Revenue Gap Meetings   104
    6. BAT Teams (Business Acquisition Teams)   104
    7. Team Meetings   105
    8. Continual Process Review   105
    9. Valuing Staff   105
    10. Humor   105
The Coach's Corner: 24 Strategies for Teamwork
    and Collaboration   106
    1. Shared Vision   108
    2. Trust Among Members   108
    3. Expectations and Guidelines   109
    4. Communication Skills and Conflict Resolution   109
    5. Systems Thinking   110
    6. Personal Leadership   111
    7. Appreciation of Differences   111
    8. Accountability and Consequences   112
    9. Ongoing Learning and Recognition 113
    10. Mentor Others   113
    11. Meeting Mastery and Meeting Menace   114
    12. Snapshot Management: "The One Hand Rule"   116
    13. Meeting Menace Checklist   118

14. Team Meetings   120
15. Guidelines for Running a Great Meeting   122
16. How to Establish Roles Within a Team Meeting   122
17. "Stand-Ups"—Short Team Meetings   123
18. The Meeting Checklist   124
19. "Nails" Teambuilding Activity   131
20. "Performance and Accountability" Teambuilding Activity   135
21. "Expectations" Activity   138
22. Team Assessment   140
23. 100 Leadership Check-In Questions   142
24. Teamwork Ingredients Survey   148
Star Performer Action Plan   150

CHAPTER FOUR: DEVELOPING OTHERS TOOLS AND STRATEGIES

CHAPTER FOUR: DEVELOPING OTHERS TOOLS AND STRATEGIES   153
What Is the Developing Others Competency?   153
Emotional Intelligence Research Examples   153
Are You a Star Performer in Developing Others or Just Average?   155
Star Profile: Mark French, University of California at Santa Barbara (UCSB) Head Coach, Women's Basketball Team   156
13 Secrets & Current Practices of Mark French— Star Performer   159
   1. Leader's Point of View (POV): Basketball as a Metaphor for Life   159
   2. Practice   160
   3. Bonding and Team Meetings   161
   4. Recruiting Stars   161
   5. Building Effective Relationships   163
   6. Self-Assessments and Goal Setting   164
   7. One-on-Ones   164
   8. Supportive Learning   165
   9. Timely Feedback   166
   10. Focus on Strengths   167
   11. Take Personal Responsibility   167

12. Performance Review 168

13. Briefings Before and After the Game 170

The Coach's Corner: 12 Strategies for Developing Others 171

1. Hiring Stars: Emotionally Intelligent Leaders Are More Likely to Be Hired and Become Stars 172

2. Behavioral Questions List 173

3. One-on-One Meetings 186

4. Soaring with Strengths 190

5. Input + 1 191

6. Circle of Influence 192

7. Performance = Potential – Interferences or P=P–I 196

8. Delegation 196

9. Coaching for Performance 199

10. Scaling Questions 202

11. Motivation Skills Matrix 203

12. Development First 208

Star Performer Action Plan 210

CHAPTER FIVE: COMMUNICATION AND EMPATHY TOOLS AND STRATEGIES 213

What Is the Communication Competency? 213

Emotional Intelligence Research Examples 214

Are You a Star Performer in Communication or Just Average? 214

Star Profile: John Davies, CEO and Founder, Davies Public Relations 215

11 Secrets & Current Practices of John Davies— Star Performer 217

1. Touch the Heart 217

2. Understand What People Want 217

3. Find Your Passion 218

4. Find Your Uniqueness 219

5. Read People 219

6. Acknowledge/Do Not Offend 220

7. Summarize and Integrate 221

8. Be Prepared 221

9. Training and Personal Growth   222

10. Quality in All   222

11. Finding the "Needle in the Haystack"   223

The Coach's Corner: 12 Strategies for Enhancing Communication and Empathy   225

1. Empathy Skills   226

What Is the Empathy Competency?   227

Emotional Intelligence Research Examples   227

Are You a Star Performer in Empathy or Just Average?   227

2. Listening and Rapport-Building Skills   233

3. White Space Issues   237

4. Intention/Interpretation Gap   240

5. Power of Language: Metaphors, Stories, and Words   244

6. Clarity: Connecting the Dots to a Better Future   250

7. Giving Feedback: SSBIR   252

8. Assumption Ladder: Arriving and Delivering Communication   257

9. Balancing Inquiry and Advocacy   263

10. The Left-Hand Column   265

11. Dialogue vs. Discussion   266

12. Dialogue Roles   268

Star Performer Action Plan   269

CHAPTER SIX: THE GAME PLAN   271

The Coach's Corner   271

The Plays   273

Keeping Score: Your Leadership Scorecard   279

RESOURCES   283

NOTES   287

REFERENCES   297

ABOUT THE AUTHOR   305

INDEX   307

ACKNOWLEDGEMENTS

I would like to first thank my family—my wife, Juli, for her creative touch, warmth, enthusiasm, love, and support; my son, Dillon, for his curiosity, cleverness, creativity, and critical eye on parts of the book; and my daughter, McKensey, for her creative spark, story listening, big heart, and love for people.

To my main men, Lux and Gregg, for being on the Board, for their humor, ideas, ski trips, and for helping me to keep my perspective of what is really important in life.

A sincere thanks to the executives profiled in *Leaders' Playbook*—Henrik, Paulette, Mark, and John—for their time sharing their life stories and the help they gave in weaving together the fabric of what makes them Stars.

I also want to thank all of the executives and companies who have allowed me to learn and practice my ideas, and who continue to teach me how to be effective in the corporate and organizational world.

Thanks, too, to my colleagues at the College of Executive Coaching (CEC) and Jeff Auerbach, for the stimulating conversations about the theory, research, and practice of developing Star Performers. Also to all of the students at CEC who gave me feedback, ideas, and support for the tools presented in *Leaders' Playbook*.

To my other esteemed colleagues: Nick Rothenberg, for his insightful feedback, camaraderie, and support of these tools; Steve Roberts, for his facilitation expertise, creativity, and ease to work with; Patricia Schwartz, for her help with the manuscript and enthusiasm; and Michelle Loomis, for her excitement and encouragement for this book.

I want to thank the Emotional Intelligence community. To Daniel Goleman, for his initiative, leadership, and integration of all of the theory and research. To Richard Boyatzis and the Hay Group, for their expertise in identifying and developing competencies and for the creation of the Emotional Competency Inventory (ECI). To Bill Tredwell of the Hay Group, for his ideas, enthusiasm, and support for this book. In addition, I want to thank all of the other EI enthusiasts who have been my colleagues.

Thank you to my friends and colleagues at Outward Bound and the Association of Experiential Education, who gave me the "best practice field" to learn about Star Performance as well as an abundance of tips, strategies, and tools.

To my Confluent Education mentors—George Brown, Stu Shapiro, and Mark Phillips—for teaching me about Emotional Intelligence before it was formally named.

To my extended family—Nancy, Larry, Michael, Katherine, Van, Martine, and all the Nadlers and Hayeses—for their years of support and love.

To Ilene Segalove, for her clarity, insight, and support, all of which are evident throughout these pages.

To Ellen Reid and the Star book team of Laren Bright, Patricia Bacall, Brookes Nohlgren, and Natalie Gibency—for their expertise, perfection, calmness under fire, and professionalism in creating this book. To Julie Simpson for her proofreading and attention to detail.

To the UCSB students who contributed to the creation of this book—Ian Farr, Steve Hall, Tony Muna, Martin Young, and Brenton Gieser.

And lastly, I want to thank my friends Roger, Charlie, the Santa Barbara bunch, and the Paramus crowd for teaching me the foundation, specifics, and practice of Emotional Intelligence.

PREFACE

As a psychologist doing executive coaching, leadership development training, and consulting in organizations, I have found the research, concepts, and application of Emotional Intelligence (EI) to be a powerful selling tool and validation for this important work. What CEO or organization doesn't want more Star Performers—successful leaders—in their ranks? But as I began using the EI research and the Emotional Competence Inventory (ECI) tool, I identified a significant gap between the big concepts and how to apply them. Like you, leaders, managers, trainers, consultants, and coaches want to know what will make them more successful today and are less interested in the rigmarole of organizational and personality theory. Simply put, when I began training people in EI, I heard a lot of, "I think the concepts and goals are great. Now, what can I do today to help raise my Emotional Intelligence?"

Numerous books and papers have been written on the topic, but most are either too general or too superficial. I needed a resource that was practical, accessible, and filled with specific strategies that could easily be applied to help executives and their direct reports raise their Emotional Intelligence without a lot of fuss or muss. When I read a business or leadership book, I want to get one or two "hard-hitting" actions that I can immediately apply. If successful, these strategies can enrich the individuals' and organization's life and effectiveness. In addition, then I have a tried-and-true practice I can use in my next consulting engagement.

Not finding this kind of book, I was inspired to create *Leaders'
Playbook* to fill the gap between theory and practice. This book, I
hope, will raise Emotional Intelligence for you, your direct reports or
clients, and your organization. It will add strategies and actions to
your toolbox, augment your work, and promote Star Performance in
all of your endeavors.

Over the last 30 years I have worked with more than 15,000
leaders in corporations, organizations, groups, and teams, always
looking for what works to separate the great from the good. What
are the specific endeavors that make them successful? Here you will
read the secrets of Star Performers, plus have me as your coach to
move into the top 10% of your field.

Leaders' Playbook is the first in a series of resources for leaders
to use to improve Emotional Intelligence. Future resources and
Playbooks will explore other competencies and the secrets of Stars
and coaches.

Leaders' Playbook allows you to discover the secrets of Stars
from a cross section of different industries and helps you use the
powerful strategies of a seasoned executive coach. Like a successful
coach's playbook from professional sports, this book should become
well-worn and guarded from your competitors!

—*Reldan S. Nadler, Psy.D.*

INTRODUCTION

WHY EMOTIONAL INTELLIGENCE?

We have all watched football coaches pacing the sidelines of an exciting game, avidly referring to their well-worn playbooks. A playbook is a compilation of vital strategies developed to utilize each player's unique capabilities and strengths, as well as the team's synergy, to win games and have a successful season.

Coaches constantly refer to their playbooks to choose the best solutions for each situation. How do they pick just the right play to highlight an individual's performance? What goes into motivating a diversity of players into working together as a powerful team? How do coaches manage their emotions while influencing others? When does a coach step up or back off to let his or her players lead?

> *A playbook is a compilation of vital strategies developed to utilize each player's unique capabilities and strengths.*

Like most coaches in the world of professional sports, leaders* in business also need an official playbook to assess their players' performance and provide just the right strategies to enhance their success, both as individuals and as part of a winning organization. Great leaders, like superior coaches, know their players and need to have access to specific strategies to increase Star Performance. Whether you are a CEO, manager, coach,

*The term *leader* is used in this book to describe a vast cross section of roles including but not limited to individual performers, managers, coaches, trainers, and consultants. "Leaders" are either leading themselves or others to maximize their potential and capabilities.

trainer, or consultant, *Leaders' Playbook* is the official hands-on guide that takes you and your team to the leading edge.

Some of the practices in this book were developed over the many years I worked closely with a variety of executive clients; others were gleaned from organizational, success, and peak performance literature. They are listed under "Coach's Corner." Filled with specifically designed resources, tools, strategies, stories, and practices, *Leaders' Playbook* informs and inspires you to increase your Emotional Intelligence. It also features a selection of what I call "Star Profiles." These condensed interviews with important leaders illustrate a set of principles and practices that help each Star shine in one or more areas of Emotional Intelligence. Often Stars are not cognizant of exactly what they are doing that makes them so effective, and through the interview process these actions became more visible.

Leaders' Playbook focuses on *five* of the 20 key competencies of Emotional Intelligence: Self-Confidence, Teamwork and Collaboration, Developing Others, Communication, and Empathy. A competency is a learned ability, and each one contributes uniquely to making a leader more effective. I have chosen to focus on these five competencies because they are the ones I find executives consistently want to master first. I also believe these five competencies give leaders tools that not only help them but also guide and inspire those they lead. (See page 15 for the list of 20 competencies.)

EI VS. IQ

"Emotional Intelligence" was first coined in 1990 by Peter Salovey and John Mayer and became popularized by Daniel Goleman in his 1995 book, *Emotional Intelligence.* There was a time when IQ was considered the primary determinant of success, but our IQ-idolizing view of intelligence is far too narrow. Instead, "Emotional Intelligence" is now considered the strongest indicator of success in the work world.

IQ, or Intelligence Quotient, and technical expertise help you get your job. EI, or Emotional Intelligence, is what makes you a

Star Performer. IQ contributes only 4-10% toward a leader's success. But the higher up you are in an organization, the more Emotional Intelligence determines your leadership success, contributing as much as 85-90%.[1]

EI can be defined in terms of understanding yourself, managing yourself, understanding others, and managing others. People who possess high Emotional Intelligence are the ones who truly succeed in work—building flourishing careers and long lasting relationships as well as having a balanced work/home life.

STAR PERFORMERS SHINE AND SO CAN YOU

The corporate world became enamored with EI, which led to Goleman's writing of a second book, *Working with Emotional Intelligence*. As EI research and theory grew in popularity and impact, Goleman helped found the creation of the Consortium for Research on Emotional Intelligence in Organizations with Cary Cherniss; Richard Boyatzis, from Case Western Reserve University; the Hay Group, a consulting firm; and others who collaborated on in-depth research. Goleman, Boyatzis, and the Hay Group developed a useful application, a 360-degree assessment to measure Emotional Intelligence, called the Emotional Competence Inventory (ECI). The research generated from these sources is rich, compelling, and invaluable. It is now possible to confidently identify what the key competencies are that make Star Performers. A Star Performer is defined as a person performing in the top 10% of an organization, while the average performer makes up 60-80% of the workforce.[2]

A Star Performer is defined as a person performing in the top 10% of an organization...

Star Performers bring a tremendous amount of value to their organizations. Here are some brief examples describing the critical benefits of developing Emotional Intelligence:

For 515 senior executives analyzed by the search firm Egon Zehnder International, those who were primarily strong in Emotional

Intelligence were more likely to succeed than those who were strongest in either relevant previous experience or IQ.[3]

"Analyses done by dozens of different experts in close to five hundred corporations, government agencies, and non profit organizations worldwide have arrived at remarkably similar conclusions…all point to the paramount place of emotional intelligence in excellence on the job—in virtually all jobs."[4]

"The research distills with unprecedented precision which qualities mark a star performer. And it demonstrates which human abilities make up the greater part of the ingredients for excellence at work—most especially for leadership."[5]

"In general the higher a position, 85 percent of their competencies for success were in the EI domain."[6]

Competency research in over 200 companies and organizations worldwide suggests that about one-third of this difference is due to technical skill and cognitive ability, while two-thirds is due to emotional competence.[7]

The executives selected based on emotional competence were far more likely to perform in the top third based on salary bonuses for performance of the divisions they led: 87% were in the top third. In addition, division leaders with these competencies outperformed their targets by 15-20%. Those who lacked them under-performed by almost 20%.[8]

Richard Boyatzis and Annie McKee in *Resonant Leadership* talk about Great Leadership, which is synonymous with the Star Performer defined here. They state: "Great leaders are emotionally intelligent and they are *mindful*: they seek to live in full consciousness of self, others, nature, and society. Great leaders face the uncertainty of today's world with *hope*: they inspire through clarity of vision, optimism, and a profound belief in their—and their people's—ability to turn dreams into reality. Great leaders face sacrifice, difficulties, and challenges, as well as opportunities, with empathy and *compassion* for the people they lead and those they serve."[9]

WHO IS THIS BOOK FOR?

This book is for everyone who wants to move up or perform better in his or her role by applying Emotional Intelligence strategies and tools.

If you are:

- An Individual Performer, you can use *Leaders' Playbook* to see what competencies you need to focus on to become a Star Performer. You don't have to supervise someone else, but can use the tools to improve your own performance in a safe, well-paced manner.

- An Executive or Manager in an organization, you usually have development plans in place for the people you supervise to bring them to the next level. The problem arises when you don't have the training, experience, or time to help your people know *what* to do differently after helping them identify their development areas. *Leaders' Playbook* provides you with a map and proven tools to support positive changes as you guide your direct reports toward becoming Star Performers.

- A Coach of any kind—whether working with business executives and leaders or life, personal, and career coaching— you can effectively use all of the tools in *Leaders' Playbook* to enhance your work. The strategies included will raise the Emotional Intelligence of your clients and will promote Star Performance in all of your respective fields of work.

- A Trainer or Consultant who wants to bring Emotional Intelligence concepts into your organizations, you will find ideas and practices that will instantly integrate into your established practice or curriculum.

WHAT YOU'LL LEARN TO DO

Following are the key benefits you will receive from *Leaders' Playbook*.

- Assess yourself (and your direct reports or clients) to determine how you rate in all 20 key competencies necessary for being a Star Performer.

- Identify possible derailers for yourself (and your direct reports or clients) on various career paths.

- Review the research that validates and supports specific Emotional Intelligence competencies to become a Star Performer.

- Read Star Profiles of successful leaders and discover their secrets and daily practices in particular areas of competency.

- Select specific development actions for yourself, your direct reports, or your clients to start the Star Journey.

- Present materials to your teams or clients to raise their Emotional Intelligence.

- Become more conversant in giving solid and specific answers to the following leadership questions as you mobilize toward becoming a Star Performer in your chosen field:

  ▲ How can I become more effective as a leader?

  ▲ How do I develop my people to be our next leaders?

  ▲ How can I communicate to be more successful?

  ▲ What can I do at my next team meeting to improve morale and performance?

  ▲ How do I increase my confidence to take the steps to be Star?

GETTING STARTED: THE IDEAL PLAN

Here is an overview and plan to enhance your Emotional Intelligence and that of the people you work with.

- First read Chapter 1: Are You a Star Performer or Just Average? to understand what Emotional Intelligence is all about.

- Then take the two self-assessments in Chapter 1 to evaluate your current Star Performance:
  - ▲ The EI Star Profile
  - ▲ The Derailer Detector
- Fill out the Star Performer Action Plan, highlighting your strengths.
- Choose one of the following four chapters featuring the five competencies that you or your clients/team need today. You need not work in chronological order!
  - ▲ Chapter 2: Self-Confidence
  - ▲ Chapter 3: Teamwork and Collaboration
  - ▲ Chapter 4: Developing Others
  - ▲ Chapter 5: Communication and Empathy
- Read and re-read the *Secrets & Practices* of a Star Performer and review the *Coach's Corner* of Star strategies in your chosen chapter. In this section you will learn a number of tools and action steps to improve your performance. It is written as if I were your coach, helping you face-to-face. All the plays, or strategies, are compiled in the Table of Contents and Chapter 6, with page numbers to allow for easy searching.
- Choose two or three strategies outlined from *Secrets & Practices* of a Star Performer and the *Coach's Corner* that you believe will help raise your or your clients'/team's Emotional Intelligence.
- Focus on these actions for one to two months until you develop mastery. Then integrate other strategies that will benefit you.
- Read, practice, and practice some more.
- Share your plan with a peer, which will help solidify your commitment and immediately engender support for your goals.

- If you are working with a leader, show him or her your Star Performer Action Plan and set aside time to review your learning and experiences with him or her.

- You can write your responses to the questions in the book or use a notebook to record your work.

CHAPTER ONE

ARE YOU A STAR PERFORMER OR JUST AVERAGE?

W hat follows is an overview of basic concepts and practical applications of Emotional Intelligence exemplified in a collection of Star Profiles, interviews and analyses of well-known Star Performers such as Rudy Giuliani, President Clinton, Meg Whitman (CEO of eBay), Jeffrey Immelt (CEO of GE) and USC's football coach Pete Carroll, plus many more. You will learn more about why it is so important for leaders to develop their EI and how you and your direct reports or clients can develop it as well. This is followed by a more in-depth discussion of the four cluster areas of EI and the key competencies necessary to be a Star.

An EI assessment called the "EI Star Profile" is included to help you and your direct reports gauge your current abilities. The influence of leaders is depicted in the section "Are You or Your Boss Debilitating?" It is followed by the Derailer Detector assessment to identify in you or in other key players behavior that may lead to derailment. You are also invited to complete your own Star Performer Action Plan at the end of each chapter.

"The headlines ring out, 'Carly Fiorina ousted,' 'Michael Eisner retiring,' 'Hank Greenberg forced to leave after becoming a target of criminal investigation.' Each day, it seems, another well-known business icon departs, forced out or pressured to retire by corporate directors seeking change."[1]

Leadership is in crisis. Criticism of corporate executives and management is at an all-time high. We see CEOs and CFOs who once marched in lockstep now undermining each other in corporate fraud trials to limit their amount of time locked up. Bernard Ebbers, past CEO of WorldCom, was found guilty on nine counts of accounting fraud, the largest in U.S. history, for $11 billion. He was sentenced to 25 years in prison. Dennis Kozlowski, past CEO of Tyco International, was found guilty on 22 counts of fraud and larceny. Both claimed "it wasn't me" and were portrayed as the "Bumbling Executive." They neither knew about the fraud nor encouraged or ordered it. They maintained it was all their CFO's plan and they had no responsibility for it.

Enron, Tyco, Global Crossings, Adelphia, and WorldCom are just a handful of organizations that engender signs of executive greed and financial deception, while their companies and shareholders lose money or go broke. "As investors were losing 70%, 90%, even in some cases all of their holdings...executives and directors of 1,035 corporations took approximately $66 billion, of that $23 billion went to 466 insiders at 25 corporations where executives cashed out the most."[2] "Oracle CEO Larry Ellison settled a lawsuit by agreeing to donate $100 million to charity and pay another $22 million to attorneys who sued him for alleged stock-trading abuses, from a $900 million gain generated by selling some of his Oracle stock before the shares plummeted in 2001."[3] All the while these "leaders" were still promoting their company and its stock to the public.

In a 2002 Harris poll, only 16% of respondents had a "great deal of confidence" in the people who run major companies.[4] Jeffrey Immelt, CEO of General Electric, said, "Corporate leadership has lost the benefit of the doubt."

What we want and need from our leaders today is drastically different from in the past. In a 2006 *Fortune* article, Tom Neff, a top CEO recruiter, stated, "Companies don't want dictators or kings or emperors. Instead of someone who gives orders, they want someone who asks probing questions that force the team to think and find the right answers—a subtle technique."[5] In this "unprecedented war for top talent" that is raging in the global economy, a new profile of a leader is beckoned.[6]

Fortune has stated: "Talent of every type is in short supply, but the greatest shortage of all is skilled, effective managers."[7] Noel Tichy, a University of Michigan Business School professor and former chief of GE's leadership development program, says, "The leadership pipeline is broke."[8] Right Management Consultants, a major outplacement firm, found that "77% of companies say they don't have enough successors to their current senior managers."[9] From a survey Right also found that "the number one skill companies seek in managers is 'the ability to motivate and engage others.' Ranking a close second is the ability to communicate."[10]

All of the above data, situations, and events raise important leadership questions and point to the essential need for Emotional Intelligence answers and training.

- How are we to trust our leaders today?
- What lessons can we learn from our fallen or derailed leaders?
- What do Star Performers have to teach us?
- What plays or strategies can we follow to develop a company of Stars?
- What can we learn about Emotional Intelligence from profiles about some of our most public leaders?

Emotional Intelligence is often *the* missing piece of the skillset and behavior of today's leadership crisis. It is obviously crucial for organizations to promote the development of high Emotional Intelligence with all of their leaders to avoid serious problems such as lack of impulse control and employees underperforming because their leader is not clear, motivating, or acknowledging their efforts.

EQ, IQ, OR TECHNICAL EXPERTISE?

Just about every manager in the boardroom or conference room is smart, with a typical IQ score of 115 or above. IQ is actually an equalizer in corporate environments, and being a few IQ points above or below isn't really noticeable (although much meeting time is wasted as executives argue to demonstrate their few extra IQ points and "smarts"). As performers move up in their organizations, the truth is, no matter how smart they are, they inevitably leave their expertise behind. As they become managers and beyond, more of their success comes from leadership skills rather than from their IQ points or technical acumen. That means they need to cultivate many new abilities, including motivating others to new levels, coordinating efforts between team members and departments, managing deadlines, and resolving conflicts.

As they become managers and beyond, more of their success comes from leadership skills rather than from their IQ points or technical acumen.

There is an obvious gap between the skill set needed to be a supervisor or a manager and a leader. At DreamWorks Animation (creators of *Shrek*, *Shrek 2*, and *Madagascar*), for example, talented animators who excel in their craft have the opportunity to move up. They often leave the work they trained years to excel at and are promoted to lead other animators who were once their peers. Often they show up with little or no experience or expertise in this important new leadership position. This challenge is common in many career paths where individuals find themselves moving up the corporate ladder. What do they do? What do they need to learn to lead and lead well? This is where Emotional Intelligence can provide the skills to help them succeed in their new leadership position. The good news is EI can be learned and enhanced, where IQ is fixed. *Leaders' Playbook* will provide the plays to advance.

The good news is EI can be learned and enhanced, where IQ is fixed.

HOW TO BE A STAR PERFORMER—
NEW RULES FOR SUCCESS

	INDIVIDUAL	SUPERVISOR/MANAGER
Motivation	Self	Diverse group
Communication	Few people	Team & cross teams
Rewards	Own effort & immediate	Success of the team, longer term
Accountability	Self	Team
Quality	Self	Diverse group
Time management	Self	Team

Martin Moskovits is a good example of a man who came into his job with a high IQ and great technical skill who was challenged to rise up to a leadership position. Moskovits is the Dean of Mathematics, Physical and Life Sciences, for the University of California at Santa Barbara (UCSB). He has a Ph.D. in Chemistry and leads 13 departments, 250 professors, 4,000 undergraduates, and 600 graduate students. Fifty percent of research funding for UCSB comes to his programs, and in the last few years three professors from his departments were awarded the Nobel Prize. How much of his day-to-day work is involved with his technical expertise, chemistry? Not much anymore. But Moskovits is a great leader because he has many strengths in the competencies of Emotional Intelligence. He can manage relationships with professors and donors, has empathy for others and elicits trust, is an inspiring speaker, and knows how to use his influence to get things done.

Generation X, born from 1964 to 1978, has been documented to have lower EI than the Baby Boomers because of all the hours they have spent interacting with technology including computers, electronic games, and TV versus being in a social situation dealing with others. Also fewer and fewer X-ers are entering the workplace to

In the near future there will certainly be an "Emotional Intelligence drain."

replace the Boomers. There are 78 million Boomers retiring in the next 10-15 years and only 45 million X-ers to replace them. This data points to the beginning of a crisis phase in the corporate milieu, where Emotional Intelligence is needed for leadership at the highest positions in organizations. In the near future there will certainly be an "Emotional Intelligence drain."

Robert Kelley of Carnegie-Mellon University has interviewed people across the nation, asking this important question: "What percentage of the knowledge to do your job is stored in your own mind?" In his book, *How to Be a Star at Work*, he states that in 1986 the typical answer was "75% of the time." By 1997 the percentage had slid 15-20 points, to 55%. One company's staff members admitted that only 10% of the knowledge they needed to do their jobs was still stored in their minds![11] What does this tell us? Collaboration, teamwork, empathy, communication, networking, and initiative are vital to complete the tasks at work. The shift from IQ and technical expertise to EI and the ability to lead in many ways from the head and heart together is obvious.

THE FOUR AREAS OF EMOTIONAL INTELLIGENCE

In *The Emotionally Intelligent Workplace*, Cherniss and Goleman have identified the key competencies of Star Performers. This model has changed over time and is constantly being updated to correspond with current research on exactly what makes a Star. The following list is from Cherniss and Goleman.[12] A Star, again, is defined as someone who is in the top 10% of performance. The easiest definition of *Emotional Intelligence* is "exhibiting a good balance of personal and social competencies in four distinct areas or clusters:

Self-Awareness—Understanding yourself

Self-Management—Managing yourself

Social Awareness—Understanding others

Relationship Management—Managing others"

Again, the goal is not to be a Star in every competency inside of each of the four clusters, but to have a good balance of competencies across the four areas listed above. Typically having 11 or 12 competencies across the four clusters is what it takes to be a Star Performer.[13] The following diagram represents the four distinct areas and lists the 20 competencies:

THE 20 COMPETENCIES
OF EMOTIONAL INTELLIGENCE [14]

PERSONAL	SOCIAL
Self-Awareness	**Social Awareness**
Emotional Self-Awareness	Empathy*
Accurate Self-Assessment	Organizational Awareness
Self-Confidence*	Service Orientation
Self-Management	**Relationship Management**
Emotional Self-Control	Influence
Trustworthiness	Inspirational Leadership
Conscientiousness	Developing Others*
Adaptability	Building Bonds
Achievement Orientation	Teamwork and Collaboration*
Initiative	Conflict Management
	Communication*
	Change Catalyst

*You'll notice that these five competencies are addressed in this book. Self-Confidence, Teamwork and Collaboration, Developing Others, Communication, and Empathy were chosen because they are the key areas executives ask for support with first and foremost. They are also core abilities that will help you successfully introduce

EI into your organization. Although these five will also help create resonance in others quickly, all the competencies are important.

PROFILES OF STAR PERFORMERS

The following profiles feature leaders who are Star Performers. You will have a chance to examine a diagram of their successes (and weaknesses) by reviewing how they exhibit their EI strengths on the key clusters. You will see not only what competencies have contributed to their successes but also which competencies have led some to derail and become fallen heroes. Sometimes you will notice that a competency overused can become a weakness. So that you can identify them more easily, many of the competencies are pointed out in parentheses inside of the profile and at the end of each profile.

Because of the person's visibility and potential impact on others, one derailer can undermine a whole set of EI competencies.

All of the leaders profiled have many Star competencies; otherwise, they wouldn't be as successful in their careers. What is interesting to note, though, is the power and influence of their particular derailers. A "derailer" is defined as a behavior or attitude that curtails an individual's performance or advancement. It gets that person off the track to success. Because of the person's visibility and potential impact on others, one derailer can undermine a whole set of EI competencies. These "fatal flaws" must be attended to and ameliorated for a leader to sustain his or her success.[15]

OFFICIAL DISCLAIMER

The determination of what competencies these leaders excel in is from a variety of sources written about them. The depictions are inferred rather than established from interviews or assessments. The aim is to illustrate, inform, and match which behaviors to focus on to be a star in your organization.

Everyone has different opinions of public figures, and you may disagree with how these leaders are profiled on the EI competencies. The goal is to look at them through the lenses of Emotional Intelligence competencies and assess which behaviors are effective and which aren't, irrespective of your political persuasion and their ideology. Behavior is always interpretive, and with high-profile leaders we have an opportunity to know more about their behaviors and patterns than we do with other leaders, even though these portrayals are highly influenced by the media. My hope is that the specific behaviors of Stars can become more salient in these profiles and therefore useful to you and others in developing leaders.

In reading these profiles and the profiles of other successful leaders in this book, you will see their ability to be resilient after a failure or a derailer. These became turning points for their resurrection and return to Starhood. Pay attention to which parts of their stories impress or attract you, as that will be a sign that there is information for you and your development in that story.

RUDY GIULIANI

Rudy Giuliani, "America's Mayor," exemplifies a Star Performer in Emotional Intelligence. He demonstrates the blending of personal competencies, understanding, and managing himself with social competencies of understanding and managing others.

After the terrorist attacks of September 11, 2001, Giuliani was visible everywhere—at Ground Zero, comforting the nation, championing the firemen and police, and speaking to individuals and families who lost loved ones. He openly expressed his emotions at public funerals and did not withhold his vulnerability with the press (Empathy and Trustworthiness). Giuliani repeatedly displayed the perfect pitch for understanding and voiced what everybody was feeling. With glistening eyes he said, "We'll never know all the heroes, the people who, maybe in the last moments, comforted others when all of them knew they were going to die" (Leadership). Giuliani modulated his emotions and shared, "We have to cry. The tears have to make us stronger" (Self-Awareness and Accurate Self-Assessment). "Every time you cry, you have to remember that we're right and that they're wrong." His words, such as, "The spirit of New York City is not the buildings, the spirit of New York is its people," gave perspective and hope. Giuliani portrayed that mysterious mix of great qualities of leadership—strength, vulnerability, resolve, empathy, and inspiration (Leadership, Communication, and Change Catalyst).

HOW STAR PERFORMERS SHINE

The boxes below illustrate and clarify the components of Star Performers. Notice how Stars are able to demonstrate the personal and social competencies in each of the boxes. True Stars know and manage themselves and understand and motivate others. A ★ indicates being a Star Performer in that cluster of competencies, while an ✗ indicates being just average or that there is not information to establish the person as a Star, and a 🜔 may indicate a derailer or potential problem for the individual.

Giuliani's profile is one of a clear Star Performer in all four clusters.

EI Ratings: Rudy Giuliani - Currently

	PERSONAL	SOCIAL
Understanding	Self ★	Others ★
Managing	Self ★	Others ★

Giuliani didn't always demonstrate these competencies. Prior to 9/11 he was criticized for his bluntness, sarcasm, and temper. He talked tough, picked fights, and demanded results. New York City was safer; the crime rate was down 57% and murder down by 65%. The city was cleaner and better run. (Achievement Orientation and Initiative) Yet its constituents were polarized. You either loved him or hated him! Giuliani had typified the stern father, who was cool, demanding, and you were never sure how he felt about you. The competencies on the personal side of the clusters were not as evident.

Key Strengths/Competencies:

- Empathy
- Self-awareness
- Accurate self-assessment
- Communication
- Change catalyst
- Trustworthiness
- Achievement orientation
- Initiative
- Leadership
- Conscientiousness
- Adaptability
- Organizational awareness

EI Ratings: Rudy Giuliani – Pre-9/11

	PERSONAL	SOCIAL
Understanding	Self	Others
	⚱	✗
Managing	Self	Others
	⚱	★

Derailers:

- Low impulse control
- Low empathy
- Drives others too hard
- Lack of accurate self-assessment

What Changed?

Significant life experiences forced Giuliani to delve into the personal competencies. He had two extramarital affairs during his term as mayor, which became public and led to a messy divorce. He also was diagnosed with prostate cancer, which forced him to pull out of the senatorial race against Hillary Clinton.

Faced with public failures and experiencing human vulnerabilities that were new for him, Giuliani shifted and was forced to reassess. He reviewed his strengths and weaknesses and looked carefully at how to correct them. These hardships made Giuliani more self-aware and better able to manage himself. He publicly admitted his mistakes, took personal responsibility for getting his life back on track, and adapted, reinventing himself in the process. His introspection and commitment to change led to his becoming more understanding and compassionate with others and ultimately touching the hearts of millions of Americans. Goleman stated that one needs to focus on the personal side of the emotional competencies *first* in order to successfully enhance the social competencies.[16,17] This is exactly what Rudy Giuliani accomplished.

CARLY FIORINA

Past CEO of Hewlett-Packard, Carly Fiorina resigned February 8, 2005, under pressure from her board of directors. She demonstrates many of the EI competencies across the personal and social clusters. She was the first woman to head a Dow 30 company and the first "outsider" of HP in 60 years to take the reins of the computer giant. Hewlett-Packard today is a $72 billion company and Fiorina helped orchestrate the biggest tech merger to date, with Compaq. She set her initial objectives on building a new vision for HP as an Internet company—jump-starting its innovation and recalibrating HP's vaulted culture. *Fortune* magazine said Fiorina is "A world-class risk taker."[18] Her strategy failed, though, in the eyes of her board. The stock price during her tenure was down 50%, where Dell was only down 9%.[19]

In *Fortune* Fiorina was rated #1 of the 50 most powerful women in American business.[20] She is a charismatic leader known for a personal touch. A standard practice of hers is giving balloons and flowers to employees who land big contracts, which inspires intense loyalty and appreciation (Developing Others/ Empathy).

The *Wall Street Journal* said, "She was an alluring, controversial new breed of CEOs who combine grand visions with charismatic but self-centered and demanding style." She was decisive and had crisp presentation skills and was "accused of valuing boldness over precision and follow-through."[21] Her overused confidence may have turned into a weakness. Inside HP she was a polarized figure who could be abrupt and autocratic. Many high-level executives had quit recently and that concerned the board. Fiorina was becoming more irritated and defensive about her strategy. She failed to empower others as much as she could, and in January 2005 the board wanted to distribute her power and she initially disagreed.

Before HP, Fiorina was at Lucent Technologies, a spin-off of AT&T. She took them public and launched a flashy marketing campaign that repositioned them from a maker of phone equipment to an Internet company. She landed on *Fortune's* cover in 1998 with the caption, "The Most Powerful Woman in American Business." "Affable and strikingly confident, she is a natural leader. At Lucent, she is said to have won the hearts as well as the minds of her staff," (Confidence and Leadership) said Louise Kehoe of the *Financial Times*.[22] Fiorina always said leadership was gender-neutral.

She was selected out of 300 potential CEOs for her ability to:

- Conceptualize and communicate new strategies
- Deliver on quarterly financial goals with operational savvy
- Bring urgency to the organization with powerful vision
- Drive a new net vision through the company with strong management skills (Leadership, Change Catalyst, Influence, and Communication)

She is very customer-focused and understands that what the customer needs is not always what he or she asks for (Service Orientation). She is up at 4 a.m. to feed her birds and work out. "It's a good thinking time," she says. (Self-management)

Fiorina's father is a federal court judge and law professor. Her mother was a painter and was the strongest person she knew. Fiorina has a B.A. from Stanford and went to law school at UCLA, before dropping out. As a child, Fiorina moved frequently. "I always landed in a whole new place...You learn to be self-reliant. It didn't scare me anymore."[23]

Fiorina spends a lot of time boating with her husband of 17 years, who is retired, and she has two stepdaughters and a 3-year-old granddaughter.

Key Strengths/Competencies:

- Developing others
- Empathy
- Confidence
- Change catalyst
- Influence
- Communication
- Service orientation
- Leadership
- Initiative
- Achievement orientation

Derailers

- Confidence (overused)
- Initiative (overused)
- Drives others too hard
- Self-promotion

From above, Carly Fiorina is clearly a Star in three clusters, but her overused confidence, an inability to accurately assess her strengths and weaknesses, and not delegating authority to others may have led to her resignation. She will certainly rise again to be a Star in a new arena of her choice.

EI Ratings: Carly Fiorina

	PERSONAL	**SOCIAL**
Understanding	Self 	Others ★
Managing	Self ★	Others ★

JEFFREY IMMELT

Jeffrey Immelt was appointed Chairman of the Board and CEO of General Electric (GE) on September 7, 2001. Founded in 1892, GE is one of the most powerful and respected companies in the world, with over 300,000 employees in 160 countries, representing 11 financial, services, and technology businesses. In 2006 *Fortune* reported that GE was rated #1 in the World's Most Admired Companies for the sixth time in eight years.[24]

Immelt's initial entry into GE was challenging. Not only did he follow the legendary Jack Welch, who had been CEO for twenty years, but he also took his new position only four days before 9/11 and the collapse of the World Trade Center. His leadership has been highlighted by weathering many storms and much criticism, but Immelt has pulled through and shined because he has demonstrated many of the EI competencies in his long and distinguished career.

In 1994, when Immelt was vice president of GE Plastics American, he almost got fired for poor performance. Instead of reaching his 20% profit goal, he delivered only 7% in earnings growth with a missed income of approximately $50 million!

In an interview with *Fast Company*, Immelt recalled the dramatic subsequent events. During the annual leadership meeting in 1995, he was actively avoiding having the "tough talk" with Welch and tried to escape the auditorium. Welch grabbed him as he was slipping away and said, "Jeff I am your biggest fan, but you just had your worst year in the company. Just the worst year. I love you and I know you can do better. But I'm going to take you out if you can't get it fixed."[25] (This is a good example of tough empathy from Welch.)

"Even though I came close to being fired," Immelt added, "I never considered quitting. I knew the issues were my fault and I didn't want to let my people down." He described this experience as the most painful time in his entire career. But Immelt is highly adaptable, and he reflected, "Surviving a failure gives you more self-confidence. Failures are great learning tools—but they must be kept at a minimum."[26] (Trustworthiness, Confidence, Adaptability)

"There was only one person who thought I had a future at GE then, and it was me." He stated that at meetings people thought he was a "dead man walking." Immelt learned that no one was going to define who he was and only he could get himself out of the fix.[27] (Initiative, Achievement Orientation)

Immelt had been in training for the CEO position for 20 years. He started working at GE in 1982 and held global leadership roles in many of GE's businesses. He earned a B.A. from Dartmouth, where he also played football, and an M.B.A. from Harvard University. He worked at Proctor and Gamble in 1978, where Steven Ballmer, now CEO of Microsoft, was his office mate.

Immelt can be a firm leader but not the bully Welch was. He has fired friends, but did it in a nice way, even calling them after they left to see how they were doing.[28] (Conflict Management) Since being named Chairman-elect in 1999, Immelt also made it a point to engage a wider spectrum of people; now 50% of all senior executives and 54% of new corporate officers are women, minorities, or foreign employees.[29]

Immelt is highly optimistic and keeps his focus on the future and how to make it better. "I've always believed the future is going to be better than the past...and I believe I have a role in that."[30] In talking about how to motivate others to get through tough times, Immelt emphasizes the need to be straight with people. "You need to let them know where you are and communicate how the road looks for them."[31] (Inspiring Leadership, Change Catalyst) His father worked at GE for 38 years, and Immelt personally experienced the effects of a good or bad boss on his father's motivation and the whole family's sense of well-being. (Empathy)

Immelt spends four to five days a month with customers as well as attending two town-hall meetings per month with hundreds of customers. He initiated "dreaming sessions" with them. Together, Immelt and customers brainstorm where the business will be in five to ten years. (Service Orientation)

GE spends $1 billion a year on training and education programs. Immelt says he spends 30% of his own time teaching and coaching. This is a huge commitment to leadership development and follows a practice of Welch's, who was known to spend more than 50% of his time teaching leadership to his people.[32] (Developing Others)

Immelt's ritual around self-management and renewal includes getting up every morning at 5:30 and working out for an hour on the treadmill, stair stepper, and elliptical trainer while watching the news and sports.[33]

Below are the EI competencies for Jeffrey Immelt, shining with stars across all four clusters.

Key Strengths/Competencies:

- Confidence
- Initiative
- Inspirational leadership
- Achievement orientation
- Adaptability

- Change catalyst
- Service orientation
- Empathy
- Trustworthiness
- Conflict management
- Influence
- Organizational awareness
- Developing others

Derailers:

- No major ones noticed (...yet!)

El Ratings: Jeffrey Immelt

	PERSONAL	SOCIAL
Understanding	Self ★	Others ★
Managing	Self ★	Others ★

SERGEY BRIN

Sergey Brin is one of the founders of Google, Inc. (along with Larry Page). Google started in 1998 in a garage in Menlo Park, California, 106 years after GE began. In August 2004 Google went public in an unconventional initial public offering (IPO) at $85 and raised $2 billion, which was the largest IPO ever. In less than a year the stock was over $300 and went as high as $475 in 2006. Wall Street has valued it at more than $100 billion.[34] It is worth more than GM and Ford combined.

In reviewing Google's meteoric rise, I wanted to examine what El competencies supported its huge success and chose to profile Sergey

Brin to find out more. Much of what is determined for him is also true for Larry Page, and many of the EI competencies can be inferred from the environment they created together at Google.

Brin and Page are both listed as #16 in the 2005 *Forbes Magazine* featuring the richest Americans, with a net worth of $11 billion. They also made 1,000 of their now 6,000 employees instant millionaires with their IPO. Brin and Page dropped out of their Ph.D. programs in Computer Science at Stanford, in their words, to "'Change the world' through a search engine that organizes every bit of information on the Web for free."[35] (Inspirational Leadership)

When they first met, they found each other obnoxious. They argued constantly about random issues, but this behavior soon turned into an intellectual game with the goal of persuading each other over to their viewpoint. Finally, they discovered common ground when it came to solving one of computing's biggest challenges—how to retrieve relevant information from a massive set of data. Today, they still debate in a shared office where they make most decisions together. They also personally approve the hiring of nearly every new employee.[36]

Brin and Page's vision for the future is: "The perfect search engine would understand exactly what you mean and give back exactly what you want." They agree that it is a far-reaching vision requiring research, development, and innovation. (Inspirational Leadership)

Google is actually a noun, a number followed by 100 zeros spelled "googol," but Brin and Page were confused about the spelling and stuck with "Google." Today, Google is synonymous with the Internet and has quickly become a verb. It is used in over 100 different languages with daily searches numbering over 200 million and indexes over 8 billion Web pages.

Sergey was born in 1973 in Moscow, Russia. His father, Mikhail, has a Ph.D. in Mathematics and teaches at the University of Maryland. His mother is also a mathematician and worked as a civil engineer. The family was forced to flee Russia in 1971 because of anti-Semitism.

Sergey has been interested in computers since he received his first Commodore 64 at age nine. He was known as a "math whiz" and one of his classmates recalled that he was "quite cocky about his intellect," often challenging his teachers. He graduated from the University of Maryland with a B.A. in Mathematics and Computer Science in 1993 at the age of 19 and then earned an M.A. in Computer Science in 1995 from Stanford. Sergey is confident, fit, and outspoken.[37] (Achievement Orientation, Initiative, Confidence)

In response to a question about Google being the highlight of his career, he said, "I think it was the smallest of accomplishments that we hope to make over the next 20 years. But I think if Google is all we create, I don't think I would be very disappointed."[38] (Inspirational Leadership, Achievement Orientation)

"We run Google a little bit like a university. We have lots of projects, about 100 of them. We like to have small groups of people, three or so people, working on projects.… The only way you are going to have success is to have lots of failures first."[39] (Teamwork and Collaboration, Building Bonds, Change Catalyst)

"Obviously everyone wants to be successful, but I want to be looked back on as being very innovative, very trusted, and ethical and ultimately making a big difference in the world."[40] (Trustworthiness)

More competencies are revealed about the Google culture by looking at the 10 things Google has found to be true, listed on their website:

1. Focus on the user and all else will follow. (Service Orientation)
2. It's best to do one thing really, really well. Google does search and has applied that unique ability to new products (i.e., Google Earth and Google Maps). (Conscientiousness)
3. You can make money without doing evil. There are no ads on their search page. (Trustworthiness)
4. The need for information crosses all borders. (Service Orientation)
5. You can be serious without a suit. Brin and Page think work should be challenging and the challenge should be fun. They

put their employees first when it comes to their daily life. It is a highly communicative environment with few walls, free food at its cafeteria, subsidized massages and haircuts, and many parties. Each team member is given one day a week to spend on their own pet projects. (Teamwork and Collaboration, Building Bonds, Communication, Developing Others)[41]

Below are the EI competencies for Sergey Brin, shining with stars across all four clusters.

Key Strengths/Competencies:
- Confidence
- Initiative
- Inspirational leadership
- Achievement orientation
- Adaptability
- Change catalyst
- Service orientation
- Trustworthiness
- Communication
- Influence
- Building bonds
- Developing others

Derailers:
- No major ones noticed (…yet!)

EI Ratings: Sergey Brin

	PERSONAL	SOCIAL
Understanding	Self ★	Others ★
Managing	Self ★	Others ★

PETE CARROLL

Pete Carroll is the head football coach for the University of Southern California (USC). USC captured the nation's intrigue as they won 34 games in a row and two national championships. They were 19 seconds away from an unprecedented third national consecutive championship when they lost to Texas and its star quarterback, Vince Young. Overall they have had 52 wins and only 4 losses over Carroll's five seasons. Carroll has won numerous "Coach of the Year" awards from 2003 to 2005.

When Carroll arrived at USC in 2001, they had been 56-39-2 the eight years prior. They were 5 and 7 in 2000, the year before Carroll arrived. His record was a remarkable feat of national reemergence, teamwork, and leadership, attributable to Carroll's unorthodox coaching style, which is rife with EI competencies. He is known as a "player's coach" versus an authoritarian command, control type of coach.

A football coach focuses most of his time on developing the talent of players and their ability to function together as a highly effective team. The best corporate leader may be focusing as much as 50% of his or her time on development, but that is rare indeed. Examining the leadership of Carroll uncovers many valuable examples of successfully applying Emotional Intelligence skills and tools to sports and business.

Carroll was actually the fifth choice of coaches considered suitable to reenergize the USC Trojans. Other coaches such as Dennis Erickson of Oregon State, Sonny Lubick of Colorado State, Mike Belotti of Oregon, and Mike Riley from the San Diego Chargers either were not interested in USC or didn't work out. Although Carroll had spent 16 years in the professional football world and was head coach of the New York Jets and New England Patriots, he had a less than overwhelming 33-31 record; plus, he was fired from each head coach job. USC was concerned about whether he had what it takes to coach in the college ranks, but in his interviews his enthusiasm and concise plan for rebuilding the team were impressive. (Conscientiousness) The assistant athletic director said, "Pete was just so amazingly engaging. His enthusiasm and his energy mixed with his expertise."[42]

Carroll is confident, enthusiastic, always pushing, striving to improve, and not afraid to take risks. These traits were highlighted in the national championship game with Texas. Carroll was criticized for going for a first down with four minutes to go rather than play it safe and punt the ball. They failed and Texas received the ball and went on to win. He said, "The last thing I want to do is sit back and see what happens. I want to get it and make opportunities."[43] (Confidence, Achievement Orientation, Initiative, Inspirational Leadership)

Carroll was a defensive back in college at the University of the Pacific and won all-conference honors as a safety in 1971 and 1972. After an unsuccessful shot at the pros, he returned to graduate school at Pacific. There Carroll learned about the Human Potential movement, sports psychology, and read Tim Gallwey's *Inner Game of Tennis* and Abraham Maslow's *Religions, Values, and Peak Experiences.* These experiences and books resonated with him and opened him up to a new leadership style.

As a young coach, he applied what he learned in the classroom to the practice field. After some tough seasons, he asked his defensive backs who were having problems which coverages they felt most comfortable with and which techniques they wanted to practice more.[44] This approach was rather unconventional compared to the traditional football hierarchy, which would rarely engage players in team or coaching strategies. Carroll recalled that his players were rejuvenated by the meeting. One of his coaches, after hearing what he had done, said, "Wait just a damn minute, boy. Don't you ever ask them what they want. You tell them what they need."[45] Carroll was totally deflated by this.

This didn't last long, though, as he was quickly identified as an up-and-coming coach with special talent. In the pros, he refined his leadership style when dealing with players one-on-one, sometimes cracking the whip and other times talking to them about their life. He certainly was not the authoritarian coach of a Bear Bryant or Bill Parcells. "That can be a great way to teach, but it's not for me. I get more out of you if I connect with you. Instead of knocking you down...I'm going to build you up."[46] He tries to understand the player and figures out the best way to inspire them. (Accurate Self-Assessment, Developing Others, Building Bonds)

After three years working with the New England Patriots, Carroll was fired and took a year off from coaching to reflect. He read a book by John Wooden, UCLA's legendary basketball coach, and Wooden's concept of "knowing exactly what you want to get done" was inspiring for him. He thought about what felt natural for him as a coach and recognized it was his energy, optimism, and desire to relate directly with his players. "That's who I am." If he believed in himself he figured the players would too.[47] Carroll decided to make only fine adjustments within his leadership style and stay with his strengths. (Emotional Self-Awareness, Accurate Self-Assessment, Trustworthiness, Communication)

The successes Pete Carroll has had at USC are a great example of Emotional Intelligence in action. He stayed with his strengths and made only small micro-initiatives in his leadership that created a macro impact. It is a tribute to the competencies of knowing himself, motivating himself, developing empathy and strong bonds with his players, and creating a strong vision of teamwork and leadership that the players, the university, and the USC community have all embraced and celebrated.

Below are the EI competencies for Pete Carroll, shining with stars across all four clusters.

Key Strengths/Competencies:

- Confidence
- Initiative

- Accurate self-assessment
- Inspirational leadership
- Achievement orientation
- Adaptability
- Change catalyst
- Empathy
- Trustworthiness
- Communication
- Influence
- Building bonds
- Developing others

Derailers:

- No major ones noticed (…yet!)

EI Ratings: Pete Carroll

	PERSONAL	SOCIAL
Understanding	Self ★	Others ★
Managing	Self ★	Others ★

MEG WHITMAN

Meg Whitman is the president and CEO of eBay and was rated the Most Powerful Woman in 2004 by *Fortune* magazine. Since Whitman arrived at eBay seven years ago, the company has grown from $5.7 million to $3.2 billion in estimated revenues. As a matter of fact, eBay is the "fastest growing company in history, faster than Microsoft, Dell, or any company during the first eight years of its existence."[48]

The $3.2 billion in revenues will produce more than $1 billion in operating income this year. eBay is a company of the future, with no factories or inventories, where the customers do the work. In 2000, when revenues were $431 million, Whitman announced that eBay would reach $3 billion in 2005 (Initiative, Leadership, and Achievement Orientation). "Few investors believed in her, and even her board had doubts."[49]

Whitman was the youngest of three children and grew up in Long Island, New York. She went to Princeton University and majored in Economics and then attended Harvard Business School. She has always been driven and even had the *Wall Street Journal* delivered to her dorm room as an undergraduate. Whitman studied brand management at Proctor and Gamble and strategy at Bain Consulting. She then worked at Disney, Stride Rite, Florist Transworld Delivery (FTD), and Hasbro.

As president and CEO of FTD, Whitman had her first taste of the limelight. In 1995 she rejuvenated the brand and it became a profitable private company. She was attractive to eBay because of her consumer marketing background. Whitman demonstrated her adaptability, leadership, and change management skills numerous times at eBay. She fended off competition, hired a top technology chief at all costs, and survived a 22-hour website crash, which she called a "near death experience." eBay's purchase of PayPal was risky yet successful. Terry Semel, CEO of Yahoo!, called it "a great acquisition." (Adaptability and Change Catalyst)

eBay's success is built on service orientation. Whitman herself responds to many customer emails. The company responds to emails in 24 hours or less and maintains customer loyalty, and more than half of the eBay referrals are from customers. Listening to customers and providing for their needs has helped Whitman expand the company and maintain the "small-town feel on a global scale." (Service Orientation) Onstage before several thousand customers, she tells them, "eBay's success will always be based on your success.

eBay reaffirms my faith in humanity. eBay is proof that people are basically good."[50] (Empathy and Leadership)

Whitman is not flashy or charismatic like other CEOs, but yields her power in a folksy den mother approach where she is nurturing values. She is non-threatening, easy to talk to, and self-effacing. She called herself "frumpy but I deliver." (Trustworthiness) Terry Semel of Yahoo! says, "Meg is Meg. She is exactly who you meet. She is smart, straightforward, and to the point. She's just really nice to do business with."[51] Clearly Meg Whitman is a Star Performer in all four clusters.

Whitman's husband is a neurosurgeon at Stanford, and she recharges herself by spending time with her family, escaping a few times a year to go fly-fishing at her husband's family farm in Tennessee.

Key Strengths/Competencies:
- Confidence
- Initiative
- Leadership
- Achievement orientation
- Adaptability
- Change catalyst
- Service orientation
- Empathy
- Trustworthiness
- Conscientiousness
- Influence
- Organizational awareness

Derailers:
- No major ones noticed (…yet)

EI Ratings: Meg Whitman

	PERSONAL	SOCIAL
Understanding	Self ★	Others ★
Managing	Self ★	Others ★

BILL CLINTON

Bill Clinton, our 42nd president, exemplifies a derailed leader because of his failings on the personal competencies. He was and is extremely socially competent, capable of knowing "how to feel people's pain" and provide social services to the masses. (Empathy and Service Orientation) Clinton was one of our best and most charismatic communicators. As president, he communicated a compelling vision in his re-election campaign, with the potent phrase "cross the bridge with me to the new millennium." (Leadership and Communication) He was excellent at championing change: using his influence and persuasion skills, he built a strong team among his cabinet to react quickly and effectively to political issues. (Influence, Teamwork, and Change Catalyst)

In his first year out of office he made $9.2 million in speaking fees, charging $75,000 to $350,000 per speech. "In cold hard cash it is almost certainly the most ever. The guy still fascinates people," said Stephen Hess, a presidential expert at the Brookings Institution.[52]

In addition, Clinton signed a reported $10 million contract with Alfred A. Knopf, Inc., to write his memoirs, a deal believed to be the biggest ever for a nonfiction book. The book came out in July 2004 and was also the biggest debut for a nonfiction book, with 2.575 million copies printed.

Clinton has started the Global Initiative, which has brought together political and business leaders for humanitarian projects.

The Initiative has already raised over $2 billion for more than 200 projects around the world. His post-presidential career is emulating Jimmy Carter's, focusing on human rights. Clinton's work with AIDS is "already saving hundreds of thousands of lives and promises to save millions more."[53]

The social competencies are going to keep Clinton in the public eye and continue to make him a fortune. Yet the personal competencies derailed him. (Self Awareness, Accurate Self-Assessment, and Self-Control) He was only the second president to be impeached, when he was charged with perjury and obstruction of justice in regards to his relationship with Monica Lewinsky. The senate acquitted Clinton, but the mistakes in his personal life have forever tarnished his legacy as a president.

Clinton certainly had some blind spots in understanding and managing himself. There were gaps between the awareness of his feelings and understanding the implications of his feelings. He failed to manage his impulses and was unable to publicly admit his mistakes. One would think the charges of his having extramarital affairs during the 1992 Democratic primaries would have forced him into planning ways of exerting more self-control in the future. Why would he risk all that he had worked so hard for to have momentary pleasures? From a cognitive perspective it certainly doesn't make sense, but Clinton's lack of emotional awareness overpowered his rational side and muted all the strengths he portrays in the social competences.

In his book and interviews he states: "I think I did something for the worst possible reason—just because I could. I think that's just about the most morally indefensible reason that anybody could have for doing anything. When you do something just because you could...I've thought about it a lot. And there are lots of more sophisticated explanations, more complicated psychological explanations. But none of them are an excuse...Only a fool does not look to explain his mistakes."[54]

Key Strengths and Competencies:

- Empathy
- Service orientation
- Leadership
- Communication
- Influence
- Teamwork
- Change catalyst
- Initiative
- Adaptability
- Building bonds
- Organizational awareness

Derailers:

- Low self-awareness
- Inaccurate self-assessment
- Low self-control
- Low trustworthiness

This graph illustrates Clinton's undeveloped and Star competencies.

EI Ratings: Bill Clinton

	PERSONAL	SOCIAL
Understanding	Self ᦒ	Others ★
Managing	Self ᦒ	Others ★

HOWARD DEAN

Howard Dean is the new Democratic chairman, an almost unthinkable position since he lost 17 of 18 2004 presidential primaries. The

Democratic chairman has long been an insider, with powerful allies. But Howard Dean often breaks the mold. He has been given a mandate to shake things up, and people do rally around him as a forceful voice and formidable organizer (Leadership, Change Catalyst).

Depending on the source, "Dr. Dean is either a breath of fresh air who will make his brethren proud again or he's a loose canon who will be crushed by the Republican machine."[55] Some Democrats felt they owed him for services rendered in 2004 since he effectively set up an online money-raising operation and stumped for over 600 local candidates (Building Bonds, Service, Influence). He still sparks unease among Democrats, though, and in a 2005 CNN poll only 31% of Americans viewed him favorably.

Howard Dean grew up in East Hampton and on Park Avenue in New York. He is the oldest of four boys, the second oldest having been killed in Laos in 1974—certainly a "defining crisis" for Dean. Dean went to Yale University, skied for a year, and then became a stockbroker before going back to medical school. He had a bad back draft deferment. His father was a top executive until retiring from Dean Witter. He is married to Judith Steinberg, a physician.

Dean and his doctor/wife have very different ways of thinking. He explains, "She's very methodical, exhausting all possibilities of potential diagnosis until she gets the one that's most likely. I'm intuitive, on the other hand. I jump steps ahead. Part of what gets me in trouble on the stump is that I shorthand things. I know what I am thinking but I don't say every word of it. I was that way as a doctor. I eliminate possibilities unconsciously…It is also part of my political judgment. I often know I want to do things before I know why."

"The confidence in his gut, his disdain for process, and his tendency to get right to solutions brings to mind someone else: George W. Bush."[56] (Initiative, Achievement Orientation, Confidence)

"Dean spends nearly as much time clarifying and apologizing as he spreads his message. Even he concedes that he has a tendency to 'mouth off.' With Dean, impulsiveness and stubbornness go hand in hand. When he shoots from the hip, it takes him a while to undo the damage."[57]

"The media portrays Dean as angry, dark, and even surly." Among Democratic voters, more than 75% see him as likable but usually qualify their opinions. "Dean is no Bill Clinton. He does not pretend to spend any time feeling anyone's pain, nor does he have Bush's folksy, quick to mist up touch. He's just not likeable."[58]

"There is a different way I show empathy," Dean says. "I kind of lean into them, and I look at them, and I'll let them know I'm really paying careful attention to what they say. But I don't put my arm around them and all that stuff. Because it's true; when you present me with a problem, I want to solve the problem." He maintains a detachment and recalls how his emotions made him incapable of assisting a critically wounded nine-year-old drive-by shooting victim when he was a medical student. "What I learned from that is, if you get sucked in and you get overwhelmed, you can't do a thing for the patient." Charge: He is too liberal and he is not electable.[59]

Dean's major falling out with the American public was his lack of impulse control, either real or imagined. The image of his red face on television as he screamed into the microphone is etched into millions of people's minds and will remain there for a long time.

Key Strengths and Competencies:

- Initiative
- Achievement orientation
- Confidence
- Service orientation
- Leadership
- Communication
- Influence
- Change catalyst
- Adaptability

Derailers:

- Low self-control
- Low empathy

EI Ratings: Howard Dean

	PERSONAL	SOCIAL
Understanding	Self ✗	Others ★
Managing	Self	Others ★

CONDOLEEZZA RICE

In August 2004 Rice was named the most powerful woman in the world by *Forbes*, before she became the first African American woman to be appointed the United States Secretary of State. She is a good example of a person with a good array of Emotional Intelligence competencies.

Prior to Secretary of State, Rice was the National Security Advisor, appointed by President George W. Bush in 2001. She also served in the George H.W. Bush administration from 1989 to 1991, as Senior Director of Soviet and East European Affairs in the National Security Council. In addition, she was a Special Assistant to President for National Security Affairs. George H.W. Bush was so impressed with her that he told Soviet Leader Mikhail Gorbachev that Rice was the one who "tells me everything I know about the Soviet Union."[60] (Service Orientation, Organizational Awareness)

Before her entrance into politics, Rice was a tenured professor at Stanford University in Political Science. She was known as quietly cerebral, friendly yet formal, and very popular with students. She served as the Stanford University Provost, the chief budget and academic affairs officer from 1993 to 1999. She continued to have friendly contact with various student organizations. (Building Bonds)

Rice grew up in Birmingham, Alabama, as an only child. Her mother was a music teacher and her father was a Presbyterian ordained minister. Growing up in the South during segregation taught Rice determination against adversity and the need to be "twice as good" as non-minorities.[61] (Adaptabiity and Achievement Orientation)

At the age of 13 her family moved to Denver, where her father became assistant dean at the University of Denver and taught a class called "The Black Experience in America."[62] Rice, who could read music at age three, had the goal of becoming a concert pianist. Her plans changed when she took a class at University of Denver on international politics taught by Josef Korbel, father of the first woman Secretary of State, Madeleine Albright. Rice had her bachelor degree in Political Science at age 19 and her Ph.D. at age 26 from the Graduate School of International Studies at the University of Denver. In addition to English, she speaks Russian, French, and Spanish. To be so successful so young she had to excel on her Conscientiousness and Initiative competencies.

Rice's personal competency of Self-Control and social competencies of Influence and Conflict Resolution were severely tested during her senate confirmation hearings as Secretary of State in January 2005. Democrats could not accept some of her previous comments and record and wanted to hold her and the Bush administration accountable for the unsuccessful search for weapons of mass destruction, as well as failures in Iraq and in the war on terrorism. However, "Rice's charm and intellect outweighed these factors," resulting in her approval by a vote of 85-13.[63] The negative votes were still the highest cast against any nomination for Secretary of State since 1825.

Rice's role in the world forces her to deal with conflict, differing views, and building and rebuilding relationships that have been damaged, all while maintaining a clear vision of what the United States wants. Her intellect and technical expertise are vital, but what has allowed her to be so successful is her EI skills. This is in part why there is talk of her running for president in 2008, which she has declared she is not interested in.

Key Strengths and Competencies:

- Confidence
- Initiative
- Achievement orientation
- Adaptability
- Self-control
- Conscientiousness
- Service orientation
- Organizational awareness
- Influence
- Leadership
- Conflict resolution
- Building bonds

Derailers:

- Confidence (overused)
- Others – unknown at this point

EI Ratings: Condoleezza Rice

	PERSONAL	SOCIAL
Understanding	Self ✗	Others ★
Managing	Self ★	Others ★

STAR PERFORMERS WHO DERAILED

Dennis Kozlowski: Past CEO of Tyco

Kozlowski had extravagant spending habits, using company money for a $15,000 poodle-shaped umbrella, a $6,000 shower curtain, expensive garbage can, and a collection of artwork. His wife's birthday party was billed to the company and cost millions. Kozlowski's issues with impulse control, trustworthiness, self-awareness, and accurate self-assessment derailed his career and put him behind bars.

Harvey Pitt: Former Chairman of the SEC

Pitt had some blind spots that cost him his job. He failed to share damaging information about William Webster, who was chairman of the new Public Accounting Oversight Board. Staffers claimed Pitt had "smartest guy in the room syndrome," and he always had to one-up his peers. A brilliant lawyer, Pitt's blunt combative stance served him well as a securities lawyer. He was obviously good at initiative, achievement orientation, and confidence, but didn't demonstrate empathy, building bonds, or developing others. All in all, Pitt needed better skills with people, especially commissioners and members of Congress, to find real success.

Kareem Abdul-Jabbar: National Basketball Association (NBA) Hall of Fame player and the leading career scorer

Abdul-Jabbar is a great example of someone with IQ and technical expertise versus a strong EI. In his long career he was a superb individual performer, Coach of the Oklahoma Stars in the U.S. Basketball League, and has been trying to be an NBA Coach for many years now. He recently got hired as an assistant coach with the Los Angeles Lakers. A lot of doors closed to him after his retirement because he didn't foster the right kind of relationships with team officials when he was a player.

"For the longest time, I didn't want to talk to the press or to management; I just played. I was a dinosaur, I guess. I can look in the mirror and only blame myself for that," he said.

With 38,387 points, Abdul-Jabbar is the leading career scorer. He has the most career minutes, second most games, third most rebounds, second most blocks, six league titles, and is a six-time MVP. Abdul-Jabbar obviously has experience and expertise; what was keeping him from his dream NBA job is low EI.

LACK OF SELF-CONTROL AND THE INABILITY TO DELAY GRATIFICATION

It is apparent that lack of impulse control or self-control is a common theme for leaders who have derailed. This weakness is contradictory to our need for someone who is consistent, steady, and grounded. If a leader lacks self-control, he or she becomes unpredictable and untrustworthy. No one knows when or to what the leader may react. In primitive terms, this kind of person becomes unsafe and even dangerous to others and the organization. Today it is more and more apparent how blind spots in the personal competencies of executives' Emotional Intelligence have led to the greed, lying, and manipulations inside major corporations such as Enron, Adelphia, and WorldCom, to name a few. As a result, there will surely be more derailed executives and a line waiting to get into prison.

Today it is more and more apparent how blind spots in the personal competencies of executives' Emotional Intelligence have led to the greed, lying, and manipulations inside some major corporations.

Many of these former Star Performers who became fallen heroes had the inability to delay gratification. Goleman talks about the "amygdala hijack," a situation where your brain's alarm system overrules executive functioning in the prefrontal lobes.[64] Mike Tyson, in his 1997 fight with Evander Holyfield, exemplified a graphic amygdala hijacking. The two boxers butted heads and Tyson reacted fiercely by biting off a piece of Holyfield's ear. This move cost him $3 million of his $30 million purse and certainly provoked scathing responses on the part of the fight game and the public.

The amygdala is the brain's alarm center. It houses the ancient emotional brain, which plays a key role in reacting to emergencies. It also is the center of emotional memory and responds to threats with primitive reactions of fight or flight. The prefrontal lobes of the brain dictate executive functioning, including decision-making, planning, comprehension, reasoning, and learning. For most people, their prefrontal lobes organize around executive functioning, bringing rational thought and control to the initial amygdala reaction. But it doesn't always work that way.

THE MARSHMALLOW STUDY

Four-year-olds at Stanford Pre-school were each given a marshmallow by a researcher. They were told, "You can have this marshmallow now if you want, but if you don't eat it until after I run an errand, you can have two when I return." Some students immediately ate the marshmallow; others contrived all kinds of distractions for themselves to manage the urge to grab and swallow it. This was a longitudinal study and, 14 years later, when the once 4- but now 18-year-olds were evaluated, researchers compared the "grabbers" versus "those who waited." It turns out that the "grabbers" grew into young adults who displayed tendencies to fall apart more easily under stress, pick fights more often, and have less resistance to temptation in the pursuit of their goals than "those who waited."[65]

A surprising finding was that "those who waited" also scored an average of 210 points higher on their SAT tests than the "grabbers" did. The amygdala is the source of emotional impulse and distraction. When mediated by the prefrontal lobes—the source of the

working memory, executive function, and the capacity to pay attention to what is on your mind—a performer manifests discipline and
the ability to put off urges and stay focused with the task at hand.

The "grabbers" and "those who waited" continued to be
studied into their late 20s. The researchers discovered that "those
who waited" were more intellectually skilled and attentive, better
able to concentrate and develop close relationships, and displayed
more self-control, dependability, and responsibility in the face of
frustration.[66]

STRETCHING STRENGTHS: GOING FROM GOOD TO GREAT LEADERSHIP

There has been a convergence of thought in the last 10-12 years
that the best way to be happy and more successful is to identify
what you do well and do more of it, and get others to do what you
don't excel at. Below are some of the experts' thoughts on leadership and why focusing on your strengths is so important for your
development plan.

First, one definition of "a strength" is: "a pattern of behavior,
thoughts, and feelings that produces a high degree of satisfaction
and pride; generates both psychic and or financial reward; and presents measurable progress toward excellence."[67]

In *The Extraordinary Leader,* Zenger and Folkman studied a
database of 200,000 questionnaires completed on more than 20,000
leaders who had 360-degree feedback to examine what makes an
extraordinary leader. They discovered key findings such as:

- Great leaders make a huge difference when compared to
  merely good leaders. Leaders in the top 10% produced twice
  as much revenue to the organization as managers in the 11th
  through 89th percentiles. Great leaders also have a positive
  impact on profitability, turnover, employee commitment, and
  customer satisfaction and retention.
- "The more great leaders an organization develops, the more it
  will become an outstanding organization."

- There is a significant difference in performance when a leader is in the top 20%. Good leaders in the 40th to 80th percentile are not significantly different from one another in performance.

- The key to developing great leaders is to build strengths.

- If there are "fatal flaws" (derailers), they must be fixed.[68]

...the best way to be happy and more successful is to identify what you do well and do more of it...

Donald O. Clifton and Paula Nelson wrote *Soar with Strengths* as a result of research they did with the Gallup consulting firm. Clifton had been pursuing the following question since graduate school, over 50 years before: "What would happen if we studied what was right with people versus what's wrong with people?" Some of their key findings were:

- "Maximum productivity can be gained from focusing on strengths and managing weaknesses."

- Understanding strengths leads to knowing the difference between good and great.

- Stop wasting time working on weaknesses.

- You can make more effective decisions by studying what's right versus what's wrong.

- Strengths develop best when sufficient time is devoted to a single subject or goal.[69]

Martin Seligman, one of the fathers of Positive Psychology and the author of *Authentic Happiness,* found that the "highest success in living and deepest emotional satisfaction comes from building and using your signature strengths." His research shows that the happiest people are the ones who are using their strengths the most. "Signature strengths" are defined as strengths that are deeply characteristic of you. Seligman defines the "good life" as "using your signature strengths to obtain abundant gratification in the main

realms of your life." A "meaningful life" he defines as "using your signature strengths and virtues in service of something much larger
than yourself."

Mihaly Csikszentmihalyi is the author of *Good Business* and
creator of the term *flow* used in sports and other performances. He
states that in "creating oneself, it makes sense to build on one's
strength." People who are blessed with a particular gift will typically
pursue what comes easily to them.

Dan Sullivan coaches thousands of executives to focus on their
"unique abilities" and delegate as much as possible the areas they
are not good at.

Finally, Marcus Buckingham, who for years worked at Gallup,
describes in his new book, *The One Thing You Need to Know*, the
difference between good and great management. "Great managers
turn a person's talent into performance." He states that the three
things you must know about a person to manage him or her effectively are strengths and weaknesses, triggers, and his or her unique
style of learning. Buckingham sums it up well:

> I've found that while there are many styles of managers,
> there is one quality that sets truly great managers apart
> from the rest: They discover what is unique about each
> person and then capitalize on it. Average managers play
> checkers, while great managers play chess. The difference?
> In checkers, all the pieces are uniform and move in the
> same way; they are interchangeable. You need to plan and
> coordinate their movements, certainly, but they all move at
> the same pace, on parallel paths. In chess, each type of
> piece moves in a different way, and you can't play if you
> don't know how each piece moves. More important, you won't
> win if you don't think carefully about how you move the
> pieces. Great managers know and value the unique abilities
> and even the eccentricities of their employees, and they
> learn how best to integrate them into a coordinated plan of

> *Average managers play checkers, while great managers play chess.*

attack...Average managers treat all their employees the same. Great managers discover each individual's unique talents and bring these to the surface so everyone wins.[70]

Identifying your strengths and the strengths of the people you are developing is the *first step* in improving Emotional Intelligence. The *second step* is developing your plan. In your plan the first action is to determine how can you stretch, redeploy, or build on your strengths. The next step is to identify "fatal flaws" that could derail you if not attended to.

The EI Star Profile below can be used to clarify these strengths and to develop a plan to focus more on your strengths. Using 360-degree feedback, which many organizations do, can also help you identify your strengths so that you can understand how others perceive you. Aside from the ECI administered by the Hay Group, www.haygroup.com, you can use the Emotional Quotient Inventory (EQi) and the EQi 360 from Mental Health Systems, www.mhs.com, or the Emotional Intelligence Appraisal from Talent Smart at www.talentsmart.com to identify your Emotional Intelligence skills. See the Resources section for more information about these programs and others.

MICRO-INITIATIVES: D.O.D. OF GREAT LEADERSHIP

Discovering the "degree of difference" (D.O.D.) between good and great leadership has been the focus of many writers. Goleman, Boyatzis, and the Hay Group use the term *tipping point* to describe the behaviors that tip or move a performer into the top 10%. Using your strengths more in a disciplined fashion is the first strategy to improve performance.

In working with organizations and executives, I have found the D.O.D. is made up of doing many small things regularly. I call these "micro-initiatives." They don't take a lot of time but are crucial habits for great leaders. The average or good leaders could do them but don't, as they are often neglected and given lower priority. Zenger and Folkman found that doing five things really well put a leader in the top 10%.[71] Micro-initiatives make a macro impact. Or:

MI = MI

In cycling races or track meets the difference between the winners and the placers can be fractions of a second. Great leaders have a series of actions that separate them from the pack that take as little as 10 seconds and as long as 45 minutes to a few hours. They make the time to do these "micro-initiatives" to foster development for themselves and others. When I coach executives, I often talk about just how long these actions take because the first response of a busy leader is "I just don't have time." When we are talking about just how little time it actually takes to do these micro-initiatives, they usually agree that time isn't the real issue. What is required is commitment and discipline.

Great leaders have a series of actions that separate them from the pack...

Below are a few examples of the "degree of difference" in time and action that separates the great leader from the good leader:

Average to good leader gives feedback:

"Mary, thanks for getting the report to me."

Time = 3 seconds

Great leader gives feedback:

"Mary, terrific job on the report BECAUSE it was well-written. I appreciate you checking in with me during the process. I liked how you collaborated with others on it. It will make us and you look great in the customers' eyes, thanks."

Time = 12 seconds

Average to good leader on relationships:

Works in his or her office on a project and then takes a break. On the way to the bathroom, nods at a few people and walks past some without even looking. Heads right back to the computer.

Time = 2 minutes each time

Great leader on relationships:

Takes a break and stops at several people's cubicles to check on how they are doing. Asks about the projects they are working on and inquires about any issues or challenges they are having. The leader then asks, using the person's name, how his or her sick spouse is doing and thanks the person for volunteering for a new task. At other times during the day the leader connects in a similar way.

Time = 5 minutes each time

Average to good leader with a poor performance issue:

John is not performing as I would like him to. "John, let's make sure you do everything to get this right."

Time = 2 seconds

Great leader with a poor performance issue:

John is not performing as I would like him to. "John, let's spend time going over the next assignment together. You haven't been performing like I know you can and I want to help. You have always met expectations, so tell me what is going on here. I'm sure we can come up with a plan that will make a difference to you. When can we meet?"

Time = 18 seconds

Average to good leader on self-management:

Thinking to self: "I'd better work through lunch because I am behind and can catch up if I eat at my computer."

Time recharging = 4 minutes

Great leader on self-management:

Thinking to self: "I am feeling tired and need to recharge. Going to lunch will help keep things in perspective and I will come back refreshed and better able to deal with these next challenges."

Time recharging = 45-60 minutes

Average to good leader on managing up with the boss:

Thinking to self: "I am not sure what she thinks of me or how I am doing. I know she is very busy and probably doesn't need another interruption. I'll stay away unless she needs something from me."

Time with boss = 15 minutes informally through the week

Great leader on managing up with the boss:

Thinking to self: "I am not sure what she thinks of me or how I am doing. I will schedule some time with her and clarify expectations and make sure I am doing what she wants. It will also give me some visibility on my projects. Scheduling a weekly check-in is something that will help me. I will take the initiative to create the agenda and keep the meeting focused. I will also update her on my projects with an email status if that will help her."

Time with boss = 30 minutes weekly

Time creating email summary = 25 minutes

If you are not doing these micro-initiatives, these examples can help get you started. Add actions that will move you closer to your goals. As you can see, none of these actions are especially demanding or challenging. When done as a part of an overall leadership strategy, these micro-initiatives add up to a winning difference. Stars make a habit of doing what the average performer is uncomfortable doing.

> *Stars make a habit of doing what the average performer is uncomfortable doing.*

For many leaders a few actions will be the "degree of difference" that transforms them into Stars. I like to tell leaders that they are more than likely 85% there already. We are looking for these few actions that will push them into the 90th and above percentile. Knowing these small but crucial moves are a mere 5-7% change of habit that will put them in the top 10% makes the process seem easier and builds motivation to act and incorporate these micro-initiatives into their lives.

As you assess your Emotional Intelligence, determine what micro-initiatives you can implement to help move you into the top 10%.

Choose one or two actions from the Star Profile and *Coach's Corner* to incorporate and leap from average to Star Performance.

COACH'S CORNER ON ASSESSMENTS

This is an opportunity to rate yourself on the key characteristics of being a Star and also to see if there is any evidence of derailers. We all want to know how we measure up on key aspects of success, but you may be apprehensive about assessing yourself. Benjamin Franklin said, "There are three things extremely hard: steel, a diamond, and to know one's self." A few tips on taking these assessments:

- These assessments are strictly for your development and you don't have to share the results with anyone. The goal is to identify a few actions that will help in your development. This may mean doing even more of what you do well.

- Be honest with yourself and try not to censor your answers. "There is always a trade-off between how you want to feel and what you want to know."[72]

- Give yourself credit for what you are good at it. Sometimes people under-evaluate themselves on items.

- In filling out these assessments on direct reports, again, be as honest and accurate as you can. This will give you specific information on ways that can assist them on their development.

TAKING THE EI STAR PROFILE ASSESSMENT

You now have the opportunity to see how you rate on these EI competencies. Below are the steps you will take:

First, you will rate how important the competency is for your position or work. A "1" signifies it is a must, a "2" signifies it is important but not a must, and a "3" means it is not necessary in your position. This step helps you examine the competencies in more depth to give you a working knowledge to do the ranking.

Next, you will rate how frequently you do certain behaviors. These are behaviors Stars do regularly. To be a Star, you must do the behavior 80% of the time. Think of this as something you do most of the time. An "8" would be doing the behavior 80% of the time. Doing the behavior 50% of the time would be a rating of "5."

You will also have a chance to rate a direct report on the competencies. Choose a person you are developing to be a successor or someone you feel challenged by.

EI STAR PROFILE*

Below is a list of key competencies and behaviors of Star Performers.

- First, rate the IMPORTANCE of each element. A "1" signifies it is a must for you to be a Star, a "2" signifies it is important but not a must, and a "3" means it is not necessary in your position.

- Rate yourself on how frequently you do each of these behaviors. Remember, to be a Star you must do the behavior **regularly, or 80% of the time.** That would be an "8" for the rating. Doing the behavior 50% of the time would be a "5" rating.

- Finally, go through the assessment just as you did for yourself and rate a direct report.

COMPETENCY	IMPORTANCE	SELF	DR
SELF-AWARENESS	**SELF / DR**	**1-10**	**1-10**
1. Emotional Self-Awareness: Recognizes feelings and how feelings affect him-/herself and his/her job performance			
2. Accurate Self-Assessment: Recognizes strengths and shortcomings and focuses on how to improve			
3. Confidence: Presents in an assured, forceful, impressive, and unhesitating manner			
SELF-MANAGEMENT			
4. Emotional Self-Control: Stays calm, unflappable, and clear-headed in high-stress situations			
5. Trustworthiness: Openly admits faults or mistakes and confronts unethical behavior			
6. Adaptability: Is comfortable with ambiguities and adapts to new challenges			
7. Conscientiousness: Takes personal responsibility to make sure that tasks are completed			
8. Achievement Orientation: Works through obstacles and takes risks to meet his/her challenging goals to continually improve			
9. Initiative: Seizes or creates opportunities for the future			

COMPETENCY	IMPORTANCE	SELF	DR
SOCIAL AWARENESS			
10. Empathy: Understands others' perspectives; is open to diversity			
11. Organizational Awareness: Understands the political forces and unspoken rules at work			
12. Service Orientation: Is proactive about customer satisfaction and addresses underlying needs			
RELATIONSHIP MANAGEMENT			
13. Developing Others: Gives timely and constructive feedback; mentors			
14. Inspirational Leadership: Communicates a compelling vision; inspires others to follow			
15. Influence: Finds the right appeal to build buy-in; develops a network of influential parties			
16. Change Catalyst: Leads change efforts and champions the new initiative			
17. Communication: Effective give-and-take with others; continually fine tunes his/her delivery			
18. Building Bonds: Builds strong networks and uses them for answers and support			
19. Conflict Management: Understands all sides and finds common ideals to endorse			
20. Teamwork and Collaboration: Is encouraging and draws others into an active commitment for the collective effort			

NUMBER OF STARS RATED "8" AND OVER

CLUSTER	SELF	DR
Self-Awareness		
Self-Management		
Social Awareness		
Relationship Management		
TOTAL		

*Adapted from Goleman, D., Boyatzis, R. and McKee, A. *Primal Leadership: Realizing the Power of Emotional Intelligence.* Boston, MA: Harvard Business School Press, 2002.

ARE YOU OR YOUR BOSS DEBILITATING?

Unless you are the CEO, you have a boss. Even CEOs have a board to report to. What kind of boss are you to your direct reports? Would anyone call you Debilitating? In learning how to be a great leader, it helps to know what bad leaders do so you can avoid those behaviors. The Derailer Detector assessment follows this section so you can determine if any Debilitating behavior plagues you or someone you know.

James is an Information Technology consultant. His boss is a poor communicator. When James's boss gives James a task, he rarely expresses his expectations. At the end of a project, the boss would inevitably announce that the work was not up to par and would be overly critical. Then he'd demand that James put in extra time to fix the problem. James, of course, was rarely aware of what the problem actually was. This kind of crazy-making leadership has profound and negative impacts. Not surprisingly, James: 1) was angry with his boss and had lost all respect he might once have had for him, 2) had lost valuable personal time and resented that kind of abuse, and 3) didn't want to do his best work for his boss because he figured he would be criticized no matter what he did. James was zapped of his productive energy and emotionally deflated in his job because of the behavior of his Debilitating Boss.

WHAT IS A DEBILITATING BOSS?

A Debilitating Boss is a boss who makes his or her employees feel ineffective, inadequate, weak, lacking confidence, confused, and generally under-performing. Often unknowingly, these bosses suck the passion, soul, and energy right out of you by being negative, critical, and confusing. Instead of using your creativity and effort for superior performance, you ruminate about the injustices and unfair treatment at the hands of your boss. These stories of grievances, inequity, and negative emotions spread, expand, and lead to a toxic environment. Any commitment, dedication, or loyalty is wiped out by the Debilitating Boss.

In a study, 40% of employees who rated their bosses as poor said they were likely to leave.[73] Clearly, Debilitating Bosses leave a trail of disheartened, disgruntled, and disengaged workers behind them.

DISENGAGED WORKERS AND THEIR COSTS

The number one reason most Americans leave their jobs is they don't feel appreciated at work, predominantly by their bosses. The Saratoga Institute reports that 50% of work-life satisfaction is determined by the relationships workers have with their bosses.[74] In a survey of 4 million workers, the Gallup Poll found that 65% of Americans received absolutely no recognition for good work in their last year. The poll also found that 55% are not engaged (i.e., are just putting in time) and 19% of workers are actively disengaged (i.e., unhappy and spreading their discontent or being Debilitating to others). That totals approximately 22 million workers who are: 1) less productive and loyal, 2) more stressed-out, 3) missing more days of work, and 4) less satisfied with their personal lives. The cost to the United States is about $370 billion annually in economic performance.[75] This is an underestimation because it doesn't take into account absences, illness, and other problems that result from disengagement and bad leadership.[76]

WHAT EMPLOYEES WANT

Beverly Kaye and Sharon Jordon-Evans in their 2004 Retention and Engagement Drivers Report had 7,665 respondents. They found the top reasons people stay on the job were:

- Exciting work and challenge = 48.4% of respondents
- Career growth, learning, and development = 42.6% of respondents
- Working with great people and relationships = 41.8% of respondents

POWER OF LEADERSHIP

The Philadelphia-based Hay Group has studied leadership and its effect on the work climate. They evaluated a number of components:

- How clear is the vision of the leadership?
- What are their standards?
- What is expected of the team?
- What is the type and amount of responsibility employees can handle?
- How flexible are they in getting things done?
- What kind of teamwork, pride, and collaboration do they have?

They found that:

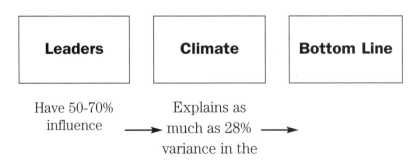

Hay Group, 2003

In some cases, where the team is small or the leader is very influential, the leader may have a 90% influence over the climate of the team or organization. That is why your relationship with your boss is one of the biggest factors in whether you leave your job or get a promotion.

Good bosses raise the "discretionary effort" of the team. Discretionary effort is the dedication, loyalty, and amount of effort put into a project or assignment.[77] Most employees fail to put in 100% on everything. But if you have a good boss, you usually want to please and do a good job for him or her, and usually you will put more into your assignment. You will check your work more often, ask the advice of others, and think about ways to work smarter. If the effort is discretionary, you put more into it than an employee with a bad or average boss. Small increases in discretionary effort, even 5-10%, can increase productivity and change good performers into great performers.

THE SOLUTION: IF YOU OR YOUR BOSS ARE DEBILITATING

There is an inoculation that can protect you from the contagion of the Debilitating Boss. You have your Emotional Intelligence competencies to build up, strengthen, and repel their impact on you, such as:

- Managing your impulses and inoculating yourself from your boss
- Communication and conflict resolution skills to interact with your boss in an effective way, to attenuate his or her impact on you, and to feel you stood up for yourself
- Confidence to prevent your boss from getting under your skin
- Achievement orientation to find ways to get your goals accomplished in spite of a Debilitating Boss
- Teamwork and building bonds skills to get others to support you and help in achieving the completion of projects

- Initiative to find yourself another job if you are unable to find your desire and motivation again in this problematic relationship
- If you are a Debilitating Boss, read on; *Leaders' Playbook* will equip you with some of the basic tools to counter the dark side.

TAKING THE DERAILER DETECTOR

Take the Derailer Detector test to see if you or a direct report are at risk for any of the key derailers mentioned. This is based on how frequently these derailer behaviors are observable to you.

The Star Performer Action Plan will assist you in developing a plan for focusing on these derailers.

THE DERAILER DETECTOR*

Rank yourself and a direct report (DR) honestly on these behaviors.

    1 = Almost never happens

    2 = Happens once every three months

    3 = Happens once a month or more often

YOU		DR

1. **"Smartest person in the room" syndrome:** Has to be right all the time, married to own ideas, and not open to or distrusting of new ideas

2. **Lack of impulse control:** Emotionally reactive, volatile, abrasive, and follows urges to an unhealthy extreme

3. **Drives others too hard:** Micromanages and takes over rather than delegates

4. **Perfectionism:** Sets unrealistic goals; rejects criticism

5. **Defensive:** Blames others; is inflexible and argumentative

6. **Risk averse:** Lacks courage to take risks

7. **Failure to learn from mistakes:** Same kind of mistakes show up

8. **Lacks insight into others:** Can't read others' emotions or reactions

9. **Doesn't ask for feedback:** Misses opportunities to include others for better decisions

10. **Self-promotion:** Is attention-seeking; overlooks others' accomplishments for own recognition

11. **Lack of integrity:** "Unhonest" with self and then others; omits and minimizes

12. **Failure to adapt to cultural differences:** Does not change leadership style appropriately

13. **Indirect with others:** Does not give the hard feedback or make the difficult decisions about people

14. **Approval dependent:** Needs too much approval before making decisions

15. **Eccentricity:** Unpredictable and odd in behavior

	16. **Mistreats others:** Callous, demeaning, or discounting to others and their needs	
	17. **Self-interest:** Acts in self-interest instead of the interest of the whole organization or larger group	
	18. **Insular:** Disregards health and welfare of group outside the responsibility of own organization or team	

Count up your number of 2's and 3's

SELF	**DIRECT REPORT**
2's =	2's =
3's =	3's =

Three or more 2's = Warning signs for derailers

Two or more 3's = At risk to you and the organization!

Now what? If you score or your direct report scores in the "warning" or "at-risk" level, make sure you read and study the next sections. Many suggestions and practices will be helpful in keeping you or your employee on track and more effective.

*Adapted from Leslie and Van Velsor (1996), Byram, Smith and Paese, *Grow Your Own Leaders* (2002); Kaplan *Beyond Ambition* (1991); Dotlich and Cairo, *Why CEOs Fail* (2002); Kellerrman *Bad Leadership* (2004); and Lipman-Blumen *The Allure of Toxic Leadership* (2005).

STRATEGIC USE OF STRENGTHS

How can you use your strengths more strategically? First, look to see if there are some obvious ways your strengths can be used or applied to help beef up some important competencies. Zenger and Folkman use the term *competency companions* to describe how one competency can enhance another.[78]

Leaders who scored in the top 10% on the differentiating behavior also tended to score very high on these supportive behaviors. We have called these supporting behaviors 'competency companions' or…'behavioral buddies.'[79]

They list mechanisms that best explain the competency companion phenomenon:

1. Competency companions facilitate the expression of their competencies.
2. Achieving excellence in one behavior helps develop a related behavior.
3. One competency is a building block or main element for another competency.
4. Developing a competency companion can change the skill level of a leader.[80]

Below are a few examples of how you can utilize your strengths to support other areas. I've often seen leaders who have great skills in one area but are blind to using the same skills in a new arena. These examples will help you think about how to stretch your strengths. These groupings have not been statistically established. Each position in an organization may require mastery in some competencies over other ones. You will still need to be skilled in what tools to use in these situations, and *Leaders' Playbook* will provide you with the answers.

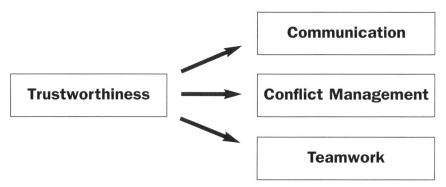

Having high trust from others gives you the equity to communicate more directly with others, especially if there is conflict. There is

an effective give-and-take. You will be given the "benefit of the doubt." Your team will better follow your leadership when they trust you.

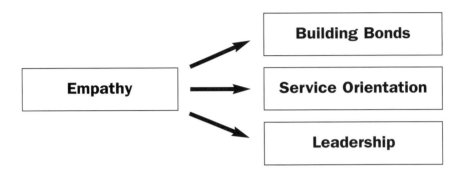

Empathy skills will help in building relationships, whether it is with internal or external customers or with peers or stakeholders. When people feel you understand and care for them as individuals they will also become more committed to you and your vision as a person or leader.

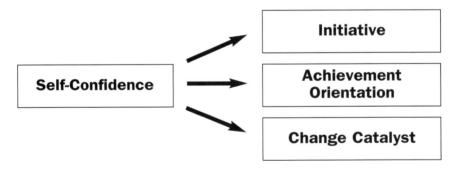

Self-confidence is important for going after and achieving your goals. Taking risks and actions for the future, anticipating obstacles, and personally leading change are all enhanced when you are confident. Self-efficacy is a strong predictor of your ability to set high goals, persist in the face of obstacles, be resistant to setbacks, and achieve the goals you set.[81]

STAR PERFORMER ACTION PLAN

Read through the EI Star Profile, the Derailer Detector, and Strategic Use of Strengths and answer the following questions to help you develop your Star Performer Action Plan.

Remember, you only need to do a few things better to go from good to great. Start with what you are already good at. Micro-initiatives can make a macro impact.

Which competencies do you currently perform as a Star Performer that you would like to improve even more?

1. _____
2. _____
3. _____

Are there any critical derailers you identified? If so, what are they?

1. _____
2. _____
3. _____

How would you bring these strengths into your development areas?

1. _____
2. _____
3. _____

What resources do you need to make this happen (e.g., training, feedback from your boss or direct reports, etc.)?

1. _____
2. _____
3. _____

Who can support you and hold you accountable?

    1. _____

    2. _____

    3. _____

What can they do to support you (i.e., specific actions)?

    1. _____

    2. _____

    3. _____

How might you sabotage your efforts and best intentions?

    1. _____

    2. _____

    3. _____

What will be your first steps in this plan?

    1. _____

    2. _____

    3. _____

Share this plan with your support people. Good luck!

CHAPTER TWO

SELF-CONFIDENCE
TOOLS AND STRATEGIES

Confidence is the fuel that ignites other actions.

T his section provides the tools and strategies to help you become a Star Performer in the area of confidence. *Self-confidence* is a building block for success throughout one's career and a key competency in the self-awareness cluster. A definition of *confidence* is illustrated with a research example about confidence-building, followed by a Star Profile of Henrik Fisker, one of the world's leading car designers. Fisker shares *10 Secrets & Current Practices* that help him shine as a confident Star Performer. He also describes some of the pitfalls he encounters from actually being overly confident!

The *Coach's Corner* adds to what you've just learned with a selection of 10 powerful proven strategies used by a cross section of top-notch executives and leaders for the development of confidence. Included are practical tools and a Star Performer Action Plan that will help you transform general ideas and concepts into tangible applications for guaranteed performance as a confident Star Performer.

WHAT IS THE SELF-CONFIDENCE COMPETENCY?

Confidence is knowing one's own abilities and having enough faith in them to make sound decisions in the face of uncertainty and pressure. A confident leader exudes a strong self-presentation and expresses him- or herself in an assured, impressive, and unhesitating manner. The confident leader will take on new challenges and hold on to his or her view, even if others disagree.[1]

EMOTIONAL INTELLIGENCE RESEARCH EXAMPLES

A variety of studies have demonstrated the positive impact of confidence on performance. A high degree of self-confidence distinguishes the best from the average performers as supervisors, managers, and executives.[2] Self-efficacy is a form of self-confidence; it is a belief in one's own abilities to take on a difficult challenge.

In a study of 112 entry-level accountants, those with the highest level of self-efficacy at the time of hiring were rated as having superior job performance by their supervisors 10 months later, showing that self-confidence is a higher predictor of performance than is skill level or previous training.[3] In another study, where more than 1,000 high-IQ men and women were tracked over 60 years, from childhood to retirement, those who possessed self-confidence during their early years were most successful in their later careers.[4] In a longitudinal study of managers at AT&T, the expression of self-confidence early in one's career also predicted promotions and success in higher management years later.[5]

ARE YOU A STAR PERFORMER IN SELF-CONFIDENCE OR JUST AVERAGE?

Stars exhibit both average and Star behaviors consistently. Where are you?

AVERAGE

- Acts independently
- Is confident in his/her own ability
- Exhibits decisiveness

STAR

- Presents in an assured, forceful, impressive, and unhesitating manner
- Takes on challenges willingly[6]

STAR PROFILE: HENRIK FISKER, CEO FISKER COACHBUILD, LLC

WHY HENRIK FISKER IS A STAR PERFORMER

Henrik Fisker is the CEO of the new luxury car company Fisker Coachbuild, LLC. After a successful career designing cars for major car manufacturers, he chose to start his own company, with a focus on designing and producing exclusive, high-end sports cars.

Fisker was Director of Ford's Global Design Studio in Irvine, California. He also served as Director of Design for the Aston Martin division at Ford Motors Company and, from September 2001 to August 2003, as Creative Director of Ingeni Design Company. Ingeni is a design studio in London that designs the merchandizing products for Land Rover, Jaguar, Aston Martin, Volvo, Mazda, Lincoln, and Mercury. In the first six months, Fisker took Ingeni from a start-up business to millions in revenue, working with employees from 15 different cultures. He was also responsible for the design and success of the $155,000 Aston Martin DB-9, the car that won the Robb Report "Best of the Best" award in 2005. Fisker also designed the show car and upcoming production car of the long-awaited Aston Martin AM-V8 Vantage.

Before being recruited by Ford, Fisker served as the president of Designworks USA, a division of BMW, where he achieved a 400% profit increase in his first year. He was the designer of BMW's limited edition Z-8 (only 400 were produced), one of the world's most sought-after vehicles that retailed close to $200,000. The car was featured in the James Bond movie *The World Is Not Enough*, was named "Car of the Year" in 2000 by the Robb Report, and won the prestigious Red Dot Award in Germany.

FISKER WAS ASKED:

- How did he learn this confidence competency?
- What does he do to be such an effective leader?

- What are his daily practices?
- What are the pitfalls he needs to be aware of?

EARLY LEARNING EXPERIENCES

Fisker stated, "I have always been good at leading people." He recalled a learning experience when he was 13 and engaged in an orienteering course to find a treasure: A group of boys were walking in the forest, and after looking at the map Fisker decided they needed to go to the right. The assigned leader and all the other boys said, no, they had to go left. Eighteen boys went to the left, whereas Fisker and one other boy went to the right and ended up finding the treasure. However, because they had split up his group didn't win, and Fisker got in trouble for leaving his team. One insight Fisker learned from this experience was to follow his convictions in spite of opposition from others. Another powerful result was learning that leaders can be decisive, but they need followers in order to be truly successful.

In his first four months as a designer at BMW, Fisker was working on a car interior with a senior designer, who asked him, "Do you want to take over this project?" Fisker had a feeling he could do it and said, "Yes," confidently, even though he didn't have a lot of experience. He saw that each time he took a risk it added to his confidence.

A role model for Fisker early in his career was Dr. Reitzle, the Development Chief of BMW, who made big decisions for the direction of the company in a very firm manner. "I saw a leader make a firm decision and the domino effect was positive. There was a wave of optimism transmitted down throughout the company." He saw that being decisive was a trait that was admired and was something he emulated.

10 SECRETS & CURRENT PRACTICES OF HENRIK FISKER—STAR PERFORMER

Read through the strategies and pick one or two to try out.

1. TAKE PRIVATE TIME

Fisker takes an hour and a half at lunchtime to work out and think through problems. He states that this dedicated period is "a hundred times more valuable than staying at work" where interruptions are the norm. He plays things over and over in his mind and explores many different scenarios and solutions. This is when Fisker gets a "feeling" for what he wants to do.

2. GET THIRD OPINIONS

Fisker believes in getting different opinions in order to have more information on certain issues. He knows what he thinks, but listens to other people's viewpoints for opinions and perspectives on the issue at hand. Fisker uses his networking skills to acquire multiple perspectives from many different sources.

3. EVALUATE CAPACITIES

Fisker evaluates the strengths and weaknesses of his team during his private time and gets a good feeling for what they can and cannot do. This allows him to gauge their window of capacity, builds trust, and helps him determine what challenges and risks he wants to present and to whom. When his team comes to him for a decision, Fisker has already evaluated what sorts of capabilities they possess and ultimately empowers them as he assigns his tasks.

4. SHOOT FROM THE HIP

Fisker prefers quick, firm, and empowering decisions. He also understands that most people don't like being managed and wants them to feel they are following their own motivation. The perception is that he makes these decisions because of blind trust. The person feels the motivation to work hard in order to demonstrate that he or she deserves that trust. Fisker captures the drama of the moment by seizing the decision-making power rather than waiting and thinking it over, which becomes anticlimactic and less empowering.

He likes to say, "Yes, go make it happen," knowing full well the positive effect this kind of response delivers. While his decisions may appear as "shooting from the hip," this is actually not the case at all. It is a much more calculated system, because of the time Fisker dedicates to Secrets #1, #2, and #3. His quick decisions are well-timed and create an optimum of emotional energy for his team.

5. GO WITH THAT GUT FEELING

Fisker takes pride in "going with his gut." For a designer, the look and feel of a car are more emotional than logical and, many times, beyond what we can put into words. Throughout his career he has depended on developing this visceral skill. Like many executives, Fisker has refined this ability, which allows him to make quick decisions when he needs to.

Cars make us feel a certain way, and this feeling comes from the amygdala, that small walnut-shaped area in the center of the brain. "Every experience we have an emotional reaction to, no matter how subtle, seems to be encoded in the amygdala."[7] There are nerve pathways that run from the amygdala to the internal organs, and thus the "gut feeling" comes from the brain.

6. TAKE INITIATIVE

Fisker believes in putting his "gut feeling" into practice and making decisions from it. After getting the "gut feeling," he assesses the risks and goes for it if appropriate. He feels this is an important part of being a leader. Fisker actualizes what leadership guru Warren Bennis, in his portrait of leadership traits, called "a bias toward action."[8] Fisker wants to take action and likes that quality in his direct reports. Taking initiative is the hallmark of a Star Performer in the confidence competency.

7. IDENTIFY YOUR STRENGTHS AND WEAKNESSES

Fisker believes that leaders should be aware of their "weak side." He defines this as "things you could do, but don't like to do."

Preferring to generate power from his strengths, he chooses to have others assume the tasks he likes the least so that he can focus on what he is good at. He knows that when he does what he likes, he remains energized, creative, and competent.

8. TAKE RESPONSIBILITY FOR YOUR MISTAKES

Fisker believes you have to be honest with yourself and admit mistakes, so you can learn and move on. He tells the story of getting a ticket for going 112 mph in London, where any speed over 70 means the loss of your license. Aston Martin wanted to hire a lawyer for him, but Fisker decided to represent himself before the judge. Fisker admitted he had made a mistake and confessed that he was speeding because he was simply too busy. He added that he had already altered his schedule to fewer appointments as a way to admit his initiative to change. He took responsibility for the ticket, stated what he had learned, and was allowed to keep his license after paying a small fine.

9. REINFORCE PEOPLE

Fisker believes it is important to read your people and keep them motivated. He does this by being genuinely engaging with them, by asking questions to find out more about how they think and what they do. Fisker then acknowledges and supports their efforts.

10. BE WILLING TO MAKE DECISIONS THAT ARE EXCEPTIONS TO THE RULE

Fisker states that a leader needs to identify the consequences of a decision, decide if it is worth it, and then act on it. Many of his examples focus on paying less attention to time-consuming bureaucratic procedures. If he feels it is the right decision and that he can cope with the consequences, he goes ahead without all of the red tape. Fisker counts on being successful and believes that not following procedures all of the time is minor compared to the potential successes of his decisions to take action.

PITFALLS: WHAT FISKER NEEDS TO BE AWARE OF

- For Fisker, there is the danger of overusing his self-confidence. Fisker admits he can overpower people with it and adds, "You have to use your confidence appropriately and be able to back off strategically where there is the least impact and let things go." He is sensitive to not overruling people if at all possible.

- It is important for Fisker to know his audience and encourage them to have their area of expertise. It is also important that he invite his team to openly ask questions.

- Fisker needs to remember to pace his decisions and actions, never assuming that he is on the same mindset or wavelength as others. He admits that he "wants to keep people in sight" and not leave them behind.

- If Fisker feels he is putting out a lot of fires, he knows he is losing touch with the organization. There needs to be an infrastructure through which he can quickly get information and slow down his speed if necessary. Feedback from the management team is crucial.

ACTIONS: REVIEW FISKER'S CURRENT PRACTICES

Look at what you have checked. What practices can you glean from Fisker's story and employ in order to be a Star Performer in Confidence? Which ones do you want to add to your Star Performer Action Plan?

1. _____
2. _____
3. _____

THE COACH'S CORNER: 10 STRATEGIES FOR SELF-CONFIDENCE

Below are 10 proven strategies you can use to improve your confidence. Confidence is the fuel to take risks, try new things, and make the micro-initiatives necessary to become a Star. As you read through the list, be aware of what you are already doing and what actions you could do more of.

Read through the strategies and pick one or two to try out.

1. BEING ON YOUR CASE VS. BEING ON YOUR SIDE

Many leaders have "faulty evaluation systems." They are rarely satisfied when successful and are overly critical of their performance even if they win and win big. This can become a rigid pattern. In the past it may have driven them to great successes, but over time it can become a burden. They tend to continually try harder and often fall short in their own eyes, often sense that they are torturing themselves, and still fall short in their own eyes. These leaders will readily admit that they are hard on themselves, but they believe it is the only way to push themselves to their best performances. It is as if they have a calculator that is defective, but they do not realize it is always off one digit. When evaluating themselves, the calculator should read 1,000, but instead it reads 100. They get upset about the reading, but don't realize their evaluation system is faulty or broken.

...they have a calculator that is defective, but they do not realize it is always off one digit.

There are three major unintended consequences of Being on Your Case rather than Being on Your Side:

- These leaders are never satisfied with their performance, and their self-confidence is affected.
- Because everything seems to be less than they had hoped, they are miserable, tense, and unhappy.
- Unconsciously they treat others the same way they treat themselves—overly critical, picky, negative, and never satisfied.

Most leaders who are hard on themselves are blinded to the problems inherent in their leadership style. Sometimes they require strong language (!) to alert them to the serious impact this kind of pattern has on their ultimate performance and well-being. If you recognize yourself in the above profile, answer a simple question: What percentage of the time are you on your case instead of on your side? Use a scale of 1-100. You can tell if you or others have a faulty evaluation system if after every performance you establish that you should have had:

- Better effort
- Higher quality
- Faster delivery

The manifestation of this kind of attitude is typically feeling scolded by yourself for failing to live up to your abilities. It's almost like you take out your whip and begin snapping yourself into shape. You may even say or think: "How could I be so stupid? When am I going to finally learn? What is wrong with me?" More, better, faster, more, better, faster…becomes an automatic negative self-evaluation system.

ANDREA'S STORY

Andrea was an executive in an agency and constantly felt she was behind in everything she was doing—emails went unanswered, voicemails were not returned, one-on-ones with staff were cancelled or rescheduled. Her evaluation system was harsh and unforgiving in spite of many of the positive things she was initiating at the agency. Andrea often spent her first moments with an employee apologizing for something she had failed to get around to. Her confidence was affected and her negative self-evaluation started to influence others. Perhaps she wasn't as competent as they had thought she was?

In one of our coaching sessions, Andrea achieved a breakthrough when I pointed out that she had apologized three times in 30 minutes.

It was obvious she was overly critical of herself. She became painfully aware of how automatic this evaluation system was and, more importantly, recognized that it was quite possibly inaccurate. Andrea also became aware of how pervasive this pattern was in all of her interactions and that it undermined her leadership abilities as well.

Andrea started out saying she was on her own case 80% of the time. Through talking about this pattern's impact and building awareness, she was able to get it down to about 40%. It was important for her to understand that she was not trying to eliminate Being on Her Case, but rather reframing it into Being on Her Side. With some real commitment and practice, she developed the ability to catch the pattern faster and redirect it from Being on Her Case to Being on Her Side.

Changing our self-evaluation greatly improves how confident we feel and allows us greater awareness of how we evaluate others.

Andrea became more On Her Side and, as a result, was less demanding of her staff and more on their side as well. She even encouraged her staff to be more realistic about the amount of tasks they were handling and to cut back on their commitments. In order to help her track this pattern, in each successive meeting I would ask what percentage of the time she was Being on Her Case versus Being on Her Side.

Changing our self-evaluation greatly improves how confident we feel and allows us greater awareness of how we evaluate others.

REDIRECTING QUESTIONS

The best way to change from Being on Your Case to Being on Your Side is first to notice how you behave and then turn the evaluation into a learning and action plan. Following are some examples of whipping statements and statements that will help you redirect yourself to Being on Your Side.

"On Your Case" Whipping

- How could I be so lame?
- Don't I know better than this?
- I'm an idiot for doing this!
- Why didn't I start this sooner?
- I could have done a much better job!
- What is wrong with me?
- I should have known better!

"On Your Side" (Phrases that redirect your habit)

- Which parts of this performance went well?
- What didn't turn out the way I wanted it to?
- What exactly didn't work out here?
- Which part is under my influence?
- Is there anything I could have done differently?
- What will I have to do to accept this performance and not beat myself up?
- What can I learn from this performance?
- What will I have to improve next time?
- Is there any learning, training, or help I need to improve my performance?
- What will be my next step?
- How will I make sure I stay on track?

Notice the quality of the statements above and their effect on you. It is important to first acknowledge what went well, in order to establish the proper perspective in your evaluation and curtail the "more, better, faster" pattern.

The following chart shows the difference between the two types of self-evaluations.

Circle the terms you experienced as a result of your self-evaluation.

	ON YOUR CASE	ON YOUR SIDE
Quality	Demanding	Respectful
	Damaging	Constructive
	Irrational	Rational
	Over-generalized	Realistic
Results	Dissatisfied	Encouraged
	Less confident	Action plan for future
	Overwhelmed	Energized

QUESTIONS AND ACTION APPLICATIONS:

- How accurate is your evaluation system?
- On a scale of 1-100, what percentage of the time are you on your case?
- How do you feel after you've been on your case?
- What are the consequences for you and others for being on your case?
- Do you treat others as harshly as you do yourself?
- Is this an effective pattern for you to continue with?
- If you don't change this, what do you stand to lose or miss out on?
- Keep track of the times you have stopped being on your case and then redirected yourself to being on your side.
- What is most difficult about being on your side?
- What helps you to be on your side?
- Keep track in your planner of the percentage of time you are on your side each day, 1–100.

2. REFLECTIONS ON THINKING

When we reflect on our thinking, we usually ask ourselves a series of questions, such as: What am I going to do about this project? Why is my co-worker so uncooperative? Why did I get passed over at the last promotion?

This is an unconscious process that stimulates the answers. The brain has been compared to a computer, even though it is far more complex. When we ask ourselves a question, our brain runs through its files to bring up an answer on our screen of awareness. We take this answer as a fact and move forward without questioning the process. If we ask ourselves poor or unconstructive questions, we will get answers that are negative and not helpful or proactive.

Part of being more confident is to be awake and aware when you ask yourself internal questions. When you pay more attention, you may notice that the questions often catalyze a cascade of negative responses and a familiar pattern of Being on Your Case. Your questions can "lead the witness" with inferences that a judge wouldn't allow in a court of law. The famous "When did you stop beating your wife?" is an example of getting stuck in a nasty loop. Unfortunately, when we ask ourselves self-deprecating questions we rarely come back with an "objection" to the kind of negative answer that comes up. Nor do we consider the fact that this knee-jerk answer may not be true and is simply a reflection of how we have programmed ourselves in the past.

ARE ANY OF THESE QUESTIONS FAMILIAR?

- Why am I always screwing up?
- How come I'm not good enough?
- How could I be so stupid?
- Why didn't I say something smart at the meeting?
- When will I finally learn?

The brain searches your history and comes up with pat answers such as: "I have always been a slow learner," or "I am not as smart as others," or "I am always making stupid mistakes," or "I'll never get ahead." These programmed responses make you hang your head and lose confidence. It's time to take control of the programming of negative self-talk. Let your brain search its files for a more positive, constructive, and useful answer. The questions and actions below can help you in this process.

QUESTIONS AND ACTION APPLICATIONS:

- Be more aware of the questions you ask yourself. Write them down and collect them over a week.
- Ask your questions out loud. Listen, and then evaluate what you are really asking your brain to search for.
- Are your questions positive or negative?
- What kind of answers are you getting?
- Evaluate the biases in your questions. Are you leading the witness? Are you setting yourself up for failure? Would a judge allow your questions?
- Are you using over-generalized words such as "always" and "never"?
- Using the following five questions will consistently lead to better answers. Think of a situation for reflection. Now use the questions to generate positive confidence-building answers:
  - ▲ What can I learn here?
  - ▲ How can I be more on my side?
  - ▲ What do I feel good about here?
  - ▲ How do I best deal with this situation?
  - ▲ How do I bring all my resources to this issue?

3. BUSTING PERFECTION: CREATING REALISTIC EXPECTATIONS

Success-driven people always set goals for themselves, but often these goals set them up for failure or frustration. Why? Because the goals are unrealistic to start with and constitute a pattern that is a setup for failure. This can lead to Being on Your Case and becoming dissatisfied with performance.

There are three key reasons for this pattern:

- These expectations are made automatically without the benefit of critical thinking.
- Once made, the expectations are no longer examined for their accuracy or realism.
- These unrealistic expectations are adhered to as the Golden Rule and clung to tenaciously.

Striving for perfection, a characteristic which once served as a standard for effort, quality, satisfaction, and acknowledgement, now operates as a carrier of the "more, better, faster" self-evaluation cycle. If left unexamined, perfection changes from a motivating driver to a relentless torturer.

THE PERFECTION LOOP

The Perfection Loop is a behavioral diagram that illustrates this now-familiar debilitating self-evaluation cycle. How much does it reflect your behavior or the behavior of those around you?

This pattern occurs unconsciously, repeatedly, and quickly. Before you know it, you are in it. The goal of identifying this loop is to:

- Become aware of the unproductive pattern
- Understand the steps that cause it and how they influence behavior and performance
- Know what to change to get different results

SIX STAGES OF THE PERFECTION LOOP

1. Perfection as an Expectation

The goals you set are very lofty and made without the benefit of critical thinking or truly examining their feasibility. "Perfection" rationalizes that you need to stretch and push yourself, so you set goals that are extreme, unrealistic, unattainable, and without the slightest margin of error. A thorough assessment of what it takes to reach them is not made, and you are doomed to complete the loop. Most of the time the effort, resources, and training you need to accomplish the goals are not taken into consideration.

In *Pure Genius*, Dan Sullivan talks about the differences between ideals and goals and how we often evaluate ourselves against the ideal and always fall short. He uses the example of the horizon, which, even though we can see it, doesn't really exist. If we chase the horizon, it keeps moving back and we never reach it. Sullivan recommends that we ask ourselves where we have come from and assess our progress in achieving our goal. This evaluation will leave us feeling better about our progress. If perfectionism is not curtailed, it will thrust you into the endless Perfection Loop, which is like being thrown into rapids where the force of the water controls where we go.

2. Stress and Pressure Going into the Task; Procrastination

Extreme expectations influence your state of achieving this goal. Pressure, anxiety, and stress accompany the preparation for the task and can have an impact on the focus and creativity needed to move toward the unattainable goal. On an unconscious level, you know that the task is overwhelming and that you have set yourself up for failure. This only adds to your anxiety. One typical response is procrastination disguised as giving yourself time to get ready. It's going to take all your effort so "planning" is actually worrying, "preparing" is actually avoiding, and "resting" is actually putting off. All of this leads to more procrastination. This stage of the loop compounds your performance even more.

Procrastination's Seduction

SEDUCTION	RESULT
"I better really plan."	Unproductive worry
"I have to carefully prepare."	Avoiding doing anything
"I better rest to ready myself."	Putting off effort
"If I had only had a little more time, I would…"	More worry, less effort

3. Less-Than-Expected Performance

The task is completed, and of course it is not at the level you expected. You could have done more, done a better job, started it sooner, and finished it faster. Repetitive "more, better, faster, more, better, faster" is a sign of a faulty evaluation system.

4. On Your Case, on Others' Cases

Your self-talk has pulled the whipping stick out. It is easy and habitual, and many leaders don't realize that their internal talk turns into the same conversation, but it can show up out loud when you communicate with your direct reports.

- "Why didn't I get this done sooner?" becomes "Why didn't you get it done sooner?"
- "How could I be so stupid?" becomes "What were you thinking?"
- "I am not cutting it and should have done a lot better" becomes "You are not cutting it or meeting my expectations."

Inside your own mind you are usually unaware of how harsh this kind of negative self-talk sounds. When you speak that way to others, your harshness can be very demotivating and detrimental. These automatic responses become who you are to the people you lead and have unintended negative consequences and repercussions.

5. Less Confident About Yourself and Others

There is less self-trust and trust in others as the loop continues and the estimation of success is less likely. Confidence is reduced.

6. Must Do Better Next Time

As a solution for stress and frustration, a leader makes the decision that, next time, "I'll try harder, start sooner, and do better." Now there is another setup put into place for the next task, which will unfortunately generate the same unrealistic expectations…and the loop goes on.

HOW TO COUNTER THE PERFECTION LOOP

To counter the debilitating effects of the Perfection Loop, you have to develop new behaviors early in the first or second steps—before the momentum sucks you in. Small changes at the beginning and throughout will help you break this pattern. To begin, think of a current expectation and answer the following:

- How realistic and attainable are your expectations?
- Do you thoroughly assess your expectations and plan for what it will take to get the task done?
- Rate yourself on a 1-10 scale with 10 representing your most realistic expectation. What is your rating?
- To what degree does perfection run your life or have control over you? Rate yourself from 1-100%.
- What is the first step you need to gain some control?
- Look at the Procrastination's Seduction chart (page 86). Which rationale do you use the most?
- What would be the best counter to the statement, "No, I need to develop a realistic plan and get something started now"?
- Is your evaluation system faulty?
- How is it faulty? (e.g., too rigid, uncompromising, etc.)
- What percentage of the time are you on your case after a performance?
- Refer back to some of the strategies from "Being on Your Case vs. Being on Your Side" on pages 77-81 to redirect your evaluations and self-talk.
- Once you have turned your evaluation into a learning experience, what is your plan for not getting into the Perfection Loop next time?
- How can you get others to support you?
- Who can give you feedback when they see you stuck in the loop?
- How will you know that you are listening?

4. SUCCESS RULES: WHO IS RUNNING YOU?

In this strategy, the objective is to become aware of your rules for being successful. All of us have them, but often they were made a long time ago and are outdated, too rigid, or over-generalized. It is like we have a nine-year-old inside of us who dictates what we should do and how. That is the age when we were becoming more on our own and trying to manage ourselves to get the best results. We made guidelines for ourselves such as:

- "Stay out of trouble."
- "Be polite to others."
- "Don't say anything stupid."
- "Don't make others upset."
- "Don't ever be satisfied."
- "Confidence is bragging."

When you were nine, these guidelines for good performance were probably very effective. Because you were successful, you kept using them. The problem occurs when:

- These guidelines become rules.
- Rules become calcified and are too rigid.
- Rules translate to everything, and you didn't realize how you abstracted them to cover all situations.
- You fail to update these rules to integrate your new learning and resources.

It's like you have an old version of software, let's say AOL 2.0, and are very happy knowing how everything works. It was once the best program available. Now with AOL 9.0 or higher, your email possibilities are far greater. The new version offers more services and is faster and simpler to use. You may hold on to outdated rules or programs without even realizing they are outdated. These unexamined rules leave you feeling unsatisfied and often like a failure. This little nine-year-old sits behind the steering wheel of your life, barely able to see the road, clipping parked cars along the way. How can you change and upgrade?

QUESTIONS AND ACTION APPLICATIONS:

Write down the rules you live by as answers to the following: "What must happen for me to really feel successful?"

Feel free to write as many rules as come to mind.

Here are some sample answers to get you started: "To really feel successful…"

- "I have to be the president of whatever I do."
- "I have to be the smartest in the room."
- "I must earn…"
- "I have to have answers when people ask."
- "I must have the best house, car, etc."
- "I have to control everyone and everything around me."
- "I must feel happy every minute."

Next to each rule you list, write #1, #2, or #3 if true for that particular rule. It's fine to have up to three numbers per rule.

#1 = It is outdated

#2 = It is too rigid

#3 = It is over-generalized

NOW, ANSWER THESE QUESTIONS:

- How many of your success rules are outdated? Too rigid? Over-generalized?
- What is the price for holding on to these rules?
- What is the first step to take in rewriting some of your success rules?
- If you were to refresh this particular rule, how could you make it more helpful and constructive?
- What will be the benefit for you in rewriting your rules?

- How will you know when rewriting these success rules actually makes a tangible difference?

5. SUCCESS LOG

Another strategy to enhance confidence is to write a log of past successes, broken into a chronology by age bracket. We all have had many successes in our life, which are easy to forget or minimize. These successes can leave footprints for future successes. And, you can build your confidence by simply reviewing the list.

ACTION APPLICATIONS:

Think of successes, activities, or events when you were proud of what you accomplished. These are the building blocks for confidence.

Age in Years

0-5

6-10

11-15

16-20

21-25

26-30

31-40

41-50

51-60

61+

Go through your life from the time you were a young child and write down key successes for each age bracket. For example, you had a best friend in kindergarten, you had a lead role in a play in school, you won a Little League baseball game with your pitching, you received an award for a story you wrote in school, you were selected to give an orientation speech to incoming students, you were the editor of your high school yearbook, you were a cheerleader, you had good grades and won an award in college, you were selected team leader in your first job, you presented at a conference, you got an advanced degree, you started your own company, you wrote a book, and so on.

Now analyze your successes by answering these questions:

- What efforts did you make to achieve this success?
- What was your preparation?
- What obstacles did you have to overcome?
- How did you feel about yourself afterward?
- What did people say about your achievement?
- How do you minimize your successes?
- What patterns or themes emerge from reviewing these successes?
- What key best practices or guidelines emerge for use in future endeavors?

6. CURRENT SUCCESS LOG

As an outgrowth of creating your Success Log, keep a current log of daily or weekly successes and achievements.

After a few months, analyze these successes by answering the same set of questions:

- What efforts did you make to achieve this success?
- What was your preparation?
- What obstacles did you have to overcome?
- How did you feel about yourself afterward?
- What did people say about your achievement?
- How do you minimize your successes?
- What patterns or themes emerge from reviewing these successes?
- What key best practices or guidelines emerge for use in future endeavors?

7. THE FIVE PIVOTAL PEOPLE IN YOUR LIFE

A useful tool in building confidence is based on the notion of Phillip McGraw, also known as Dr. Phil, that each of us has five pivotal people in our lives who represent positive forces—people from our history who shaped our sense of self-worth and confidence.

QUESTIONS AND ACTION APPLICATIONS:

Who were these five key people in your life? Write them down and then respond to the following for each key person:

- What capabilities did this person see in you?
- What did he or she say or do to motivate you?
- How did you feel in this person's presence?
- What are the main insights you received from this person?
- What have you internalized from this person?
- What have you rejected or minimized from this person?
- If this person was here today, what would he or she tell you?
- How are you sharing this learning with others today?

8. VISUALIZATION

The power of visualization has been well-documented in sports and theater performance. To improve your confidence, a regular visualization of mastering your most challenging situations will be helpful. You imagine yourself in the situation, performing exactly the way you want to perform. This kind of pre-practice informs your nervous system and helps create neural pathways to make the performance more natural.

ACTION APPLICATIONS:

- Find a quiet time to preview your day and the challenges you will encounter.

- Take five minutes to quiet yourself, take some deep breaths, and focus on the outcome you want.
- See it happening just the way you would want it to happen.
- Picture what others are saying to you, how you are feeling, and how it feels to be successful in the endeavor.

9. DECISIVENESS

In 1983, Quaker Oats bought the slumping sports drink Gatorade. CEO William Smithburg paid $220 million for Gatorade and turned it into a $3 billion business. When he came to his board to purchase Snapple in 1994, it seemed like a no-brainer. The acquisition, though, proved to be one of the most unsuccessful in American history. It cost Smithburg his job, and Quaker unloaded Snapple for $300 million in 1997 after having paid $1.8 billion for it.[9]

How could the Gatorade purchase be so successful and the Snapple deal be such a failure? The answer is: it is easy and natural to rely on old data to give us insight about a current decision. It is in our human nature to rely on historical precedent. We have a selective memory and recall what is recent or most traumatic and neglect subtle details or results.

KEY STEPS FOR DECISION-MAKING

Strong leaders do not act as the group's brain, but rather as consensus builders. When team leaders express their opinions too early in a decision-making discussion, the group generates fewer ideas and often makes poorer decisions. But when the leaders hold back and act mainly as facilitators of the group's process, without imposing their views until the end of the discussion, the outcome is a better decision.[10]

Lee Iacocca, who rebuilt Chrysler into a world-class auto company, states, "If I had to sum up in one word the qualities that make a good manager, I'd say that it all comes down to decisiveness...

In the end you have to bring all your information together, set up a timetable, and act."

In making decisions it is crucial to:

- Cross-examine every precedent
- Clarify assumptions
- Have others challenge your thinking
- Not rely only on precedent
- Develop a disciplined process[11]

QUESTIONS AND ACTION APPLICATIONS:

- What is your decision-making process?
- What kind of information, how much time, and what conditions do you need to make your best decisions?
- When you made your best decisions in the past, how did you do it?
- When you made your worst decisions, how did you do it?
- What patterns do you see?
- Do you tend to distort or over-generalize any specific type of information?
- How often do people consciously challenge your decisions?
- What could you do to make sure you get enough input? Do you play devil's advocate?
- On a scale of 1-10, how effective are you at using reflective time to mull over your major decisions?

10. THIN-SLICING

Malcolm Gladwell wrote *Blink: The Power of Thinking Without Thinking*, which immediately became a *New York Times* best-seller. The book gives fascinating examples and stories about how people make snap judgments in their decision-making, often without knowing why. He calls this "thin-slicing." Thin-slicing is "the ability of our unconscious to find patterns in situations and behavior based on narrow slices of experience."

Thin-slicing, snap judgments, and intuition all describe this phenomenon that happens unconsciously, behind the "closed door."

Researchers from Harvard suggest that people can intuitively sense, in the first 30 seconds of an encounter, basic impressions they have about a person. People watching 30-second snippets of teachers giving a lecture can assess each teacher's proficiency with approximately 80% accuracy as well.[12]

"In a study of three thousand executives, with regard to decision-making, those at the top in various fields were most adept at utilizing intuition in reaching their decisions."[13]

This nonlinear type of knowing is a good complement to the tried-and-true systematic thinking prevalent in traditional problem-solving. (See more about thin-slicing in Chapter 5.)

QUESTIONS AND ACTION APPLICATIONS:

- Do you know when you are having a gut reaction?
- How good are you at identifying your gut reactions, on a scale of 1-10, 10 being the highest?
- How good are you at honoring your gut reactions, on a scale of 1-10?
- What helps you get in touch with and listen to your gut?
- How often do you communicate these gut reactions to others?
- What do you need to do to utilize your intuition more?

STAR PERFORMER ACTION PLAN

The Star Performer Action Plan helps you integrate some of the learning from this chapter's *Star Secrets* and *Coach's Corner* into your overall development plan.

Read through Fisker's Star Profile and the list of other strategies that you noted to develop your confidence. Answer the following to help you make your plan.

Micro-initiatives can make a macro impact.

Which competencies or practices are you already doing that you want to continue?

1. _____
2. _____
3. _____

What are some new practices you want to incorporate?

1. _____
2. _____
3. _____

What resources do you need to make this happen?

1. _____
2. _____
3. _____

Who can support you and hold you accountable?

1. _____
2. _____
3. _____

How might you sabotage your efforts and best intentions?

1. _____
2. _____
3. _____

What will be your first steps in this plan?

    1. _____

    2. _____

    3. _____

Share this plan with your support people. Good luck!

Remember, spend a good month working with your new behaviors and actions. Don't try too much and end up getting stuck in the PERFECTION LOOP. When you are ready, pick another competency chapter to explore, practice, and integrate.

CHAPTER THREE

TEAMWORK AND COLLABORATION
TOOLS AND STRATEGIES

It is easy getting the players; getting them to play together is the hard part.
—Casey Stengel, Famous Yankee Baseball Manager

This section provides tools and strategies to help you become a Star Performer in the area of Teamwork and Collaboration. It begins with a profile of Paulette Jones, Director of Technical and Strategic Business Development of NMB Technologies Corporation. Jones is a Star Performer who shares *10 Secrets & Current Practices* that help her shine as a successful team leader and player. The profile is followed by the *Coach's Corner*, which presents a series of 24 strategies and activities you can implement with your team right away to increase Star Performance in teamwork and collaboration. These include: 7 tools to improve your meetings, 2 Experiential Teambuilding Exercises, 2 Team Activities, and 100 Leadership Check-in Questions. To augment the process, take the Teamwork Ingredients Survey, which monitors positive changes.

WHAT IS THE TEAMWORK AND COLLABORATION COMPETENCY?

Teamwork and Collaboration are competencies that contribute to building an atmosphere of friendly and cooperative relationships within a team. Members are drawn into active, committed, and enthusiastic participation and exhibit respect and helpfulness. There is a team identity and an *esprit de corps*, which members work hard at developing and protecting.

EMOTIONAL INTELLIGENCE RESEARCH EXAMPLES

As noted in Chapter 1, for many years Robert Kelley of Carnegie-Mellon University has been asking people in various companies the following: "What percent of the knowledge for doing your job is stored in your own mind?" In *How to Be a Star at Work*, Kelly stated that the typical answer was 75%. By 1997, the percentage had slid to about 55%, and in one company it dropped as low as 10%. It is obvious that the group mind knows more than the individual mind and that teamwork or collaboration brings about better decisions than working alone.

Cambridge University Business School explored this topic further. They set up an experiment with 120 simulated management teams who were asked to make important decisions for a mock business. Some teams consisted exclusively of high-IQ members. Surprisingly, these high-IQ teams performed worse than other "less brilliant" teams. Why? The members of the high-IQ teams spent too much time debating issues and trying to outshine each other. They failed to attend to the necessary practical parts of the job, such as communicating information and coordinating a game plan.

In another study, the Center of Creative Leadership evaluated top American and European executives whose careers had derailed. It revealed that the main reasons for executive failure were the inabilities to build and lead a team. Lastly, in a study of 60 work teams operating in a large American financial services company, the behaviors that mattered most for team effectiveness came down to how members interacted and connected. Clearly, the demand for team skills will only grow in the years to come, as more and more work is done at a distance and in cross-functional project teams that form and dissolve depending on the task.

ARE YOU A STAR PERFORMER IN TEAMWORK AND COLLABORATION OR JUST AVERAGE?

Stars exhibit both average and Star behaviors consistently. Where are you?

AVERAGE

- Cooperates
- Expresses positive expectations
- Solicits input

STAR

- Encourages others
- Builds team spirit[3]

STAR PROFILE: PAULETTE JONES, DIRECTOR OF TECHNICAL AND STRATEGIC BUSINESS DEVELOPMENT, NMB TECHNOLOGIES CORPORATION

WHY PAULETTE JONES IS A STAR PERFORMER

Paulette Jones from 1998 to 2002 has held a variety of leadership positions, from Director of Marketing and Sales of Keyboards in North America to General Manager of Keyboards. When I interviewed her in 2001, she was responsible for the management of an 18-person computer keyboard team, a 30-member engineering group, and a 6-person audio team. Jones's direct activities included product and program management, customer service, quality assurance, and factory coordination. She had full profit-and-loss responsibility for the company's keyboard business in the United States. Jones and her teams were successful in growing the Keyboard business by 300% from 1998 to 2004 and increasing the Audio sales by 566% during the same time period. Jones earned a B.S. in Computer Sciences, and she holds an MBA from Pepperdine University. She is a member of Mensa, is listed in International Who's Who of Business professionals, and held a Top Secret security clearance with the U.S. Navy.

Paulette Jones has one of the best initial greetings I have ever experienced and makes you feel appreciated and welcome. She has a quick sense of humor, can be self-deprecating, and makes everyone on her team feel special.

JONES WAS ASKED:

- How did she learn this Teamwork competency?
- What does she do to be such an effective leader?
- What are her daily practices?
- What are the pitfalls she needs to be aware of?

EARLY LEARNING EXPERIENCES

"It seems that all of my life I have expressed [the Teamwork] competencies. I was president of my class in high school, and these leadership qualities have always seemed to be natural for me.

"Demonstrating these competencies has never been a conscious effort on my part. I can't ever remember a time in my life when I did not use them. Perhaps my perspective comes from the fact that I was one of six children growing up. (I was the fifth born out of the six children.) My father died when I was three years old and my mother raised all six of us by herself. We had to work together as a unit, and lack of teamwork was just not an option. We all learned that our strength and security lay in our numbers. It was 'us' trying to survive and we had to stick together to do it. That was my mom's message."

10 SECRETS & CURRENT PRACTICES OF PAULETTE JONES—STAR PERFORMER

Below are strategies that Jones and other managers at NMB use to be Stars. Read through the strategies and pick one or two to try out.

1. START THE DAY WITH "AN ATTITUDE OF GRATITUDE"

"As I drive to work each day, I mentally walk through a list of things that I am grateful for (e.g., my family, health, and job). I also specifically think of individuals on the team who I am particularly grateful for. By the time I have gone through this exercise, I am ready to start the day feeling uplifted."

2. FOCUSED GREETING OF PEOPLE

"I believe it is important to greet people in such a manner as to indicate that you are glad to see them and that you view this individual as an important person. A strong handshake, direct eye contact and a display of genuine interest in the person conveys the message that 'I am truly glad to see you.' I never actually thought about this 'skill' until it was brought to my attention. This has never been a conscious choice on my part."

3. COMMUNICATION

"It is absolutely essential to present the team with accurate and up-to-date information regarding our financial performance, achievement of stated goals, etc. We have placed a bulletin board in a central location that contains easy-to-read graphs and charts. These graphs and charts document our revenue, expenses, profitability, and inventory value compared to our budgets and goals. All members of the team have been trained in how to read and interpret these graphs and all team members share a common vision. Everyone knows how we are performing to goals at any time. In addition to these tools for tracking our performance, the bulletin board also includes easy-to-read charts that indicate the status of our sales efforts to introduce new technologies to our major customers."

4. RED FLAG MEETINGS

"Daily red flag meetings are held in the team area and are attended by all team members. These meetings are 'stand-up' meetings that usually last anywhere from 5 to 15 minutes. The purpose of these meetings is to raise red flags and to quickly identify resources to address the issues raised. These meetings are the *lifeblood* of communicating with the team members and are an essential tool for quickly sharing critical information."

5. REVENUE GAP MEETINGS

"These meetings are held immediately after the red flag meetings and are also 'stand-up' meetings that last no longer than 5 or 10 minutes. Their purpose is to identify the current revenue for each customer, the individual customer forecast for that month, and any specific actions needed to close the 'gap.' These meetings are critical for ensuring that revenue opportunities are not lost due to oversight or administrative errors."

6. BAT TEAMS (BUSINESS ACQUISITION TEAMS)

"BAT teams consist of 4 or 5 members each and are drawn from the keyboard team at large. Each team is assigned a major strategic account target. The objective of the team is to document specific information about their account. The team studies the account and identifies the decision-makers and their individual contributions to the purchasing decision, the competitors and percentage of the business they each hold, the important purchasing criteria, the customer product road map, a strategic statement that will guide our dealings with the customer, and specific milestones that are needed to achieve our objective.

"In addition to delivering a valuable account profile and specific actions, the benefits of forming the BAT teams are apparent to those who participate. Participation in these BAT teams by members who do not normally engage in sales-related activities offers an opportunity to become involved in processes that many people in customer service, program management, and factory coordination would otherwise never be involved in. It gives the team members a sense of ownership and a valuable learning experience."

7. TEAM MEETINGS

"Held twice per month, attendance by all team members at these meetings is mandatory. They provide an opportunity to share information that is not normally shared during the daily red flag meetings. These learning experiences for the team, such as practicing Covey's *The 7 Habits of Highly Effective People* over a 3-month period, are valuable ways people learn and bond together. Whenever a team member demonstrates one or more of the habits, the team recognizes them during our daily red flag meetings. The team meetings are also used to provide detailed product and financial information and provide opportunities to bring up other important issues during the 'round robin' portion."

8. CONTINUAL PROCESS REVIEW

"All processes (MRP, sales forecast, etc.) are subject to constant review and refinement and all departmental processes are well-documented and available to anyone who cares to view them. When problems are identified, a team consisting of stakeholders within that process is formed, the process is reviewed, and modifications are made by the people who will be working with that process."

9. VALUING STAFF

"I believe in the value of each individual on the team. Whenever I return from a business trip, I make it a point to go around to each and every person on the team and check in with him or her. It only takes a few minutes, but people sense that I do care about them and it sends a message that they are valued."

10. HUMOR

"I am amazed at how well the prudent application of humor can relieve tensions and bring the group closer together. We use humor constantly to build a sense of camaraderie. It's a great stress-reliever."

PITFALLS: WHAT JONES NEEDS TO BE AWARE OF

"I am aware that I may have an emotional response to a business situation. Due to real or imagined slights, my feelings may get hurt and my ego may become bruised. When this happens, I may have a tendency to want to impose my position on the business unit. I really don't like myself when I do that and I feel that it compromises my ability to be an effective leader."

ACTIONS: REVIEW JONES'S CURRENT PRACTICES

Looking at Jones's current practices, what practices can you incorporate to become a Star Performer in Teamwork and Collaboration?

Which ones do you want to add to your Star Performer Action Plan?

1. _____
2. _____
3. _____

THE COACH'S CORNER: 24 STRATEGIES FOR TEAMWORK AND COLLABORATION

OVERVIEW

Most organizations talk a lot about teamwork, but their approach is often simplistic and superficial. A group of workers is dropped together, told "You are now a team," and expected to act like one. This so-called team is marched onto the performance field of business without the skill sets to collaborate successfully. Becoming a functional and effective team that works and communicates well together is no slam dunk! It takes a great deal of discipline, planning, and practice and certainly isn't easy.

Although they desperately want it, it is uncommon in today's organizational environment for leaders to prioritize teamwork and collaboration. Take a quick look at the focus of a professional sports team or dance troupe compared to a typical organization. In the corporate world, only about 5% of an individual's time is devoted to off-line learning. Compare that to the athletes' or dancers' commitment: 95% of their time is spent practicing, standardizing routines and movements, identifying roles and responsibilities, improving communication effectiveness, and practicing coordination, alignment, and teamwork. To thrive, it is paramount that leaders devote the same kind of time and intention to teambuilding that athletes or performers do. Leaders need to help their employees practice their skills, enhance their strengths, and improve their weaknesses. Unfortunately, the crisis of the day tends to take precedence over dedicating this quality time.

10 KEY INGREDIENTS TO MASTER COLLABORATION AND TEAMWORK: TEAMWORK IS AN UNNATURAL ACT

There are 10 key ingredients organizations must incorporate to master the competency of Collaboration and Teamwork. Each needs to become a discipline that is practiced, reinforced, and refined. Only then does Star Performance become a habit and a solid foundation for superior teamwork. The following combine to help you develop high-performance teams.

Average performers do what is easy and NATURAL. By that I mean they do what is obvious, effortless, and painless. Star Performers do what is UNNATURAL and difficult on a regular basis to develop their teams. By that I mean that, despite the pain, they do what is necessary in an organized, ritualized, and disciplined manner.

Notice how each of the 10 ingredients illustrates an "Average" as well as a "Star" approach, and gives specific actions designed to help you make your team succeed.

Star Performers do what is UNNATURAL and difficult on a regular basis to develop their teams.

1. SHARED VISION

AVERAGE: Holds a blurry vision of where the organization is going and does not share this vision often enough throughout all of the departments.

STAR: Creates a clear and inspiring vision for the future that is communicated regularly, understood by all members, and reinforced in numerous ways.

ACTIONS to do the unnatural and be more effective: Leaders maintain a clear picture of their vision with a deliberate plan to communicate it to the team. Below are some suggestions.

- Communicate your vision at least four times a day.[4]
- Communicate what needs to be done to implement the vision and explain how the vision supports the team.
- Use the word *because* to help explain the connection between the vision and the individual team members.
- Include others, from all levels of the organization, and invite them to offer comments and clarifications. It is important to get everyone's "fingerprints" on the projects at hand. Remember, involvement equals commitment.

2. TRUST AMONG MEMBERS

AVERAGE: Relies only on him- or herself or on his or her particular department and does not expect much from others.

STAR: Develops an interdependency with others characterized by high trust and risk-taking.

ACTIONS to do the unnatural and be more effective: Leaders develop trust by trusting their people. Below are some suggestions.

- Develop trust by being vulnerable and admitting your mistakes.
- Make and keep small promises.

- Set high expectations for your team and encourage risk-taking and direct feedback.

3. EXPECTATIONS AND GUIDELINES

AVERAGE: Assumes that co-workers are on the same page and that they can read minds and so understand the desired results.

STAR: Is deliberate in clarifying reciprocal expectations and establishes guidelines for working together effectively.

ACTIONS to do the unnatural and be more effective: Leaders encourage members to co-create their expectations for themselves and communicate that they value the input. Below are some suggestions.

- Leaders and the team decide how they are going to make decisions (i.e., by majority, minority or content expert, unanimous, or consensus).

- Expectations are clarified from the leader to the team, from the team to the leader, and within the team. (See team Expectations exercise on page 138 for how to do it.)

- Meetings and team guidelines are established that flow out of agreed-upon expectations, such as "One conversation at a time," "Stay focused," and "Defer judgment." (See more about meetings beginning on page 114.)

4. COMMUNICATION SKILLS AND CONFLICT RESOLUTION

AVERAGE: Avoids conflict, jumps to conclusions, and may fail to effectively communicate his or her thoughts. Communicates the same way to everyone.

STAR: Makes thinking known and heard, identifies assumptions, acknowledges and resolves conflicts. A Star treats each person as a "chess player" with unique talents and varies his or her communication to fit the person.

ACTIONS to do the unnatural and be more effective: Leaders give the team specific tools for communication and working through conflict; otherwise, the strongest, loudest, and most senior voice tends to prevail. Below are some suggestions.

- Teach communication skills such as how to listen better, inquiry versus advocacy, and summarizing what is said.

- Appreciate differences and then communicate uniquely to each person to fit that person's style.

- Assign a devil's advocate to enliven conversations and protect against "group think."

5. SYSTEMS THINKING

AVERAGE: Focuses on his or her own department to the exclusion of thinking large, across departmental boundaries. Believes his or her team's action has limited impact on others across the organization.

STAR: Looks at the big picture and recognizes how his or her department's actions affect others. Knows that customers, co-workers, vendors, and family are also intertwined as stakeholders and can have unintended impact and consequences.

ACTIONS to do the unnatural and be more effective: A leader helps the team see the big picture. Below are some suggestions.

- Make sure all sides of a situation are examined by assigning advocate roles in the conversation to customers, employees, managers, and vendors. Team members take on the roles and concerns of each of the above stakeholders.

- Encourage the team to elaborate on all possible consequences before rushing to make decisions.

- Counteract limited thinking and organizational learning disabilities such as "I am my position" and "The enemy is out there."[5]

6. PERSONAL LEADERSHIP

AVERAGE: Stays in his or her comfort zone and only takes "safe bet" risks.

STAR: Takes risks that are consistent with values. In order to become a change leader, stretches and encourages others in spite of doubts and fears.

ACTIONS to do the unnatural and be more effective: Leaders know that the team is the playing field to try out their Emotional Intelligence skills and also the place to receive feedback on their performance. Below are some suggestions.

- Cultivate a developed point of view of your leadership style and know where you are going.
- Be aware of the different styles and preferences of your team and vary your style to meet and challenge each individual.
- Be a role model for development by sharing your current areas of focus. Ask for support and feedback from the team.
- Wear all of the hats on the team and know which hat to wear when. Key roles are initiator, coach, model, facilitator, and negotiator.
- Read the team's emotional state and create balance through attention, humor, and empathy.

7. APPRECIATION OF DIFFERENCES

AVERAGE: Values team members with similar backgrounds and opinions.

STAR: Embraces differences and creative tensions to generate better solutions and raise the "Team IQ."

Treats team members as chess players, not checkers. Matches each person's unique talents to his or her best-fit position.

The team IQ is a great indicator for the group to evaluate themselves. The IQ should be higher than the IQ of any one individual.

IQ is 100 points, plus or minus 15 points. Above 115 is high average, 85-115 is average, and below 85 is low average.

ACTIONS to do the unnatural and be more effective: The leader is a powerful role model for dealing with differences. Below are some suggestions.

- Spend time thinking about and conversing with each individual, establishing his or her unique talents and deciding how that talent can best be used for the team.

- Hold a conversation with your team about their team IQ. Rate it, talk about it, and take actions to raise it.

- Encourage the team to stay with ambiguity, creative tension, and dialogue as long as possible. (See Dialogue Skills in Chapter 5.)

- Do not rush into a decision.

- Embrace differences and recognize that holding opposite and contrary ideas long enough can lead to breakthrough ideas.

- Integrate differences and transform them into innovations.

8. ACCOUNTABILITY AND CONSEQUENCES

AVERAGE: Feels disappointed with the efforts of team members, but fails to hold anyone accountable.

STAR: Discusses accountabilities and consequences up front, before a project gets underway, and reviews them throughout the project.

ACTIONS to do the unnatural and be more effective: Leaders provide the road map for dealing with obstacles before they arise. Below are some suggestions.

- Help individuals define their roles and responsibilities and make sure everyone is clear about them.

- Define and clarify what success looks like.

- To eliminate problems later, converse about accountabilities and consequences as part of the team's formation.

9. ONGOING LEARNING AND RECOGNITION

AVERAGE: Completes a task, possibly congratulates the team, and moves on to the next item on the "to do list."

STAR: Takes time to reflect to discover if what worked can be used again. Learns what not to do next time, decides who needs to know this information, disseminates it, and designs formal and informal celebrations for the win.

ACTIONS to do the unnatural and be more effective: Leaders look for every opportunity to learn and improve. Below are some suggestions.

- Hold sessions to crystallize learning and "spread the news" to the right people.
- Recognize individuals' efforts and contributions, which increases discretionary effort and raises morale.
- To keep performance focused, give timely and specific feedback.

10. MENTOR OTHERS

AVERAGE: Gets caught up with the urgent crises of the day and does little mentoring or training of key employees or colleagues.

STAR: Takes time to train and mentor others to be better performers. Keeps motivation high with career development, learning, and succession planning.

ACTIONS to do the unnatural and be more effective: Leaders enhance strengths and develop plans to improve the weaknesses of their team members. Below are some suggestions.

- Hold one-on-one meetings with your direct reports to coach and mentor. (See Developing Others for more tools on how to do this.)
- Encourage team to share core competencies by cross training.
- Spread your knowledge and develop your successors.

MORE COACHING TOOLS

11. MEETING MASTERY AND MEETING MENACE

In reading Paulette Jones's Star Profile you probably noticed how many of her actions revolve around the types of meetings she holds. Meetings are the primary tools of a leader. They are the executive playing field where leadership is most on display. In many organizations, over 50% of an executive's time is spent in meetings. When used well, meetings can increase the performance of your team and build your credibility as the leader. When used poorly, in an undisciplined way, meetings can waste the organization's time and money and derail leadership.

> *Meetings are the primary tools of a leader.*

THE MEETING MENACE: FRANK'S STORY

I have attended many corporate meetings, either facilitating or observing, and I would say that most could run better and that the members could participate more effectively. This story features "Frank," a composite of many leaders I have worked with or witnessed. I call his kind of leadership "Menacing."

Frank is a senior member in his organization and has been there for almost 10 years. He is known to have a temper that occasionally flares up. In one meeting, he was so upset about the direction his boss was taking on a particular project that he angrily tossed a wad of paper across the room, swore loudly, and shouted, "This makes absolutely no sense!" His boss happened to be at the meeting and an awkward, uncomfortable silence prevailed. No one seemed to know how to deal with him or the situation.

Frank has a history of being short and gruff. In the past, others had talked to him about his inability to be a team player, but his style continued to be confrontational. At meetings he would ask piercing questions and put others on the defensive. He would then calmly make his counterpoint, and people would feel embarrassed and humiliated. Because he is so critical and often volatile, Frank is negatively affecting the project deliverables and undermining any teamwork.

In a meeting with a cross-functional action team, Frank got overly excited and put another member of the team on the spot by asking endless questions about an interpretation of what a customer really wanted. Frank proceeded to engage others by asking them to comment on what they remembered happening in past meetings. Members stammered through their responses, and most felt and behaved anxious or uncomfortable.

Frank's boss talked to him numerous times about his temper and how it affected others, but Frank refused to apologize. Things would usually settle down, until the next blowup a few months later. Frank didn't realize how devastating these blowups were to his credibility and trustworthiness as a leader. He was unpredictable. Everyone wondered if he or she would be next to feel his wrath.

How would you deal with Frank if you were his boss? If you are Frank, it is important to realize the fear you are instilling in others and the harm you are doing to yourself. Take time to reflect and then apply some of the practical tools in the section.

QUESTIONS AND ACTION APPLICATIONS:

- Did you see yourself portrayed on any level in Frank's story?
- How aware are you of your impact on others in meetings, 1-10, where 10 is totally aware?
- How would you rate your impact on others in meetings, 1-10, where 10 is very valuable and effective in meetings?
- Would you be willing to ask others about your impact?
- Did you see someone else you work with reflected in Frank's story? If so, would it be beneficial to talk to him or her about it? How might you approach this person? (e.g., take the person aside and tell him or her about the impact of his or her behavior and give suggestions for alternatives)

- Read the Snapshots below, which you may be creating, and the actions you can take.
- Take the Meeting Menace Checklist on pages 118-119 and establish actions to work on.

12. SNAPSHOT MANAGEMENT: "THE ONE HAND RULE"

Most of the time that members of your organization spend with you is at meetings. It is here that your image as a leader gets crystallized. It exemplifies what I call "Snapshot Management." Members quickly make positive or negative fixed impressions of you as a leader. If your behavior, posture, and style are similar in three to four meeting snapshots, you can count it on "One Hand." Then you get "thin-sliced" as "that is you." People don't take time to understand your intentions or rationale. They want to know quickly if they can trust you or not. If you are unpredictable, you are untrustworthy in their eyes. Certainty, even if wrong, is more comfortable than ambivalence. These snapshots may not be accurate portraits of who you are as a leader, but unfortunately they stick in people's minds and become "reality."

If your behavior, posture, and style are similar in three to four meeting snapshots, you can count it on "One Hand." Then you get "thin-sliced" as "that is you."

If your snapshot image is positive, your colleagues and boss will give you the benefit of the doubt if you miss a deadline or make a mistake. The problem occurs when these snapshots are negative, because once the impression is made it is almost impossible to change. If this impression was created because you have been unpredictable or impulsive in your behavior, your direct reports, peers, and boss are constantly poised for that same behavior. They can't trust that you can control yourself. Even if you make considerable changes over 6-12 months, if the same impulsive behavior happens again, in most people's minds you haven't changed at all. They think, "There goes Frank again."

I have been in meetings with executives talking about the performance of an individual victimized by Snapshot Management. The question discussed was, "If this person actually made positive changes, would the executives see and recognize him?" Original snapshots are so powerful that they can blind people to the multifaceted sides of a person. All of the person's wins, strengths, and capabilities in different settings with different people can blur the original fixed snapshot, but it is a very slow process and doesn't always stick. It is crucial to become acutely aware of how you present yourself in meetings and important to learn how to manage the snapshots you give people.

> *Original snapshots are so powerful that they can blind people to the multifaceted sides of a person.*

The goal is to counter the one hand of snapshots with a "collage" of all your successes and efforts. That may mean communicating more than you feel is necessary about what you have accomplished. Many executives say, "I don't want to toot my own horn" or "They will see my results." In taking the initiative to communicate in an informative and respectful way what you have been doing, you can ensure that your co-workers and boss "see" more of you than just a few snapshots. Otherwise, you are leaving your image management more in the hands and minds of others. Being more visible has been a strategy for many executives I have worked with, especially if they have negative snapshots ingrained in the minds of their supervisors or co-workers.

For example, here are some micro-initiatives you can say without boasting:

"I feel very comfortable with our progress thus far in…"

"The team is really performing well with…"

"I am very proud about…"

"I am excited with our direction with…"

QUESTIONS AND ACTION APPLICATIONS:

- Do you have snapshots of people that are limiting how you see them?

- Can you inquire about other successes they have had and multiply or expand your snapshots of them?

- What are the snapshots of you? Are they more positive or negative?

- Are you taking the opportunities to present the "collage" of your successes and efforts?

Next, take the Meeting Menace Checklist to raise your awareness of the behaviors that can handicap your pursuit of being a Star Performer.

13. MEETING MENACE CHECKLIST

Check the box if you notice the behavior in yourself, a direct report, or a peer at least one time in a two-month period.

☐ 1.   Gets irritated, upset, or angry in a meeting.

☐ 2.   Interrupts people frequently during a meeting.

☐ 3.   Uses questions like weapons. They are not really questions, but disguised statements.

☐ 4.   Over-talks issues advocating only one's own ideas.

☐ 5.   Prevents people from managing or interacting with him or her. Says, "I just have one more thing to say," and then continues to talk on.

☐ 6.   Makes disagreements a grand performance.

☐ 7.   Fails to build on others' ideas.

☐ 8.   Refuses to acknowledge others.

☐ 9.   Puts others on the spot and urges them to express an opinion about a conflict.

☐ 10. Indulges in debating but doesn't realize others are uncomfortable and might see it as conflict or confrontation.

☐ 11. Is unprepared. Asks questions that have already been covered.

☐ 12. Interrogates others about their points of view in a condescending manner.

SCORE: If you made three or more checks, you are (or your direct report or peer is) a Meeting Menace.

QUESTIONS AND ACTION APPLICATIONS:

What are one or two things you can do that would help you break out of being a Meeting Menace? For example:

- Take time to prepare for the meeting.
- Decide what outcomes you are looking for with each statement you make.
- Ask clarifying questions before advocating your point.
- Get a coach to help you deal with what might be blind spots and to learn new strategies.
- Work with a colleague to give you feedback if he or she notices any of the "menacing behaviors."
- Work with your supervisor on these development issues and have him or her give you feedback if he or she notices any of the behaviors.

Stars have a disciplined system for using meetings and maximizing their use. They are prepared for each meeting and appreciate the visibility that a meeting casts. Employing some of the following actions will bring about the degree of difference (D.O.D.) that moves your performance from good to great!

BECOME A MEETING MASTER

Employing the following collection of meeting tools, tips, and insights will make you a Meeting Master. This chapter focuses on

Team Meetings and shorter Stand-Up Meetings. You will discover information about how to orchestrate other kinds of meetings in the Developing Others and Communication and Empathy chapters.

14. TEAM MEETINGS

Team meetings are usually held weekly or bi-weekly. They are more frequent when you are involved in a big project. After 9/11, Rudy Giuliani held a daily morning meeting with the top 20 department heads. It was his key management tool to make sure he and everyone else knew what was happening and how they needed to respond after the tragedy.

HOW TO SET UP AND RUN AN EFFECTIVE TEAM MEETING

Here are the *key tasks* that should occur before, during, and after a team meeting:

Before

The leader or meeting owner should:

- Define the purpose and objective of the meeting.
- Select participants.
- Secure the room and equipment.
- Prepare the agenda and send it out ahead of time. Ask if there are items people want on the agenda and include them.
- Make a final check on the meeting room.

During

The leader or meeting owner should:

- Start promptly.
- Select a scribe to take minutes.
- At the start of the meeting, prioritize the agenda with time frames and then manage the time.
- Follow specific team guidelines you have created. (See page 122.)

- Hear from everyone. Use the Leadership Check-in Questions as a way of beginning a meeting. (See page 142.)
- Limit or encourage discussion.
- Clarify actions to be taken.
- Summarize results.

MEETING PROCESS CHECKS

Here are various ways to make sure your meetings are effective. It is good to vary the way you perform the process check.

- On a 1-10 scale, how effective or satisfied are you with today's meeting? (Use the lowest scores to state what the team thinks needs to be improved.)
- What was good, what was bad, and what needs to be improved regarding this meeting?
- On a 1-10 scale, rate how on track the meeting was. What needs to be improved? (Use this at the halfway point of the meeting, asking each person to answer.)

After

The leader or meeting owner should:

- Restore the room.
- Make sure the scribe sends out minutes.
- Evaluate meeting and meeting feedback.
- Take agreed-upon action.
- Prepare next steps.
- Evaluate the effectiveness of the meeting. Focus on content and process. Most meetings are only content-focused, and yet what goes wrong in meetings usually has to do with "process"—the "how" versus the "what" of the meeting. By not focusing some time on the process of the meeting, you miss the critical variables to improve the meeting. (See the Meeting Checklist on pages 124-125).

15. GUIDELINES FOR RUNNING A GREAT MEETING

Following are guidelines for making meetings more effective. Have your team look at the list and add any other specific points that would be helpful. So that everyone is on the same page, hold a short meeting to discuss these guidelines.

Consider:

- Which guidelines will be hardest to comply with?
- How can you hold the accountability if someone isn't following the guidelines?
- What is the most effective way to administer these guidelines? Consider having a facilitator who rotates from meeting to meeting, or come up with other suggestions. Here are some sample guidelines.
  - ▲ Arrive on time.
  - ▲ Be well-prepared.
  - ▲ Be concise. Stick to the point.
  - ▲ Make "I" statements.
  - ▲ Don't hold sidebar conversations.
  - ▲ Participate in a constructive manner.
  - ▲ Seek first to understand before seeking to be understood.
  - ▲ Make your thinking visible.
  - ▲ Don't interrupt.
  - ▲ Other guidelines specific to your situation.

16. HOW TO ESTABLISH ROLES WITHIN A TEAM MEETING

To make a meeting run effectively, it is valuable to assign key roles within the meeting. Before the meeting, identify who will do what. Decide if a facilitator or another person will be the time-keeper. Also establish if people need more training in their roles before proceeding.

FACILITATOR:

Your role is to keep the meeting going and to follow the agenda. State the purpose and end result of the meeting. Go through the agenda. Enforce the guidelines. Consider using a "latecomer's jar" to fine someone if he or she is late. Stop people if they go off on tangents. Honor the time limits or appoint a timekeeper to do so. Ask how much time people need on new topics. Use a "parking lot" for items that are not part of the agenda but need to be discussed at another time.

SCRIBE:

Your role is to take notes (minutes) of the meeting so the facilitator can focus on the content and process. Document key issues and decisions made, with actions highlighting responsible parties. Make sure the minutes are distributed to all the participants within a 48-hour time frame.

PARTICIPANTS:

All participants are expected to add value to the meeting and follow the guidelines. If you can't make it to a meeting, it is your responsibility to notify others.

17. "STAND-UPS"—SHORT TEAM MEETINGS

Short 10- to 15-minute meetings are a powerful means to promote teamwork and communication. Paulette Jones referred to them as "red flag meetings" in her Star Profile. Other people call them "huddles." The stand-ups are done standing up, thus the name. This is not time to get comfortable. Instead, your team stands in a circle, and each person has an opportunity to say something or pass. This is not a problem-solving meeting. (Use your team meeting for that.) Make sure that tangents are curtailed and topics between only two people are taken off-line.

Acceptable topics are:

- Information that will be helpful for everyone to know (e.g., a customer is coming today; he or she will be at an all-day meeting tomorrow).
- "Red flag issues" (e.g., someone needs everyone's help to get a rush product order out the door).
- What he or she is working on, or information or knowledge that is new to others.

As a leader, you can use these meetings to:

- Clarify the vision or deliverables.
- Acknowledge others.
- Celebrate small wins.

18. THE MEETING CHECKLIST

Use this checklist on a regular basis to make sure each meeting improves upon the last.

Team _____

Meeting owner _____

Date of meeting _____

Rank each item from 1 to 10 points, with 10 being the best or most productive meeting you have participated in.

1. Leadership of the meeting:

☐ The agenda was clear and explained up front.

☐ The meeting owner stated the overall purpose.

☐ Time frames were honored.

☐ Overall

2. Accountability

☐ Individual team members were prepared for the meeting.

☐ Actions had a clear assignment, owner, and time deadline.

☐ Resources for the assignment or task were clarified.

☐ Other stakeholders' involvement and impact were considered.

☐ Overall

3. Communication

☐ Assumptions and interpretations were made explicit.

☐ People asked good questions and listened well.

☑ Risk-taking and challenging the process occurred.

☑ Tension and disagreements were aired, reduced, and resolved.

☐ Overall

4. Summary

☐ A summary of the decisions made was communicated.

☐ Actions and the people responsible for them were summarized.

☐ Next steps or considerations for the next meeting were stated.

☐ People evaluated the meeting and talked about improvements.

☐ Overall

5. What one thing do you want to change or improve for the next meeting?

_____

_____

_____

EXPERIENTIAL TEAMBUILDING EXERCISES

This section focuses on two experiential teambuilding exercises that you can do with your team. They are designed to give you all the information you need to set up, conduct, and process the activities successfully.

What follows is a brief rationale for experiential training. When you enter into an organization, you may be asked to explain why you believe experiential exercises have value and impact.

Whether you are a manager, coach, or trainer talking to an HR Director or giving your boss an overview of some of the exercises you will do with the team, your ability to understand and explain the power and value of these exercises will help to get buy-in.

WHY EXPERIENTIAL TRAINING?

"The premise is simple: that we have all been brainwashed by the cultural myth that learning occurs 'in our heads,' not in all of us, and that, until we challenge that belief, our capacities for any sort of deep learning are severely limited...Our learning is 'in our heads' but we don't seem to get it out, and apply it."[6]

Experiential training is quite different from traditional training. It involves whole-body learning and engages the physical, mental, behavioral, and even spiritual dimensions of a person, rather than focusing solely on the person's mind. Because the activities are generally unknown and unfamiliar, they can lead to unexpected outcomes and surprises, creating situations of crisis and chaos. In this way, experiential activities are a metaphor for work itself, mirroring the ups, downs, and unexpected twists and turns that take place on a daily basis.

Experiential training is a "practice field" that allows learning to happen in a setting where cause and effect are closely linked in time, and knowledge is generated to improve teamwork, communication, and collaborative problem-solving. Experiential training helps a team project their decision-making process and group intelligence onto the experience to be successful. The team has to organize itself to deal with time constraints, ambiguity of the directions, changing resources, leadership, follow-through, and vision, again mirroring a variety of work projects.

WHY EXPERIENTIAL LEARNING WORKS:
12 UNIQUE CHARACTERISTICS

1. Equality: It provides a common yet novel experience, where all participants are equal in their knowledge about the tasks or projects. One year or 20 years with the organization doesn't help an individual solve these problems.

2. Relationships Build Quickly: This is accomplished by the communication, collaboration, cooperation, and physical effort needed to solve these exercises. Participants are in close proximity all day and interacting in new ways. The end result is that they have to rely and depend on each other in clear and significant ways, which builds trust in an accelerated manner. People get to know each other more in a day than they have over the last one to two years.

3. Disequilibrium: Because of the unknown and unfamiliar quality of the challenges, participants are put into a state of disequilibrium or disorder. They are stripped of their normal status, roles, and defenses. Prior experience isn't relevant here. This creates a pure learning environment as the group has to self-organize around the challenge.

4. Projective Technique: In organizing instability or disequilibrium, the group projects their problem-solving, project management, and leadership style onto the experience. The experience provides a "gotcha" where participants are "caught" in doing what they typically do, in spite of knowing better. The learning is profound, revealing, and presented in a more meaningful and relevant way than would come from an organizational assessment. This window into their process provides unlimited information to shape team learning. This is one of the prime reasons experiential learning is an excellent "laboratory." Other methodologies don't provide such a rich projective technique.

5. Decreased Cycle Time: The space between project initiation and outcomes is compressed, so consequences of organizational decisions can be examined and improved. Typically, there is more of a time lag and more variables must be considered, so learning by doing is diluted and delayed.

6. Meta Learning: In this "learning laboratory," as the projections shed light on the managerial process, the group is asked to step back and evaluate itself. The learning is about themselves, their leadership, problem-solving skills, teamwork, communication, and ability to manage change. This time to reflect and develop lessons learned after studying themselves and their processes is usually not done with the same intensity within the organization.

7. Chaos Management (in a Safe Environment): Teams are able to experience chaos, disorder, and changing requirements for success in a safe environment where the consequences for failure are limited. The groups develop strategies or best practices to manage the change back at the work site.

8. Kinesthetic Imprint: Experiential learning anchors cognitive material. Participants have a kinesthetic imprint or whole-body learning of cognitive principles, because the learning is graphic as it involves physical, mental, behavioral, and even spiritual dimensions.

9. Common Language/Story-Making: The experience provides common language, story, and imagery that can be transferred to the workplace. This language becomes a shortcut in communicating a shared vision or "learning disability." The intense experience is storied in such a way that the participants see themselves and others in a new light. This story then becomes the catalyst for continuing the same theme, but taking it into the organization.

10. Encourages Risk-Taking: The experience allows participants to take risks, try on new roles, and make mistakes with few costs to the organization. Risks are perceived versus actual. Each person taking a risk vicariously pushes others to try something outside of their circle of comfort. In this environment, there are always individuals who shine and whose leadership hasn't been noticed at work.

11. Diversity of Strengths: The activities include physical and mental challenges requiring the resources of the whole team. Differences become necessary strengths for solving challenges. Just like on the job, one person alone could not complete most of the challenges, so the interdependencies of the team are emphasized.

12. Fun: Experiential learning provides a fun way of learning how to become a high-performance team. Fun also helps participants learn more, because they are more open to the experience and are typically more creative.

WHY TRAINING FAILS

In today's world, learning is the critical advantage that separates an organization from its competition. One reason learning needs to be improved is found in the systems perspective. Often, the learning or training is not embraced or reinforced back in the real world. Many times, the training is a solution to an undefined or complex problem. It may be a Band-Aid doomed to fall off and reopen the existing wound. Here are eight of the main barriers to the transference of learning. They are presented in rank order, with the first being the biggest impediment:

1. Lack of reinforcement at the work site
2. Interference from others (e.g., customers, co-workers, supervisors)
3. Non-supportive organizational climate
4. Training seen as impractical and irrelevant
5. Participants uncomfortable with the amount of change needed to implement the learning
6. Leaders or trainers not present as support mechanisms
7. Training perceived as poorly designed and delivered
8. Pressure from support group to resist making significant changes

CORPORATE TRAINING PRINCIPLES

Experience-based training and development as a field is continually growing and incorporating new skills and activities. As we innovate the way in which Corporate America and the international market-place are learning and growing, we must keep in mind the basic premises of working with adults. These five principles are adapted from the *Creative Training Techniques Handbook* by Bob Pike:

1. Adults are like kids in big bodies. Like kids, adults learn the best through hands-on experiences.

2. The more you get others involved, using their own projections as the learning material, the more it stays real and relevant.

3. The more fun your participants have, the more they will learn.

4. No learning takes place until behavior changes. Everyone must learn to "walk the talk."

5. Learning has ultimately taken place only if participants can teach each other what you have taught them.

Using these experiential methodologies along with traditional training will make the entire process more lively, engaging, and fun. In the future, managers and trainers share the same bag of tricks to help develop strong and high-performance teams.

PROVEN EXPERIENTIAL EXERCISES

The following two activities are presented with instructions, materials needed, and process questions. They are designed for a team leader, outside consultant, or trainer to use for team development.

- Nails
- Performance and Accountability

These exercises can be used:

- To help "break the ice" for the team.

- To focus the team on the problem at hand, rather than doing it by yourself.
- As metaphors for how the team is working together. Leadership, teamwork, and communication prowess will be immediately evident.
- To assess strengths and weaknesses of the team and develop action plans for improvement.

19. "NAILS" TEAMBUILDING ACTIVITY

 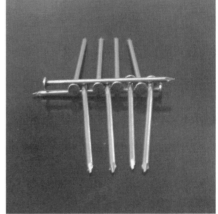

RESOURCES:

- 11 3-inch 10-D nails with a head
- A small piece of wood with one nail in the center (See photo above for the answer.)

TEAM SIZE: small groups of 2-3 people

INSTRUCTIONS AND GOAL:

Read these instructions aloud or print them out and hand them to the team:

- You have in front of you a bag with 10 nails and a piece of wood with one nail.

- Take the nails out of the bag.
- Your objective as a team is to get all the nails to rest self-contained on the top of the nail in the piece of wood.
- There is a configuration or pattern to make this possible.
- All you can use are the nails and your ingenuity.

GUIDELINES:

- The piece of wood must remain flat and can't be turned on its side.
- No nails can touch the wood.
- No nails can touch the neck of the nail in the wood.
- Do not use extraneous tools to hold the nails together (e.g., hands, string, paper, cup, etc.). Use only your ingenuity!

TIME FRAME: 12 minutes

PROCESSING THE ACTIVITY

GOAL:

- To help your team master teamwork and collaboration
- To make your team more cohesive and high-performing
- To reach consensus on the key ingredients of a Star team
- To assess your team on these key ingredients
- To affirm your team strengths
- To pick a few key areas to focus on for team improvement

TIME FRAME: 2 hours

MATERIALS NEEDED:

White board or flip chart and pens

PROCEDURE:

Focus: After 12 minutes ask the small group how they felt doing the exercise, especially if they were not successful.

- What did the curve of their energy and focus look like?
- Was it:
  - ▲ Constantly going up?
  - ▲ Did it plateau?
  - ▲ Did it dip and go down?
- Would they want their team or staff to respond in this way to a hard project?

Metaphor: Have each small group recreate the design or pattern in front of them, even if they didn't get the answer initially. (Usually you will have to create it and have them copy it.) Ask: "What do you notice about this pattern?"

Sample responses:

- It is a picture of interdependence.
- One definition of a team is a group of people who "hang together well," just like you see with this design.
- Each nail can represent your team members or your departments and how they fit or "hang together," relying on one another.

Consensus Exercise: If the nail in the wood represented the key foundation or ingredient that holds the whole team together, what does that nail represent?

- Have each person individually write his or her "top three ingredients for a high-performance team" on a piece of paper.
- Then ask each small group to get a consensus and come up with their "top three ingredients for a high-performance team."
- Have one person report for each group. He or she writes the answers on a flip chart.

- Go around to each group and hear one ingredient from each team until you have all the key ingredients.
- Look at your list and consolidate any of the ingredients, where possible. The ideal number should be around seven. If you have many more, it will be cumbersome for the next steps.

Team Assessment: Have each group write all the key ingredients you have on the flip chart onto their paper.

- Now have each group assess your whole team on these items. "Where is the team today, on a scale of 1-10, where 10 is high?"
- Give the small group 10 minutes to discuss it and come up with a score on each ingredient you have on the flip chart. The whole team will have to reach a consensus on each one.
- Pick one ingredient and get each group's score for it.
- Then ask for more details about why the group selected that number from both the highest score and lowest score.
- Continue this process for each item. Then get an average of the small groups' scores for each key ingredient.

Team Actions:

- As a whole team, look over your list and find where you are highest and lowest.
- Pick the two highest scores and ask two small groups to each take one strength and come up with actions to enhance it. (You may have more than one group work on an area if they have a lot of members.)
- Pick the two lowest scores and ask two groups to each take one ingredient and come up with actions to improve their weaknesses.
- Each group reports their actions to the whole team.
- Collect all the actions on the flip chart.

- Decide which actions would get you the biggest results. Remember the 80/20 rule: 20% of your efforts yield 80% of your results. You can vote if you have too many; ideally you should have two enhancers and two development areas to begin with.
- Each action team should have an owner, a key deliverable, a small team, and a time frame. Plan to report on progress in a few weeks.
- Schedule the follow-ups so you continually support the efforts.

Follow-ups:

- Have each action team report their progress.
- Ask how you can support each team's effort.
- Plan small win celebrations and spread the news.

20. "PERFORMANCE AND ACCOUNTABILITY" TEAMBUILDING ACTIVITY

RESOURCES:

20-30 soft kush balls or any kind of small, soft ball

TEAM SIZE: Ideal size is 8-12

GOAL:

To forecast how many balls you will catch and assess how successful you were.

GUIDELINES:

- Catch as many balls as you can.
- The balls must be thrown up in the air at the same time.
- Say, "Ready on the outside?" "Ready on the inside?"

TIME FRAME:

Go until you finish. Depending on the size of your group, it will take 10-15 minutes.

PROCEDURE AND INSTRUCTIONS:

- Distribute the balls in such a way that everyone has at least two balls.
- Everyone gets into a circle.

Round One:

▲ Ask for two volunteers from your group to come into the middle of the circle.

▲ Have them give their balls to others.

▲ Ask them to decide how many balls between them they will catch. They will announce their forecast.

▲ Have the rest of the group throw the balls all at once and count how many were caught.

▲ Let the group self-organize. Only reiterate the guidelines; they must decide how to proceed.

Round Two:

▲ Same as above with two different volunteers.

Round Three and On:

▲ Continue as above with as many rounds as you need until you have only two people left.

Last Round:

▲ Now say that you received a message from the corporate office: "You now must catch all the balls. The balls represent your customers, and you can't afford to let even one fall through the cracks."

▲ If successful, the two people in the middle will receive a bonus of 25% of their salary.

▲ If balls are dropped, both people in the middle will be fired (again, let them self-organize, and reiterate only the guidelines).

PROCESSING THE ACTIVITY

TIME FRAME: 20 minutes

QUESTIONS:

- What did you notice?
- What roles did you see?
- What assumptions were there?
- How did things change when you had stiffer consequences?
- Did you use any of the innovations from other groups?
- How creative were you in using your resources?
- What did you notice about your role?
- How assertive were the individuals who offered ideas?
- Were there any ideas that were not heard? Why not?
- What would the team need to do better to make sure all inputs are heard?
- How does this experience relate to what happens at work?
- What are some of your insights and applications back at work?

KEY POINTS IF NOT BROUGHT UP BY THE GROUP:

- Unclarified assumptions in your team can be a poison and can curtail your ability to innovate.
- All ideas have to be heard for a maximum of creativity.
- It is easier to go along with others and be unsuccessful than it is to be a change leader and challenge the process.
- Leadership is not about having all the answers, but rather utilizing all the resources effectively.
- "Thinking outside the box" requires that people challenge the process, take initiative, and get buy-in from others.

TEAM ACTIVITIES

Below are three activities you can do with your team to foster teamwork and collaboration. Each one is laid out to assist you in leading the 1.5- to 2-hour session. The topics will help you clarify expectations, assess your team on specific Star ingredients that the team created, and establish what stage of group development your team is in. Specific actions help keep the momentum to develop a Star team.

The Leadership Check-in gives you or the leader 100 key questions to jump-start your meeting. The questions also help to keep past training or learning ever present.

At the end of the chapter, there is a Team Ingredients Survey, followed by a Star Performer Action Planning sheet.

21. "EXPECTATIONS" ACTIVITY

"Sixty percent of business problems come with unclear expectations." – Stephen Covey

GOAL:

- To help your team become more cohesive and high-performing
- To make your expectations as the leader visible and clear to others
- To hear from your team what they expect of you as their leader
- For your team to clarify expectations of each other

TIME FRAME: 2 hours

MATERIALS NEEDED:

White board or flip chart and pens

PROCEDURE:

- Ask the leader to prepare ahead of time a list of what he or she expects from the team (e.g., open and honest communication, they come to you with recommendations versus problems, they give above and beyond the call of duty).

- Have your team prepare their expectations of you and each other. Send out an email or tell them about this exercise a week before the meeting.

- Read your list slowly to the team. Let them ask questions and try to engage them in a dialogue about your expectations.

- Now, have each person state one expectation of you and write it down on the flip chart. Stop when more clarification is needed and get examples, where possible. Go around the room until you have heard from everyone.

- Look at the list and give your comments. Is there anything on the list that you can't do for some reason? Tell the team you'll work on meeting their expectations.

- Then have the team share their expectations of each other (e.g., get back in touch with each other within 24 hours for emails, support each other in meetings). Things that get repeated often can be guidelines for your team.

- Again, hear from one person and go around the group as many times as needed to finish hearing all the expectations from everyone. Encourage discussion and clarification. If things were communicated negatively, have them give an example and ask what they would rather see.

- Send out the notes so everyone has a copy of the expectations.

- Within two months check back on how you and the group are living up to meeting the expectations.

- Go through each item and ask, "How are we doing on this one?" Use a scale from 1-10 to get a measurement. If someone gives it a 5, ask what it would need to get it a 6. Look for small wins.

22. TEAM ASSESSMENT

GOAL:

- To help your team become more cohesive and high performing
- To reach consensus on the key ingredients of a Star team
- To assess your team on these key ingredients
- To affirm your team strengths
- To pick a few key areas to focus on for team improvement

TIME FRAME: 2 hours

MATERIALS NEEDED:

White board or flip chart and pens

PROCEDURE:

- Have each person write his or her "top three ingredients for a high-performing team."
- Break up the team into groups of three and ask each group to "Come up with your top three ingredients for a high-performance team." Have one person report for each team.

  Go around to each group and hear one ingredient from each team until you have all the key ingredients. Write the ingredients on a flip chart.

- Look at your list and consolidate ingredients where possible. The ideal number should be around seven. If you have many more it will be cumbersome to get to the next steps.

- Now, have each group assess your team on these items. "Where are we today on a 1-10 scale, where 10 is high?" Give the group 10 minutes or so to discuss it and come up with a score on each ingredient you have on the flip chart. The team will have to reach a consensus on each one.

- Pick one ingredient and get each team's score for it.
- Then, from both the highest score and lowest score, ask for more details about why the group selected that number.
- Continue this process for each item. Then get an average for each key ingredient.
- As a whole team, look over your list at where you are highest and lowest.
- Pick the two highest scores and ask two groups to take one strength each and come up with actions to enhance your strengths. (You may have more than one group work on an area if your team has many members.)
- Pick the two lowest scores and ask two groups to take one ingredient each and come up with actions to improve your weaknesses.
- Each group reports their actions to the whole team. Collect all the actions on the flip chart.
- Decide which actions would get you the biggest results. Remember the 80/20 rule. 20% of your efforts yield 80% of your results. You can vote if you have too many; ideally you should have two enhancers and two development areas to begin with.
- Each action should have an owner, a key deliverable, a small team and a time frame. Plan to report on progress in a few weeks.
- Schedule the follow-ups so you continually support the efforts. Ask, "What can you as their leader do to support each team's effort?"
- Plan small win celebrations and spread the news.

23. 100 LEADERSHIP CHECK-IN QUESTIONS

GOALS:

- To give team leaders and trainers a tool for starting meetings, setting the tone, and reinforcing the learning gained from the structured experience back at the work site
- To give team members opportunities to select the check-in
- To give the leaders across the organization a similar way to lead their meetings
- To warm up the group and get everyone to say something; this helps the team to get to know each other better and develop camaraderie
- To specifically focus on topics you want *to breathe life into* and continue the ongoing leadership focus and learning
- To have a process check during the meeting or at the end; to gauge effectiveness and what needs to be improved

TIME FRAME:

Takes place at the start of your meeting and should take only fifteen minutes.

MATERIALS NEEDED:

A copy of the Leadership Check-in topics on the next page.

PROCEDURE:

The following questions are to be used as warm-ups to start your meetings around a leadership topic. It is best to do a "round," meaning to go around in a circle and hear everyone's response to the question. Passing is always an option. The responses should be brief. Keep the process moving briskly.

LEADERSHIP CHECK-IN TOPICS:

TEAMWORK

- Complete the statement: "The best team I have been on is… And what made it so good was…"
- How did a member of your team help you last week?
- What have you done to foster collaboration with others?
- Give an example of systems thinking you have done.
- Give an example of a small win you created for your team.
- How have you "walked your talk" regarding your team?
- Have you given an appreciation to the person on your left or right for something you have thought or felt but never mentioned before?
- On a 1-10 ranking, how effective is your team? How could it improve?
- In the forming, storming, norming, and performing stages of team development, where is your team today, and why?
- Complete the statement: "Our team's main strength is…"
- Complete the statement: "One area of weakness for our team is…"
- Give an appreciation to the person on your left.

RISK-TAKING

- How do you challenge the process, confronting or improving the status quo?
- What experiments or risks have you taken in the last week? What have you learned from them?
- What have you done to empower your co-workers or subordinates to take risks?
- In what ways have you rewarded others for their accomplishments?
- Who is a hero or heroine in risk-taking for you, and why?

- How do you best prepare for your risk-taking?
- What is a risk you are most proud of?

RELATIONSHIP-BUILDING

- What is the value of building better relationships with others?
- What have you done recently that contributed to your relationship with a customer?
- What have you done to contribute to the relationship with a team member?
- What has someone else done with or for you that contributed to building your relationship? Be specific, especially if the person is present.
- From your perspective, what is the best thing someone else can do to build a better relationship with you?

PASSION/VISION

- What is the most meaningful part of your workday? Give an example.
- What have you or others done to envision an uplifting future for your team or organization?
- Where do you see the team or organization in 3-5 years?
- What do you see as your contribution to the team and the organization?
- What do you truly get excited about at work and outside of work?
- What was one of your earliest dreams of what you wanted to do with your life?

TRUST

- Fill in the blank: "For me to trust you, you should _____."
  Give at least four answers. For example, "For me to trust you, you should not talk behind my back."

- For which team member do you have a great deal of trust, and why?
- On a 1-10 scale, how do you rate your team regarding trust?
- What could you do to increase your rating one point?
- What actions must someone undertake for you to feel that he or she is trustworthy?
- Share a trust story about someone or about an incident at work.

LEADERSHIP

- Who is a role model for you as a leader? What is it that you admire about this person?
- Can you give an example of something you did recently that exemplified your leadership?
- What has someone else done that demonstrates leadership to you? Why?
- Which Kouzes and Posner[7] leadership attributes or practices do you feel you use the most?
  - ▲ building a shared vision
  - ▲ being a role model
  - ▲ taking risks and challenging the process
  - ▲ encouraging and empowering others to act
  - ▲ acknowledging the accomplishments of others
- In which leadership attribute or practice do you feel you need the most practice?
- Complete the statement: "As a follower, what I look for in a leader is…"

EMOTIONAL INTELLIGENCE SENTENCE COMPLETIONS

- The person I know with the most Emotional Intelligence is… His/her impact on the people in his/her life is…

- What surprises me the most about the Emotional Intelligence concept is…
- Of the Emotional Intelligence clusters—Self-Awareness, Self-Management, Social Awareness, and Relationship Management—I am best in…
- The area I am working on now is: Self-Awareness, Self-Management, Social Awareness, or Relationship Management
- The best way to have influence with me is to…
- The way I deal with adversity is…
- The best change leader I have seen is…because…
- An example of how I or others leveraged self-awareness is…
- I am most positive when _____ happens.
- The best way to acknowledge me is…
- The best way to motivate me is…
- When there is conflict I usually…
- I think our meetings are…
- My greatest strength is…
- What is most inspiring for me is…
- A person I know who builds bonds well is… And how he/she does it is…
- The best way to develop discretionary effort in me is…
- I know someone is confident when I see him/her…

VALUES/MISSION

- Pick one of your team's or organization's shared values you used at work last week. Select a different value for different meetings.
- What is your top personal value, and why?
- What is a value that you avoid or move away from (e.g., rejection, humiliation, embarrassment)?
- Which value is the easiest for you to demonstrate?

- Which value is the hardest for you to show?
- Give an example of how you actualized the organization's mission with a customer.
- Give an example of living the organization's vision with your people.
- Give an example of demonstrating the organization's vision for the business.

SELF-AWARENESS SENTENCE COMPLETIONS

- You know I am under stress when...
- I am most motivated when...
- The biggest challenge of the day is...
- I feel at my best when...
- Something I learned this week was...
- A mistake I made last week was...
- I am most happy when...
- What I fear the most at work is...
- I am most frustrated when...
- What I like most in others is...
- Most people don't know that I...
- I try to avoid...
- My biggest highlight this week was...
- When I am angry I...
- What irritates me the most in the workday is...
- I feel one of my strengths is...
- One development area for me is…

SELF-MANAGEMENT AND RENEWAL HABITS SENTENCE COMPLETIONS

- I am at my peak when I…
- The way I recharge myself is...

- The last "Amygdala Hijack" I had was…
- When I'm about to lose control, I manage myself by…
- What brings me balance in my life is…
- What I do to move into the gap between stimulus and old reactions…
- Once in the gap, I…
- My way of saying no to doing more is…
- What is hardest about saving time for myself is…
- If I don't sharpen the saw, I feel…
- The value of self-renewal is…
- My best trick for time management is…
- How I end up wasting the most time is…
- My goals for the next three years are…
- The biggest initiative I have ever undertaken is…

24. TEAMWORK INGREDIENTS SURVEY

For each of these questions, please rank on a 1-5 scale as follows.

1 = *it never happens*

2 = *it happens infrequently*

3 = *it happens occasionally*

4 = *it happens frequently*

5 = *it always happens*

Never	Infrequently	Occasionally	Frequently	Always
1	**2**	**3**	**4**	**5**

1. Our team has a shared vision that we understand and accept. ☐

2. There is high trust among team members. ☐

3. Communication is open, thinking is made visible, people listen well, and differing ideas are encouraged and accepted. ☐

4. Conflict is dealt with openly and resolved. ☐

5. Our team is able to establish, prioritize, and work on what is most important. ☐

6. Risk-taking and being proactive are encouraged and supported among team members. ☐

7. Collaboration is high and team members seek win-win solutions. ☐

8. Our team maintains a "one-team" perspective (i.e., all individuals and departments are one big team). ☐

9. Our team is constantly learning and trying to improve. ☐

10. Leadership is participative, shared by all, and no one person dominates. ☐

11. Our team has established values and guidelines for how we operate. ☐

12. We are able to hold each other accountable for the performances. ☐

13. I receive recognition or praise for good work within every seven days. ☐

14. My opinion counts at work. ☐

15. I am clear about what is expected of me at work. ☐

NARRATIVE QUESTIONS

16. Which items from the 15 above work well on your team?

17. Which items from the 15 above do not work on your team?

18. On a 1-10 scale where 10 is the highest, how would you rank your teamwork?

19. From 1-10, how would you rank the leadership on your team?

20. What could your leaders do to improve your teamwork?

21. What are a few things you would like to see changed that would significantly improve the way your team performs?

22. Other comments?

STAR PERFORMER ACTION PLAN

Read through the Star Profile and *Coach's Corner* to develop your teamwork and collaboration skills. Now, answer the following questions to help you make your plan. Remember, micro-initiatives can make a macro impact.

Which competencies or practices do you already do that you want to continue?

1. _____
2. _____
3. _____

Which new practices do you want to incorporate?

1. _____
2. _____
3. _____

What resources do you need to make this happen?

1. _____
2. _____
3. _____

Who can support you and hold you accountable?

1. _____
2. _____
3. _____

What will be your first steps in this plan?

1. _____
2. _____
3. _____

How might you sabotage your efforts and best intentions?

1. _____
2. _____
3. _____

Share this plan with your support people. Good luck!

CHAPTER FOUR

DEVELOPING OTHERS
TOOLS AND STRATEGIES

Keep away from people who try to belittle your ambitions. Small people always do that, but the really great make you feel that you too can become great. —Mark Twain

This section provides the tools and strategies to help you become a Star Performer in the area of Developing Others. It begins with a profile of Mark French, Head Women's Basketball Coach for University of California at Santa Barbara. French shares *13 Secrets & Current Practices* that help him shine as a Star Performer. The profile is followed by the *Coach's Corner,* which presents a series of 12 strategies and activities you can implement with your team right away to increase developing others in your organization.

WHAT IS THE DEVELOPING OTHERS COMPETENCY?

Developing Others is a key component in leading others to become Star Performers. It is the process of identifying the strengths and potential of others and then designing and implementing a plan to help them succeed. It provides support, timely feedback, and mentoring to bolster their career development.

EMOTIONAL INTELLIGENCE RESEARCH EXAMPLES

Strong coaching and mentoring, two methods of developing others, help the individual and the organization in many ways, including better employee performance, higher levels of loyalty and job satisfaction, more opportunities for promotion and pay increases, and lower rates of turnover.[1]

Developing Others is a vital skill for all levels within your organization, but a study of supervisors, managers, and executives in 12 large companies reveals that the greatest impact is with supervisors and also affects both sales people and line staff.[2] Research shows that as managers and executives move up in their careers, they spend a greater amount of time away from the line (and their specific job skills) and their leadership skills become more essential.

In superior managers, excellence in Developing Others is second next to team leadership.[3] Star Performers understand the value of this competence. The relationship with one's boss is one of the best predictors for how long a person stays at a job, and an essential part of that relationship is the sense that your boss sees your potential and wants you to succeed. Spherion and Lou Harris Associates found that only 11% of the employees who rated their bosses as "excellent" said they were likely to look for a different job in the next year. However, 40% of those who rated their bosses as "poor" said they were likely to leave. So, people with good bosses are four times less likely to leave than are those with poor bosses.[4]

One of the questions I ask in many of my leadership trainings is about a person's best boss. What did he or she do and say? How did he or she influence you? It is always enlightening to hear the specific practices, some micro and some macro, that have had a powerful impact on these individuals. After asking these questions of hundreds of leaders, a pattern has emerged. The individuals adopt the practices of their "best boss." Their thinking is, "It worked well for me and should work well for others I supervise." Typically these are essential practices like the ones we are discussing here. The fact that people remember and repeat these practices illuminates the power and influence every leader has on his or her people. If you start doing a few micro-initiatives right now, not only are you having an immediate impact on your people but you are also influencing the next generation of leaders who will pass your practices on to their followers.

In *The One Thing You Need to Know*, Marcus Buckingham states that great managers make a point of discovering the uniqueness in each of their workers and then capitalize their findings. He identified the three things that great managers need to know about their people:

- What are their strengths?
- What are their motivators or triggers?
- What is their particular style of learning?

As noted, the average manager views his or her employees like generic checkers on a black-and-red board—all basically the same and able to move only one space at a time in only one direction. Stars see their employees as "chess players," each with unique skills and talent who can move in different ways and cover more territory than one space at a time. The challenge is to discover your "chess-playing" employees' uniqueness and then learn how to implement their strengths for the sake of the organization as well as the development of the individual.

ARE YOU A STAR PERFORMER IN DEVELOPING OTHERS OR JUST AVERAGE?

Stars exhibit both average and Star behaviors consistently. Where are you?

AVERAGE

- Expresses positive expectations
- Provides support

STAR

- Gives timely feedback
- Acts as a mentor[5]

STAR PROFILE: MARK FRENCH, UNIVERSITY OF CALIFORNIA AT SANTA BARBARA (UCSB) HEAD COACH, WOMEN'S BASKETBALL TEAM

WHY MARK FRENCH IS A STAR PERFORMER

Why a basketball coach as the Star Profile? Most leaders have a difficult time focusing on developing others. They are juggling their own meetings, deliverables, as well as administrative and operational tasks. Depending on their role, they may spend as little as 25% of their time on development, some possibly a tad more. A college coach's success is totally dependent on his team's performance. It makes sense that a smart coach would devote a great deal of time to developing others. Approximately 75-80% of French's workload is built around nurturing the talents of each person, in practice or conversation, focusing on performance issues, stretching each team member to his or her physical and mental limit, and orchestrating his or her unique abilities to create one high-performance, winning team. Mark French's 25 years of experience and secrets are a goldmine of information and inspiration for leaders to study and practice.

French has been a Division I head basketball coach for 25 years and has 494 career wins and is soon to cross the 500 victory threshold. He has taken UCSB to 10 NCAA appearances and nine straight Big West titles. In the 2003-2004 season, they made it into the Sweet 16 in the NCAA finals, losing to the eventual winner, University of Connecticut. Coach French has been the Big West Coach of the Year seven times and in 2002-2003 was the WBCA District Coach of the Year and the Naismith National Coach of the Year finalist.

French is very proud that UCSB players have a 98% graduation rate and that 63% of the players go on to graduate school. There are even five graduates who play or played in the Women's National Basketball Association. More than 20 of French's players were recognized as Big West scholar athletes, tops in the conference. He states,

"I'm more of an educator than a coach," and he is more concerned that his players "have world-class people skills and be good people than just excel on the basketball court."

As an athlete, French was a two-sport letter winner at University of California at Santa Barbara. He was an all-league pitcher for the baseball team and played two seasons on the basketball team. French earned a B.A. in Political Science from UCSB and received a master's degree from the University of the Pacific in Physical Education.

In looking over the 20 Emotional Intelligence competencies, Coach French added, "Most of our star players have a lot of these."

COACH FRENCH WAS ASKED:

- How did he learn the Developing Others competency?
- What does he do to be such an effective leader?
- What are his daily practices?
- What are the pitfalls he needs to be aware of?

EARLY LEARNING EXPERIENCES

"Both of my parents were teachers. My mother taught English and my father was a baseball coach. My mother helped me understand the value of language and how to talk about my feelings. She constantly told me it was okay to share how I felt and convinced me I'd be more successful and satisfied if I were really in touch with other people. I think that's why I'm particularly successful coaching women. My father was an old school coach for 41 years and was highly organized and competitive. I spent a lot of time watching and learning from him. I believe I had the best of both influences."

Coach French had great role models for many of the EI competencies. His father demonstrated conscientiousness, initiative, leadership, and achievement orientation, while his mother taught empathy, communication, accurate self-assessment, and emotional self-awareness. This blend of utilizing and integrating both logical and emotional aspects of the brain continued in his formative training.

As a graduate student at the University of the Pacific, French became the pitching coach for the baseball team. The head coach, Tom Stubbs, a lot like French's father, was very efficient and organized. He knew all the relevant statistics of the players and the game and was quite structured. In his graduate classes, Coach French was learning about coaching theory, sports psychology, and the body-mind connection.

Fortunately, Coach Stubbs was a strong believer in developing others, and he let Coach French teach and practice visualization, meditation, and progressive relaxation with the pitchers in particular. The team won games and, as French remembers, "The players felt like I really cared." His experimenting and risk-taking were paying off.

Coach French was building a philosophy and practice for educating the whole person—physical, mental, and emotional—and he received immediate positive feedback on his techniques. The success of the team's performance, the intimate relationships he was developing with the players, and the constant commitment to development truly put Coach French on the road to becoming a Star.

In 1978, French was asked to be the head coach of the women's basketball team at University of the Pacific. He took the job and found, "I really liked working with the women, and it fit me better. Women value other things than just being the star. They are there to be a part of a team." In his first season the team won 16 games and lost 11. The second season they were 20 and 7, and Coach French proclaimed, "I can do this."

Another key influence for Coach French was Stephen Covey's *The 7 Habits of Highly Effective People*. It helped him in his personal life, and he was able to integrate the practical habits into his coaching philosophy as well. To be an effective coach or player he learned, "You have to win the inner battle and work interiorly first to become trustworthy and confident." This is in line with focusing on the personal competencies of Self-Awareness and Self-Management before addressing the social competencies of Social Awareness and Relationship Management.

13 SECRETS & CURRENT PRACTICES OF MARK FRENCH—STAR PERFORMER

Coach French took his early learning experiences and created a successful coaching philosophy and strategy, not just for basketball players but also for being Star Performers in all aspects of life. You are probably not developing Star basketball players in your role, but season after season Coach French has honed the development process, and you can borrow some of his strategies.

Think about these practices and how to apply them to your own business or setting to help develop and guide your Stars. Read through the strategies and pick one or two to try out. (Note that each secret is followed by a set of business applications you can use for your organization.)

1. LEADER'S POINT OF VIEW (POV): BASKETBALL AS A METAPHOR FOR LIFE

Coach French says, "Basketball helps my players learn about themselves." A recent NCAA study states that the average woman athlete spends 3,000 hours with her sport, but only 4% of her time dedicated to playing the game itself. The other 96% revolves around "What we are really about," as Coach French says. "That's communicating, bouncing back from adversity, and dealing with stress."

When asked, "Is this journey better if you are the Star or the 14th player," French smiles. "Our program is for both." French focuses on this philosophy every day, to help his players develop "habits of excellence." (A Covey term.) "We are what we repeatedly do." This organizing principle helps Coach French keep perspective and inspires how he communicates his program to new prospects and the community. A Leadership Point of View is incredibly important because it is the cornerstone of how you perceive and practice developing others.

BUSINESS APPLICATION:

- As a leader, what is your POV regarding work and fellowship?
- What is your leadership POV in developing your people?
- Do they know your POV?
- How often do you talk and act on your POV?

2. PRACTICE

Practice is a critical piece in the development of people and teams. This is the one big difference between sports and the business world. In sports, people spend 95% or more of their time practicing and only 5% of the time performing. In the business world it is the exact opposite, where 95% if not more is spent performing and very little time practicing. As mentioned in Chapter 3, we can learn and adopt a great deal of useful techniques from sports and the performing arts regarding practice.

During the season, Coach French's teams practice two to three hours a day, and he assigns a specific focus for each session. During practice, French studies the development of each player and also builds individualized training programs to improve each player's game. (For example, some may need to work on their defense, others on rebounding and boxing out.) He feels his players shine at game time because they focus on staying with what they do best rather than letting the opponent dictate what they do.

BUSINESS APPLICATION:

- How prepared are your people for their meetings and presentations?
- Do you regularly have "dry runs" or practice sessions for important presentations or meetings? (Most organizations do not.)

- Are your people clear where they are in their learning curve and when they must perform?

- How are your people encouraged to try new risks and practice something that will pay off for them and the organization in the future?

3. BONDING AND TEAM MEETINGS

At the start of every season the team has a bonding weekend. To help the players get to know one another, they participate in a variety of teambuilding and community events. Coach French has each of them talk about themselves, their past, family, and current aspirations. He encourages starting the season with meaningful activities. Many have done rope courses, spent time at community soup kitchens, and then spent the night together sleeping on the basketball court. These rituals are created to help individuals get to know each other as people as well as basketball players. One of the most positive results is a heartfelt commitment each player feels toward one another and to the team as a whole.

BUSINESS APPLICATION:

- What rituals do you have to bring your team together?

- How do you encourage your team to get to know each other?

- Do you have a team formation process to start a new project or orient new players to each other? (See Chapter 3, *Coach's Corner* for some ideas of things to do with your team.)

- What is your process for orienting new employees? Are they able to quickly feel connected to people and your company's culture?

4. RECRUITING STARS

In the business world, hiring the wrong person can cost a company three times his or her annual salary. For UCSB's Women's

Basketball team, the wrong player can affect the team chemistry and the success of the season. The coaching staff has an elaborate process for selecting and recruiting their future Stars. They have to be able to have "successors" for all the positions, and naturally they go after their recruits in a focused manner. The pinnacle of the recruiting effort is the home visit. According to NCAA rules, a prospective player can only have five home visits from universities or colleges. UCSB is competing with Stanford, Virginia, Georgia Tech, and other top-tier basketball schools for these players. The visit is limited to two and a half hours and is highly orchestrated.

In order to structure their visit, the coaching staff spends a great deal of time researching the specific recruit to understand what is important to the recruit and his or her family. The research results in a three-page outline for each visit, followed by role-playing the visit while videotaping it. To cap thing off, they review their efforts. A win for Coach French results in the family having had a positive experience and saying, "This was a nice visit and a great conversation."

Some families wonder if their child can keep up with the academics at UCSB. Coach French and his top assistants will talk about "special admits," support available, and the overall grade point averages. Understanding Coach French's philosophy or point of view (POV) is important. Many times he is the differentiator who influences the recruit to select UCSB.

The home visit is the playoff game for using Emotional Intelligence. Reading their audience, coming prepared, using empathy, asking questions, having a good give-and-take, inspiring the family, building bonds, and developing a trusting relationship are paramount in this game. Getting their recruits to enroll at UCSB is the ultimate win.

BUSINESS APPLICATION:

- What kind of Stars do you need in your organization?
- Is your interviewing and hiring method as clear and practiced as Coach French's?

- What do you need to do to enhance your process of hiring Stars?
- How capable are you at understanding the needs of new employees and providing challenging positions to meet their needs?
- Are you able to paint the picture of what your culture is like and what is expected of them as employees? (Strategies for hiring are found in the *Coach's Corner* on page 172.)

5. BUILDING EFFECTIVE RELATIONSHIPS

Coach French understands that to develop his players he needs to build a relationship with them. One solid way to do so is to act as a mentor, one of the Star competencies. French states that women often define having a good relationship with him as "Knowing he is someone I can talk to." This description is far different from what male basketball players find important, such as top-notch facilities, details about the schedule, and being informed about the amount of playing time they will have.

One key in building a real relationship is to support the women as they deal with their "inner battles," an issue that affects their performance and life in general. Some of these battles include lack of confidence, parental pressure, or the boyfriend back home. French works with the women to solve these conflicts so that they feel cared for and can then focus more intently on their performance on the court.

BUSINESS APPLICATION:

- How are your relationships with your co-workers?
- Do you know your direct reports very well?
- Do you have an open and honest relationship with each one?
- Do you know what is causing your direct reports' performance to be less than desirable?

- Do your direct reports trust you to share their real concerns?
- Do your direct reports feel you care about them and that their opinion counts?

6. SELF-ASSESSMENTS AND GOAL SETTING

Coach French uses the Myers-Briggs Type Indicator and Strong Campbell Interest Test with all the players. They share their results to determine what they need to work on as individuals and also as a team. Each player is encouraged to acknowledge that she needs help in specific areas. "Athletes don't learn this naturally," French states. Some of the goals may be developing "trustworthiness, selflessness, patience, tolerance, or leadership." The players are then encouraged to reach out to each other to provide support in these key areas.

BUSINESS APPLICATION:

- Do your team members know the strengths and weaknesses of each individual person?
- Have you encouraged them to help each other?
- Do you know your direct reports' strengths?
- Do you know what each of your people's career aspirations are?
- As a leader, do you know what motivates your reports to their peak performance?
- Do you know each of your people's specific learning style?
- What style assessments do you use to help determine your people's uniqueness?

7. ONE-ON-ONES

Each week in season and out, Coach French meets with his players individually. These one-on-one conversations provide the place for French to act as mentor to help his players deal with their "inner battles." He uses a Socratic approach where he asks questions and lets the player explore her own answers. He also takes opportunities to give feedback on each player's progress. This is an anchor to his program and contributes greatly to truly knowing and developing each player year after year.

BUSINESS APPLICATION:

- Do you come to one-on-ones with your leader prepared and able to bring up pertinent issues to your development?

- Do you have one-on-ones with your people?

- Are there specific goals your reports are working on for their development along with the tasks for their position?

- Are the one-on-ones valuable for you and your reports?

(Read more about one-on-ones in the *Coach's Corner* on pages 186-190.)

8. SUPPORTIVE LEARNING

Ongoing learning is important to Coach French because it supports his philosophy and program. He expects his players to read and report on books such as Stephen Covey's *The 7 Habits of Highly Effective People*. He also has his players attend diversity training so that they can appreciate the differences in their teammates as well as in other people who will show up in the rest of their lives. A highlight of the year is the afternoon spent with legendary Coach John Wooden of UCLA. Coach Wooden and the players exchange questions and he reads poetry to them. Wooden discusses his Pyramid of Success, which has 15 building blocks, many identical to the EI competencies, such as confidence, team spirit, self-control, initiative, industriousness, conscientiousness, cooperation, and loyalty.

Wooden's principles are evident in all of his actions. During one of the meetings, he received two phone calls. One was from Roone Arledge, the creator of ABC Monday Night Sports as well as the ABC news division. Coach Wooden let the call go directly into voicemail because he didn't want to interrupt his visit with the players. The second call was from his granddaughter. He jumped up to answer that one!

BUSINESS APPLICATION:

- As an employee, do you have specific ideas on what training and education you want?
- As a leader, what learning do you provide for your employees?
- How are you checking in with your employees to reinforce and hold them accountable? (As their leader, your support for their training is the key to their retention and application of the training.)
- Do you pass along articles or books you think would be helpful to your employees?

9. TIMELY FEEDBACK

According to the EI competency model, Stars give timely feed-back and act as mentors. Coach French quotes a study that charts the type of feedback Coach Wooden gave in his winning history. Wooden's feedback to his players was 80% positive; while the average coach's feedback is 80% negative and only 20% positive.

Coach French thought he and his staff were pretty positive, but then he checked videotapes of the practices and scored it for positive and negative feedback. He was surprised to find out that 60% was negative! French immediately made changes and the next season he got it up to 50% positive, with the goal for the next year being to increase it to 60%.

In the business world, it is very rare for teams to examine their performance to decide what works and what they can do differently, let alone watch themselves on videotape.

BUSINESS APPLICATION:

- How often are you giving positive feedback to co-workers and direct reports?

- Is the feedback immediate and helpful?
- Is your feedback successfully received?
- How often does your team as a whole evaluate your performance?

(Chapter 3 gives specific tools for your team to assess its effectiveness.)

10. FOCUS ON STRENGTHS

Coach French makes sure that he shows film clips of the team doing their offense and defense correctly. He knows that, from a motivational standpoint, he will get more effort from them if they focus on what they are doing right.

An athlete's confidence is critical to his or her performance, and focusing on strengths while balancing negative feedback ensures a confident performer. In the business world, your performer's confidence level is also critical, although many managers don't take this into consideration when interacting with employees. It can hardly be said enough: Your *relationship* with your subordinates is the critical factor that contributes to their feeling valued and wanting to stay at the organization.

BUSINESS APPLICATION:

- Where is most of your focus with your people—on their strengths or development areas?
- Do you spend time talking about their strengths and ways to use them more?
- Are your decisions about tasks for your people dictated by what they do best and thinking about them as chess players? If not, how can you make more time to do so?

11. TAKE PERSONAL RESPONSIBILITY

Coach French said, "I would never yell at my team about something we haven't made a big deal about in practice. We never do anything in games that we haven't done in practice." If there is a mistake or letdown, Coach French looks at where he might have let the team down. French is willing to take responsibility for it.

Dean Smith, the famous University of North Carolina (UNC) basketball coach with 879 victories, more than any other coach in college basketball history, has a similar philosophy. Scott Williams, a UNC graduate who went on to win three NBA championships with the Chicago Bulls, said about Smith, "…he never took credit for our wins but went out of his way to take the blame for all our losses, claiming he hadn't prepared us properly."[6]

How often have you heard of leaders or employees taking responsibility for a mistake by admitting they had not prepared enough? Just because nobody takes responsibility for the mistake does not mean the mistake did not happen. In many organizations, the exact opposite occurs—people spend time and energy blaming someone else for the problem.

BUSINESS APPLICATION:

It is crucial to ask yourself if the following statements are heard enough in your organization.

I need help.

I don't know.

I made a mistake.

If you don't hear these often enough, you do not have the optimum climate for positive and responsible learning. Ask yourself:

- How often are these statements made in my organization?
- What would help to make them safer to say in my organization?
- How can I take more responsibility for the preparation and performance of my employees?

12. PERFORMANCE REVIEW

All of French's team games are videotaped, and then the team-work and individual player performances are studied and discussed.

Usually, the highlights are accompanied with music and humorous commentary. Typically, the team strengths are emphasized. This is immediate feedback for the team. When mistakes are shown, they are framed in a context of learning with the idea of improvement in mind, so that they will not be repeated. In addition, the coaches are always taking the players aside during practice, to talk about their performance and what they need to work on. Each coach tailors his feedback to the individual player, in terms of her unique requirements for help with motivation, confidence, or specific play instruction.

BUSINESS APPLICATION:

Athletic teams require continual reviews for daily improvement. In many business organizations, there is only one yearly review. Others expect the leader to talk to their employees every month about their performance. Because leaders are too busy responding to "the crisis of the day," this often does not happen regularly or in depth. Leaders often make uninformed assumptions that everybody is doing just fine. Here are some of the basic review practices used successfully in the world of sports that leaders can apply to their businesses:

1. Communicate and give feedback daily.

2. Tailor communication to the individual.

3. Balance strengths with development.

4. Offer experiential teaching. Make sure "correct" actions are repeated along with support and guidance.

5. Give feedback immediately after the next performance in the developed area.

Which practices can you use to improve your performance reviews?

- Are there ways you can shadow or witness a direct report's performance?

- How can you incorporate feedback from others, such as peers?

13. BRIEFINGS BEFORE AND AFTER THE GAME

BEFORE THE GAME:

Coach French always focuses on what his team does well and how they can continue to execute what they already know. He doesn't focus or worry as much on what their opponent does. Coach Smith at the University of North Carolina had a similar philosophy. Before games he would repeat the phrases: "play hard," "play together," and "play smart."[7]

AFTER THE GAME:

Coach French and the team talk about what they did well and what led to their successes. This discussion reinforces the practices and disciplines the team has employed. It is important for French to hear from his players about their perception of the game. This helps him gauge their confidence level and motivation and often begets new insights and practices. The successes are written down so they can be referred to at a later date.

BUSINESS APPLICATION:

- Do you consciously prepare your team for a new endeavor?
- Do you clarify your expectations with them and hear from your people what they think they need to succeed?
- Do you practice for this new endeavor?
- What kind of feedback do you give and get after a performance? It may be a meeting with a new client, a presentation in front of your executive team, or solving a conflict with co-workers. In many companies, this is called an "after-action review" or a "postmortem."
- Would this be helpful in your organization?
- What do you need to do to start this process for your team or organization?

PITFALLS: WHAT FRENCH NEEDS TO BE AWARE OF

Coach French identified a few of the pitfalls that can get in the way of developing his players:

- He can become too sensitive about being liked by his team, the administration, and the fans and fail to stick with his gut feelings about what the right thing to do is.
- At the risk of not being liked as much, he might not challenge the players as much as he could.
- He can be too helpful in solving players' problems instead of letting them struggle to find their own answers.

ACTIONS: REVIEW FRENCH'S CURRENT PRACTICES

Looking at Coach French's current practices, what practices can you incorporate to become a Star Performer in Developing Others?

Which ones do you want to add to your Star Performer Action Plan?

1. _____

2. _____

3. _____

THE COACH'S CORNER: 12 STRATEGIES FOR DEVELOPING OTHERS

OVERVIEW

The Center for Creative Leadership has trained and written a great deal about the development process for executives and managers. They state: "Managers are critical to the development process. They have a number of roles that they must endorse, understand, and have the skills to carry out. These include: making development real, providing development experiences, providing support and feedback, and accessing organizational resources."[8]

12 KEY STRATEGIES FOR DEVELOPING OTHERS

Below are 12 strategies I use in executive coaching when focusing on developing others. Read through each of the tools, pick one or two to try out, and then incorporate them into your plan.

1. HIRING STARS: EMOTIONALLY INTELLIGENT LEADERS ARE MORE LIKELY TO BE HIRED TO BECOME STARS

Increase your success rate by hiring executives with strong EI competencies. They are far more likely to perform in the top third based on salary bonuses for performance of the divisions they lead (87% are in the top third). In addition, division leaders with these competencies outperform their targets by 15-20%. Those who lacked these strengths under-performed by almost 20%.[9]

One of the most important activities in hiring is being clear about what the position requires. Every position is unique—some require high interaction and collaboration; others require much individual planning and effort.

Behavioral Questions for EI Competencies: Behavioral interviewing techniques are a way to relate a candidate's answers to past experiences and to develop indicators for how this candidate may respond and perform in the future.[10] Remember, the best predictor for future behavior is past behavior. Some of the benefits of behavioral questioning are:

- Spontaneity, as the candidate cannot give you a "canned, prepared" response.
- The ability to watch the candidate's thought process as he or she selects an experience to speak about.
- The opportunity to see the candidate think and communicate on his or her feet.
- Less exaggeration, as the response is tied to past concrete experiences.
- Ease in establishing his or her lack of experience in an area.

2. BEHAVIORAL QUESTION LIST

Select two or three questions from the competencies below that you feel are most important. After each set of questions is a list of assessments to help you delve deeper. When you finish each interview, rate the candidate using the Interview Rating Scale.

INITIATIVE

- Give me an example of extra efforts you have taken to get a sale. What did you do or say?
- What is the biggest initiative you have taken and championed at work?
- How did it work out? On a scale of 1-10, where 10 is the highest, how would you rate the result? What would you have done differently?

Assessment:

- Did he/she appear to take risks and initiate actions on his/her own?
- Does this seem to be a habit for him/her; does he/she regularly and consistently act this way?
- How would you rate the candidate for Initiative—Star or average?

SELF-CONTROL

- Give me an example of a time when you were very frustrated with a customer or co-worker. What did you do or say?
- What methods do you use to control yourself or keep yourself in check? How effective are you at managing your emotions, on a 1-10 scale?
- What triggers you or pushes your buttons the most with customers?

Assessment:

- Did the candidate give responses that indicate he/she responds calmly and calms others as a regular habit?

- How would you rate the interviewee for Self-Control—Star or average?

EMPATHY

- How do you read others' non-verbals?

- Give me an example of how you demonstrate that you are open to new ways of looking at things.

- Tell me of a time when a customer, co-worker, or employee was very upset with you. What did you do or say?

Assessment:

- Did the respondent give indications of understanding where the customer was coming from or why he/she was feeling that way?

- Did he/she report any empathic responses, such as "You must have felt…" or "That sounds very challenging, rewarding, exciting…"

- How would you rate this candidate for Empathy—Star or average?

BUILDING BONDS

- Give me some examples of what you do or say to build strong relationships with customers and co-workers.

- Tell me an example of an opportunity you received from networking.

- Who is the best person you know at building and cultivating relationships? What does he/she do or say?

Assessment:

- Did it appear as a habit or an irregularity that the interviewee used strong mutual relationships as a tool in influencing or selling?

- Did it seem he/she understood the importance of networking for success?
- How would you rate this candidate for Building Bonds—Star or average?

SELF-CONFIDENCE

- Give me an example of a time that you had to be very decisive. What did you do or say?
- What do you do to ready yourself for a big project, meeting, or presentation?
- What do you do to maintain your confidence?

Assessment:

- Did the candidate appear to speak and behave in an unhesitating manner?
- How confident did this person seem to you?
- How would you rate him/her for Self-Confidence—Star or average?

ADAPTABILITY

- Give me an example of a time you had to totally change or adopt a new strategy in working with someone. What did you do or say?
- What do you find to be the hardest part in dealing with change?
- Give me an example of a time you changed your strategy or ideas based on what someone else told you.
- On a 1-10 scale, how adaptable are you? What else could you do to improve?

Assessment:

- Did this candidate seem to have a tolerance for ambiguity and the ability to change as a strong habit?
- How would you rate him/her for Adaptability—Star or average?

ACHIEVEMENT ORIENTATION

- What has been the most challenging goal that you set for yourself and achieved?
- What has been your most challenging goal that you set for yourself and didn't achieve?
- What is an example of a calculated risk you have taken recently?
- Explain how you decide if you will take a calculated risk.
- In this position, what obstacles do you anticipate you will have to deal with?
- How long do you think it will take before you make a significant contribution to the team and company?

Assessment:

- Does it seem as though these behaviors are a habit for this candidate?
- How would you rate him/her for Achievement Orientation—Star or average?

SERVICE ORIENTATION

- How do you know that your customers are satisfied with the service you are providing?
- Give me an example of satisfying a customer need that was beyond his or her expectation.
- How do you find out what the customer really needs? Is there an example of providing for a need that the customer didn't initially think of?
- How well do your customers trust you, 1-10? What makes you say that?

Assessment:

- Does the interviewee seem very customer-focused?
- Do you think customers will relate well to him/her?
- How would you rate this person for Service Orientation—Star or average?

INFLUENCE SKILLS

- Give me an example of your best and worst persuasion experiences.
- What do you find is the best way to persuade someone?
- How do you deal with objections to what you are trying to sell?
- Give me an example of your strategy for selling a new idea to a client or your team.

Assessment:

- Are there indications that this person anticipates the impact of his/her words and actions?
- Are there indications of using indirect influences (e.g., others internal and external, research information, articles, and stories)?
- Are there any examples of using complex influence strategies to meet his/her goals?
- How would you rate this candidate for Influence Skills—Star or average?

TEAMWORK

- Give an example of how you dealt with someone who strongly opposed some ideas you had.
- What would be your initial strategies to build relationships?
- What kind of questions would you like to ask people?
- What is the main thing you want to convey about yourself to people on your team or to a new customer?

Assessment:

- Does it seem that this person values teamwork for getting things done or is he/she more of an individual performer?
- From your interview, will he/she solicit input from others?
- How encouraging does he/she seem of others?

- Will this person be able to build a strong team?
- How would you rate him/her for Teamwork—Star or average?

TRUSTWORTHINESS

- Tell me about a time that was challenging for you to follow your own values, when there was pressure to do otherwise.
- Tell me a time you made a mistake and how you deal with situations when you don't know or need advice.
- How would you develop your credibility in this organization?
- In many organizations, it is difficult to ask for help. How do you deal with that?

Assessment:

- Does this person seem open to admitting his/her mistakes and asking for help?
- Does it seem like this candidate would stick to his/her values or bend them under pressure from others?
- What is your gut reaction about this person?
- How would you rate him/her for Trustworthiness—Star or average?

COMMUNICATION

- Tell me about a time when you were a new leader. What things did you communicate to your team, the customer, or the organization?
- How would you describe your communication style?
- What do you find is the best way to engage your audience?
- What has been the hardest thing for you to communicate as a professional? How well do you do it? What would you do differently?
- How would you communicate differently between an internal and external customer?

Assessment:

- In your interview, was there an effective give-and-take?
- Did the candidate ask you good questions?
- Did he/she appear to have the skill to communicate in different ways for different people?
- How would you rate this person for Communication—Star or average?

ORGANIZATIONAL AWARENESS

- Give me an example of how you might use the politics of the organization to help get something done.
- What would you do to find out about how this company really works?
- How long do you think it would take you to understand the underlying structures of this organization?

Assessment:

- Does it feel as though this person is sophisticated in understanding the underlying issues of the organization?
- Did he/she demonstrate organizational savvy in getting things done?
- How would you rate this candidate for Organizational Awareness—Star or average?

DEVELOPING OTHERS

- Give me an example of how you go about developing your people.
- What is the best example of your successfully mentoring someone?
- Give me an example of the most challenging person you were developing.
- What was the most challenging part for you?
- When do you find is the best time to give someone feedback?

Assessment:

- Does it seem like the candidate is good at giving people feedback?
- Do you think he/she could be an effective mentor?
- How would you feel being mentored by him/her?
- Would people be able to relate to this person as their leader?

EMOTIONAL SELF-AWARENESS

- Give me an example of a time you had mixed feelings about something and how you sorted through it.
- Give me an example of a time your feelings had an impact on your experience or others' experience.
- Is there a specific emotional signal you have that helps identify what you are feeling?
- What are the top three feelings you most frequently have?
- Tell me about a time you had a negative feeling at work. Why did you have it and what did you do about it?

Assessment:

- How was this person's emotional vocabulary—fair, good, or excellent?
- Did it seem that he/she knew why his/her feelings occurred?
- Did this candidate demonstrate understanding of the implication of his/her feelings?
- How would you rate this person on Emotional Awareness—Star or average?

ACCURATE SELF-ASSESSMENT

- Give me an example of feedback you received at a past job and how you used that feedback.
- What goals for improvement have you made the most progress in? Least progress?
- What was the hardest feedback you ever heard from a co-worker or boss? What did you do about it?

Assessment:

- Did you feel that the interviewee is open to feedback?
- How well does this person appear to leverage feedback and awareness?
- Does he/she seem to regularly make long-term self-development plans?
- How would you rate this candidate on Accurate Self-Assessment—Star or average?

CHANGE CATALYST

- Tell me a time that you personally led a change effort. How did it go?
- What strategies did you use to get people on board?
- How did you execute the change effort?
- What was the most successful change initiative you have been involved in and what made it so successful?
- How would you rate yourself as a change agent, on a 1-10 scale, where 10 is the highest? Why?

Assessment:

- Did you feel that the candidate took full responsibility for promoting and championing this change?
- Did it seem like he/she had effective strategies for getting people involved in the change initiative?
- How effective were this person's communication strategies?
- How would you rate him/her on being a Change Catalyst—Star or average?

INSPIRATIONAL LEADERSHIP

- Describe a situation where you were the leader of an initiative.
- What strategies did you use to position yourself as the leader?
- What methods did you use to communicate your vision?

- How did you stimulate enthusiasm and make the vision compelling?
- Describe a situation where your leadership was lacking. What would you do differently?

Assessment:

- Did you feel this person took a confident and powerful role in the situation described?
- Would you feel inspired and enthusiastic, listening to him/her?
- As a follower, would you follow his/her lead into new territory?
- How would you rate this candidate on being an Inspirational Leader—Star or average?

CONFLICT MANAGEMENT

- Describe a situation at work that was conflictual for you. What did you do to de-escalate the conflict?
- Give me an example of a solution you created that was a win-win for the people involved?
- Tell me what steps you take to resolve conflicts.

Assessment:

- Does it feel to you that this person is comfortable with conflict?
- Does he/she seem to have a plan on how to deal with conflict?
- Is it a habit for him/her to de-escalate conflict and orchestrate win-wins?
- How would you rate this person on Conflict Management—Star or average?

CONSCIENTIOUSNESS

- Give me an example of a project where follow-through was very important. What systems did you employ to carry it out?

- Tell me a time that you had to personally take responsibility for getting something major done. What did you do? How did it turn out?

- Tell me a time when something dropped through the cracks in a project. How did you correct it? What would you have done differently?

- What is your method for time management? What is the most challenging thing for you with time management?

Assessment:

- Did it seem to you that this person manages follow-through?

- How easy was it for him/her to acknowledge a mistake in the third item above?

- Does this candidate seem to you to have a strong habit in taking responsibility for tasks?

- How would you rate this person in Conscientiousness—Star or average?

HOW TO USE THE INTERVIEW RATING SCALE

Below is a rating scale to help you determine which competencies are needed for each position. Rate the competencies first for importance and then rate the interviewee using a score. This is helpful because when you are talking with other interviewers you can be more specific about what you are looking for and what each interviewer's opinion is about a certain competency. The result is a focused and poignant conversation about competencies, rather than the general, "So what do you think?"

INTERVIEW RATING SCALE

Use the Interview Rating Scale for each of your employees and each of your positions.

First, RANK each of these characteristics for its IMPORTANCE to the particular position.

3 = Must have   2 = Like to have   1 = Not necessary

Next, SCORE the individual on each characteristic.

4 = Excellent   3 = Good   2 = Fair   1 = Poor

Now, MULTIPY the two numbers (IMPORTANCE times SCORE) for the TOTAL

Name:_____

Characteristic	Importance	Score	Total
Organizational Awareness			
Proactive Initiative			
Energy Level			
Self-Control			
Acceptance of Others/Empathy			
Trustworthiness/Integrity			
Communication: Internal			
Communication: External to Clients			
Intelligence			
Conflict Resolution			
Self-Awareness			
Building Bonds/Rapport			
Self-Confidence			
Accept Things as a Challenge/Adaptability			
Motivation/Achievement Orientation			
Service Orientation			
Voice of Reason in Chaos			

Leadership			
Teamwork and Team Player			
Software Tools: Microsoft Excel, Microsoft Project, Quickbooks			
Fit for Our Culture			
Influence Skills			
Technical Skills			
Developing Others			
Conscientiousness/Work Ethic			
Financial Knowledge & Experience			
Creativity			
Other Characteristics: _____			
TOTAL SCORE			

Assessment:

- What I like best about the candidate is...
- I think he/she can help us in the following areas...
- Concerns I have about the candidate are...
- Overall rating:

Don't hire!   Good.   Adds value.   We must have! (Circle One)

Gregg Butterfield, an executive project manager in Dealership Facilities Services working for General Motors, has been extremely innovative in the project development process. He uses this form and these types of behavioral questions to evaluate and select architects, engineers, and contractors for dealership development projects. He says, "I ask the questions that people are not prepared to answer in the normal interview process for this type of work. What this yields is an indication of how this person may function with other members of the team." This information about their Emotional Intelligence, paired with their experience and their bids, has allowed him to select the best teams. He has saved General Motors hundreds of thousands of dollars and untold hours of conflicts and headaches. Butterfield says, "Every project that goes wrong is usually driven by mismatched expectations. That's why this selection process is so important."

3. ONE-ON-ONE MEETINGS

This is the heart and soul of development. If you don't have one-on-ones with your people, you are missing the primary tool for moving your people from good to great.

Jim Snell is the president and COO of Shield HealthCare, Inc., a national distributor of medical products. He has one-on-ones every Tuesday with all of his direct reports. When asked about the value and content of these meetings, he replies:

"The one-on-ones are a good opportunity for me to stay current with what the department is working on and allow me to offer suggestive input on the direction of significant initiatives. Often the initiatives cross functional boundaries, and if I perceive inconsistencies between departments I can suggest the managers get together and do a reality check between them.

"We establish due dates, timelines, and significant events to determine 'go' and 'no go' decisions. These conversations go a long way in helping us learn about each other. They are essential to team-building and creating meaningful long-term business relationships."

Paul Collins is the Director of Client Services at Shield Healthcare, Inc., and has reported to Jim Snell for almost nine years. In that time he missed only a handful of Tuesday morning meetings because of vacation, sickness, or out-of-town trips. "Jim is the one who is so diligent about keeping these meetings," Paul states. "He lets you know this is our time and he is brutal at holding it."

Paul described the impact of the meeting. "It puts the onus on me to give him information I think he wants, and it gives me a valuable opportunity to see where I am." Paul also has one-on-ones with his people. He confesses, "I found out how hard it is to commit to these weekly meetings. There is always a good reason to reschedule, but I don't." It takes time, commitment, and discipline to keep meetings with your direct reports, but Jim Snell and Paul Collins see these as a mainstay to successfully developing their people and company.

Myron Jones, the president of NMB Technologies Corporation, a computer peripheral company, also uses one-on-ones as his key management and development tool. He truly believes in the value of the one-on-one.

"I know the lack of these meetings can cause misalignment in the company. In the one-on-one—I call it a Performance Review—we talk about four elements:

1. Major Job Responsibilities

Talking about the Major Job Responsibilities helps us grade the performance at that point in the fiscal year. A well-written MBO should potentially have an impact on short- and long-term company performance. Reviewing them quarterly allows more top-of-mind thinking.

2. Our Win-Win Agreement under the Covey guidelines

The Win-Win is a complementary tool to Job Responsibilities and allows me to focus on the cultural and behavioral actions of the employee.

3. Bonus Plan Progress: Performance Metrics and Management by Objectives (MBOs)

The Bonus Plan review is cool because it is a document employees typically ignore until the last month of the year. A well-written MBO should potentially have an impact on short- and long-term company performance. Reviewing them quarterly allows more top-of-mind thinking.

4. Course Corrections

Course corrections make sure there are no surprises at annual review time. It ensures that the employee and I are aligned on what is most important to the company.

These quarterly meetings can have a powerful impact because my staff members can be aligned, and then you can go into the Business Units and replicate the process."

SOME BENEFITS FROM HOLDING REGULAR ONE-ON-ONES WITH YOUR DIRECT REPORTS:

- You demonstrate you care about their development by dedicating time, your most valuable commodity.
- You truly understand what they are doing as well as what their key challenges are.
- You value them by observing and highlighting their strengths.
- You recognize their accomplishments and validate their efforts.
- You can give and clarify information about where you and the organization want to go.
- You can coach them about specific "inner battles" or "other battles" they are having.
- You can teach them about the company and its culture.
- You can have more influence and make more of a contribution with the organization by helping them be better workers, managers, and leaders.
- You can prevent crises by helping them think and plan ahead.
- You can teach about your POV and give specific data about products, customers, bosses, etc.

THE AGENDA AND TIME FRAME: You and your direct report should both create the agenda for your one-on-ones to help meet your needs. To stay abreast of their direct reports, many successful executives have their one-on-ones once a week. Some hold them every other week or once a month. You have to decide what will work best for you. You may start off with more frequent meetings and then spread them out. To make it is easy to stay focused, take notes and keep a file on each person.

KEY AGENDA ITEMS SHOULD INCLUDE:

- Progress on deliverables or tasks. Helps to get a "% completed" number.

- Challenges or obstacles they have; anything they want to add to the agenda.

- How can you help as their leader (e.g., resources, talking to department heads, training, etc.)?

- Critical information you want to make sure they get.

- Recognition and acknowledgement you can give for what they are doing.

- Identify and stretch their strengths. (See pages 190-191.)

- Feedback and coaching on issues.

- Clarity of vision and answering any questions they have.

- Stretch goals, projects, and positions for your direct reports to keep them growing.

- Next steps and actions.

The Center for Creative Leadership (CCL) has identified five broad categories of experiences that lead to growth and personal development. Here are additional topics to talk about in your one-on-ones to solidify the learning.

- Being given a challenging job was rated as the number one source of development by managers at CCL. Challenging jobs force rapid growth and development for your direct reports.[11]

- Experiences off the job such as community service, serving on boards, or leading church and youth projects can be valuable lessons in leadership.

- Learning from bosses, both "best bosses" and Dementors, can help in identifying the characteristics to emulate or avoid.

- Hardships can teach about limits, mistakes, resilience, and courage. Integrating these learning experiences can let your direct reports see themselves in a new light. Also, it can cast a new perspective on life matters.

- Traditional training classes are a means to self-development. They can give participants tips, strategies, shortcuts, and a comparison of how they stack up against others in the class.[12]

QUESTIONS AND ACTION APPLICATIONS:

- Decide how often you want to have one-on-ones with your direct reports.
- Prepare the first meeting agenda from the list above.
- See what agenda items your direct reports want and ask how you can best use the time.
- Use the time to truly explore thinking and learning on many of the topics above.
- Discuss and evaluate the meeting together. How was this meeting, what worked well, and what could be better?
- Re-establish the frequency required for the meetings to remain beneficial.

4. SOARING WITH STRENGTHS

When working with your direct reports, scan for their strengths, help them stretch them, and teach them to apply them to other areas as well. In their book *Soar with Your Strengths,* Clifton and Nelson identified five characteristics of strengths:

LISTEN FOR YEARNINGS: This is a pull or an attaction toward something. It may come from watching someone else and saying, "I'd like to do that." Leaders use yearnings as a clue for strengths. Talking about their dreams, aspirations, or future goals will help to identify these aspirations.

WATCH FOR SATISFACTIONS: "Satisfactions are experiences where the emotional and psychic rewards are great; typically they are the activities we 'get a kick out of doing.'"[13]

WATCH FOR RAPID LEARNING: When someone catches on quickly to something, this is an indication of a strength or talent. It comes easy to the person and it feels like he or she has always known how to do it.

Slow learning, where a person just doesn't get the hang of something, is also very significant. It is an indication of a non-strength.

GLIMPSES OF EXCELLENCE: Within each task there are a series of moments or subtasks where someone can demonstrate excellence. This can be a glimpse of a strength. My son and I were taking guitar lessons, and our teacher demonstrated what she wanted us to do. As I was trying to memorize the sequence, my son just listened and was able to repeat it perfectly. As I toiled away, he got it effortlessly—a glimpse of excellence.

These glimpses can be nurtured to develop the talent. Examples include an ability to know just the right time to ask for the sale, or an ability to make people feel very comfortable, or thinking on one's feet in a presentation, responding to hard questions, or an ability to simplify complex tasks.

TOTAL PERFORMANCE OF EXCELLENCE: This isn't a glimpse of excellence, but rather when the whole task is done with excellence. In sports, for example, the person may be experiencing "flow," where the performance is effortless.

Notice that the above five characteristics for strengths involve your watching and listening. You will need to listen with one ear for strengths and one for development opportunities.

5. INPUT + 1

This strategy has to do with learning theory. Do you know how each person learns? Do you know when and why people get into overwhelm? It is important for you to help stretch your direct reports by giving them new information, and thus the moniker "Input + 1." Dr. John Luckner, Director of the Low Incident Disabilities

Center at University of Northern Colorado, stresses the importance of teaching to the specific level and style of the learner. If matched well, the student will learn more and develop better self-esteem. Keeping the new material at Input + 1 is critical for this to happen.

If your direct reports are at Input + 3, they are on overwhelm and can't integrate all the information or learn well. Their eyes are glazed over, and they may be just nodding their head. They may be asking vague questions, or their results may be far from what you expected. The average performer may think it is his or her direct report's fault for not understanding. The Star Performer will take responsibility, like Coach French and Coach Smith, for not meeting the direct report's needs. The Star will figure out where the employee comfort zone lies and how to push just the right amount so that he or she can be successful. What may be Input + 3 for one person can be Input + 1 for someone else.

QUESTIONS AND ACTION APPLICATIONS:

- In your one-on-ones, assess or ask about their learning styles.

- Get feedback on how much you are stretching them. Find out if it is working.

- Use the Myers-Briggs Type Indicator (MBTI), the Kolbe, or the DISC to delineate learning styles.

- Hold conversations with your team about learning styles, preferences, and how they best take in and assimilate information.

6. CIRCLE OF INFLUENCE

This term was first used in Stephen Covey's *The 7 Habits of Highly Effective People*. It is useful in establishing responsibility and in deciding when to refocus your energy on more fruitful endeavors.

CIRCLE OF CONCERN: These are concerns that are important to you but that you don't have any control over. They begin to be a distractive noise that takes the place of truly focusing on what you can actually do.

CIRCLE OF INFLUENCE (OR POWER): These are things you do have control over and where you feel empowered. Put your energy and effort here.

CIRCLE OF FOCUS: These are the key areas where you need to focus. It is important to clarify a plan and the first steps.

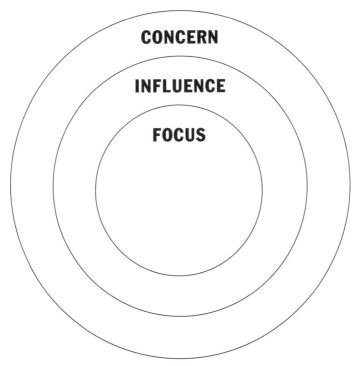

Stephen R. Covey. The 7 Habits of Highly Effective People. *Simon & Schuster, copyright 1989. Used by permission.*

USING THE CIRCLE OF INFLUENCE

When working with your direct reports, show the Circle of Influence and ask questions about their concerns. The goal is to move them from the Circle of Concern into the Circle of Influence. If people stay in the Circle of Concern for a long time, they become victims who feel helpless, powerless, anxious, and insecure. They have many concerns that can and do affect them, but they feel there isn't anything they can do about the situation. Their Circle of Influence is very miniscule, and everything is impinging on them. Their Circle of Influence can feel like the diagram that follows:

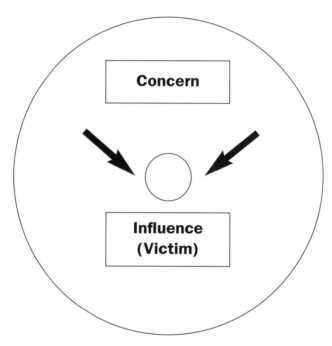

As a leader, you need to listen to your direct reports about their concerns. You need to really hear them, show empathy, and evaluate the situation. Once they feel heard, you want to shift them from areas of concern to areas of influence and power. These questions can help:

- Is there anything you can do about this situation that will help?
- Is there anything anyone else can do that would help you?
- Is there any part of this situation where you have some influence?
- Is there anything you can do right *now* about this?

If the answer to all four questions is no, you want to help them let go of the concern and focus on something else, something that is under their influence. Some of these questions may help:

- What will it take for you to let go of this concern?
- What are you getting out of putting your energy into something you can't change or influence?
- Is it your choice to put your energy on something that won't or can't change?
- Where else could you be putting your energy and focus if you weren't so absorbed in this situation, which you can't change or alter?
- What are you missing out on by staying in the Circle of Concern?

Now take your direct reports into answering some focusing questions:

- What do you have influence over that you can do now?
- What is the first step?
- What is the rest of your plan?
- What support or resources do you need to get this done?
- How can anyone support you?
- What would prevent you from taking action?

TEAM APPLICATION: Hold a meeting with your team and go over the key concerns they face. First, have each person evaluate whether each item is a concern or something he or she has influence over. Hold a discussion to talk about differences of opinion. Second, talk about what actions you can take for the areas under your influence.

QUESTIONS AND ACTION APPLICATIONS:

- How can you implement the Circle of Influence tool with your team or team members?
- Think of examples from your experience that will illuminate the Circle of Influence.

- Practice explaining the Circle of Influence to another person first before working with your whole team.

7. PERFORMANCE = POTENTIAL – INTERFERENCES OR P=P–I

In *The Inner Game of Work*, Tim Gallwey introduces a simple and effective technique he uses with professional athletes. It begins by focusing and expanding on one's strengths. Once you have your strengths identified and stretched, you can then look at the main interferences that seem to create limitations. The goal is to have performance equal potential. Examples of interferences that may limit one's performance are:

- Lack of closure
- Time management
- Not including others in decisions
- Avoidance of conflict
- Being overly on your case
- Lack of focus
- Poor listening
- Low self-control
- Not open to new ideas
- Talking down to people

QUESTIONS AND ACTION APPLICATIONS:

- In your one-on-ones, ask your direct reports to list their interferences.
- How aware are they of their interferences?
- Are there one or two things they can do differently that would have a big impact?

8. DELEGATION

Delegation is a key skill that Star Performers excel at and practice daily. The following model adopted from Covey's Win-Win Agreements has five steps that can help ensure that your delegations are clear, empowering, and effective if performed sequentially and in depth.

The "Recommend, and Then Act" and "Act and Advise" below can be used as a separate *check-in strategy*. Have both you and your direct reports fill out what they need to come to you with first with a recommendation before acting on. With these, you have to give them the green light *(Recommend, and Then Act)*. Then, fill in what they are empowered to do and just inform you on *(Act and Advise)*. The resulting conversation can be very clarifying and can ensure that your direct reports are empowered and checking in with you appropriately.

Often when I am talking with leaders, they complain that their direct reports are not taking enough initiative. Or, on the other side, their direct reports have made decisions the leader wished they had known about ahead of time. I ask, "Have you told them what they can and can't do (as explained above)?" Usually this conversation hasn't happened. This is another example of a micro-initiative that can make you a Star and separate you from the average performers.

Usually impacts don't get talked about. This gives you an opportunity to tie in the value to the greater cause of what they are doing. Employees want to know how they are contributing to the bigger picture, and the impacts of their actions give them that feedback. An example of a negative impact may be: "If you don't get this done on time, it will slow down the production line and cost the company money. Plus, you and I will be the blame and that won't work for what we are trying to accomplish. Come to me if you need more support or resources."

1. DESIRED RESULTS

The big picture, beginning with the end in mind.
- What are you trying to accomplish?
- What are the key goals or deliverables?
- What kind of relationship do you want with your direct reports?

2. GUIDELINES

More specifics, how to get it done.

- Key do's and don'ts.
- Check in with you at what points?
- Don't spend more than X amount of time or money.

LEVELS OF INITIATIVE: WHEN TO CHECK BACK RECOMMEND, AND THEN ACT:

For example: Personnel issues, changes that affect the project, budget, or timeline.

ACT AND ADVISE:

People are empowered to make their own decisions and keep you informed periodically or immediately.

For example: Daily routines, clarify up to what amount of money, time, and resources they can use.

3. RESOURCES

What people, time, money, training, software, consultants, etc., can be used to achieve the desired result?

4. ACCOUNTABILITIES

- What metrics do you have to measure the desired results?
- How will you know if they are being successful or not?
- When and where will they be measured?
- Others also act as accountabilities (e.g., executive feedback).

5. IMPACTS

What are the positive impacts on you, the team, and the individual from achieving the desired results? For example: More challenging projects, better leadership, eligible for more training, make budget, quality product, helping the team, more respect, and progress in their career goals.

NEGATIVE IMPACTS: The opposite of the positive ones given above. It's better to talk about them before negative consequences happen.

QUESTIONS AND ACTION APPLICATIONS:

- Try out the delegation steps when you next delegate.
- Get feedback on how the delegation went.
- Ask if there is a way you could be clearer in the next delegation.
- Encourage your direct reports to use the delegation steps when they delegate to others.

9. COACHING FOR PERFORMANCE

FIVE STEPS FOR DEVELOPING CAPABILITIES

This model has been used for over 15 years as a way of developing people. When coaching, it is important that you save your advice or feedback until the end of your session. Often people are not looking for expert advice, but instead want validation or acknowledgement for what they are already doing. Many teachers miss this and go right to Step Five, advice!

When I ask leaders, "How long do you wait before answering questions from direct reports?" Often they laugh and say, "If I don't interrupt them, maybe I'll wait three to five seconds."

Then I ask, "How long do you think this person thought about his or her issues before coming to you for an answer?" They usually respond, "Anywhere from one to three days."

Often people are not looking for expert advice, but instead want validation or acknowledgement for what they are already doing.

So I say, "What are the chances, with three to five seconds of thought, that you are going to be right?" and "What is the possible impact on the employee?" Obviously the longer you understand the issue, what the direct report's take is on it, and what he or she has already tried, the more accurate you can be with your advice. When you race to advise, the impact on the direct report can be negative, from feeling insulted, devalued, or not heard.

The value of not jumping to advice or Step Five until the end of this process is:

- The employee feels heard and understood.
- You will have more time to truly think.
- The employee can feel acknowledged and honored for the problem-solving he or she has already completed.
- You have an opportunity to see how your direct report thinks and problem-solves.
- Your employee can demonstrate his or her strengths to you.
- If placed at the end, your answer or advice has a better chance of being helpful and accepted.

Step One: Hear the Problem or Issue Fully

- What happened?
- When did it happen?
- Why do they think it occurred?
- Reflect back the content and emotions you have heard.

Step Two: Get More Details

- Find out what they have tried.
- How long has it been going on?
- Who has been affected or impacted by the problem?
- What does anyone else think the problem is?
- Is there something that worked even part of the time?
- Reflect back the content and emotions you have heard.

Step Three: Honor Their Ideas for a Solution

- If it is their problem, what do they think should be done next?
- What is the benefit of their idea?
- How long do they think it will take?
- What major obstacles do they see with this solution?
- What other resources will they need?
- How will they know if it's working or not?
- If there is more than one solution, ask about the merit of each. If they had to rank each answer, which is the highest, and why?

Step Four: Ask If They Want Your Feedback

- If not, just confirm what they will do.
- If you feel they really need it but don't want to hear it, offer it.

Step Five: Give Your Advice or Feedback and Make a Plan

- Don't just give the answer, but also use this as a *mentoring moment*.
- Make your thinking visible to them.
- What are your considerations for this choice?
- Why did you select this?
- What did you consider but rule out, and why?
- In a similar experience you might have had, what was the impact of that decision?
- How would you have improved on it knowing what you know today?
- What things did they *not* consider with their choice— unintended consequences, impact on stakeholders, resources needed, time needed to implement it, skills needed?

PLAN

- What will be the next step?
- When should they check back with you?
- How will they know it is working?

10. SCALING QUESTIONS

These questions ask candidates to rate where they are in various situations. It is a helpful strategy to see how people rate themselves. When you are going through your goals in the review, it will also help you see if there have been gains. Scaling questions bring some metrics to the development process, even if it is a self-report.

Ask questions from your direct reports and request that they rate themselves on a scale from 1 to 10, where 10 is the highest. When you get a number, say a 6, you want to follow with the question: "What will bring it to a 7," not a 10. This will help in getting some micro-intiatives to help them move forward. Another benefit when you review their goals with them using scaling questions is that people typically don't remember what number they gave months ago. They are surprised and encouraged when their self-report has increased.

Carl was a client who worked for a design firm, and we developed the following goals for his coaching. Here, the ratings are 1-10, where 10 is the highest:

- Be an inspiring leader = 4
- Set strategic direction = 2
- Communicate frequently = 6
- Become a better listener = 6
- Time management = 3

On two separate occasions we reviewed Carl's goals and modified his actions to continue his development. At the end of the coaching, Carl's progress on the goals was as follows:

- Be an inspiring leader = 7
- Set strategic direction = 5
- Communicate frequently = 7.5
- Become a better listener = 8
- Time management = 6

Carl was satisfied with his progress, as was I. He was very clear about what he needed to do to maintain his gains and what actions to focus on to continue his improvement in the areas listed. The scaling questions helped in identifying gains, rewarding progress, and clarifying areas for continued development. They also helped by bringing some metrics and evaluation to the coaching process.

11. MOTIVATION SKILLS MATRIX

Paul Hersey, Ken Blanchard, and Dewey Johnson have written extensively about the Situational Leadership Model. It is used in many organizations to determine the unique needs of followers or direct reports and what leadership style will engender the best results. This model looks at the task and relationship behavior of the leader and the follower's readiness level.

I have always found the model cumbersome and not as easy to use as I would like. Below is the Motivation Skills Matrix, which managers have found easier to understand and apply with their team members. There are plenty of models like this to use, and the goal is to find something you are comfortable with that allows you to identify the learning needs for each of your direct reports. To be a Star Performer, you must differentiate your leadership style to better fit each of your people.

MOTIVATION SKILLS MATRIX*

Think about your direct reports and where they are on this matrix in regards to their motivation and skills.

	Directing	Coaching	Empowering
Motivation	1	2	3
Skill	1	2	3

| | Low | | High |

Motivation = The ability to challenge themselves, meet the deliverable, internally driven, and high-achievement orientation.

Skill = The capabilities to do the job and the competencies and proficiency to do what is required.

M1, S1 = Low motivation and low skill

M2, S2 = Average motivation and average skill

M3, S3 = High motivation and high skill

LEADERSHIP STYLES

Once you determine where your direct reports fall on the matrix, you can choose the appropriate leadership style to best develop them. Where do you place your direct reports?

Directive style: M1, S1 / M1, S2 / M2, S1

Coaching style: M2, S2

Empowering style: M3, S3 / M2, S3 / M3, S2

DIRECTIVE STYLE—APPROPRIATE FOR: M1, S1 / M1, S2 / M2, S1

Be specific about what you want done, tell them the basic "how-to's," be clear about your expectations and the resources to use. Spend time determining what skills they need. Go over assignments in detail. Get their "brief back" and have them tell you what you said.

- Teach them
- Provide specific instructions
- Supervise closely
- Encourage and motivate
- Clarify when to check back with you and how far they can go

COACHING STYLE—APPROPRIATE FOR: M2, S2

Set up goals and paint the "end" of each project. Then ask them what they think should happen first. Get their recommendations. Explore their thinking. If not there yet, coach. Make your thinking visible and give "why's" and "because's." Tell what resources are available. Give them stretch goals and go over what went well and what didn't; use it as development coaching time.

- Involve them
- Get their ideas; create a dialogue
- Share your thinking about the tasks
- Encourage and acknowledge what they do
- Have them teach others
- Ask when they want to check back with you on the task

EMPOWERING STYLE—APPROPRIATE FOR: M3, S3 / M2, S3 / M3, S2

Give them an end in mind and tell them to give you their plan. Give any key "don'ts," then let them figure it out, use resources, and implement as they see fit. Continue to give stretch goals and tie into their development plan. Constantly ask if they are challenged enough and what else they want to do.

- Challenge them
- Increase what they can act on and just advise you
- Turn over responsibility and decision-making
- Delegate some of your tasks to them
- Spread the news of their successes, have them teach others

Adapted from Situational Leadership in Hersey, Blanchard, and Johnson (1996)

EXAMPLES OF MATRIX AND LEADERSHIP SOLUTIONS

Diane has been a manager of an accounting department for the last eight years. The accounting systems are complex and ever-changing. Diane used the Motivation Skills Matrix, looking at strengths and weaknesses and motivation and learning style for two of her people. It gave her useful new strategies for dealing with her employees.

DIRECTIVE LEADERSHIP SOLUTION:

Susan is a manager who has worked at the organization for less than one year. The technical knowledge aspects of the job are still very new for her. Diane placed Susan as M2, S1—average on motivation and low on skills.

STRENGTHS for Susan: She is very detail-oriented, has good focus and clarity, and can think out of the box once she understands the system or process.

WEAKNESSES: In the pursuit of understanding all the details, she will miss the big picture.

MOTIVATION: Is to be very competent and have a strong knowledge set.

LEARNING STYLE: Is to start small in a detailed manner and learn in a hands-on and visual manner.

LEADERSHIP STYLE for Diane with Susan is to be more *Directive* than she has been. She needed to go point by point in explaining new information, talk slower, and check for clarity more. Diane would step back from her expectations of Susan and do more teaching. She also decided to be more diligent about supervision and give more immediate feedback. Diane also established that her feedback and praise would be more about the competencies she noticed Susan developing and would get her to teach to others what she has just learned. She would also encourage and acknowledge any out-of-the-box thinking with Susan.

COACHING LEADERSHIP STYLE:

Martha has been a manager for the last three years. She has been working with the systems longer than Susan has. Diane placed Martha at M2, S2—average in motivation and skills.

STRENGTHS: Martha is very detail-oriented, receptive, and open to feedback.

WEAKNESSES: She has issues with follow-up and time management. Leading others also adds to more overwhelm.

MOTIVATION: Praise and acknowledgement are very important for Martha. Challenging her with support is also helpful. Giving her some space to work on her own is motivating for her.

LEARNING STYLE: Being right is important for Martha, and she likes to have a mentor whom she can ask questions, even though she knows the answers. Allowing her to be autonomous in her endeavors and check back when she feels she needs to is important. Feedback at those times is also beneficial.

LEADERSHIP STYLE for Diane with Martha is to use more *Coaching,* asking her for her opinions and recommendations. Diane wants to make sure she is very clear and then let Martha go figure things out on her own and come back when she has questions. Diane decided to back off some. She also decided to put Martha in a position where she had fewer direct reports to lower her tendency to overwhelm.

DEVELOPMENT CHART

Use this chart to organize the information about your direct reports and to clarify the best ways to lead them.

Name: _____

Motivation Skills Matrix placement:

Strengths:

Weaknesses:

Motivations:

Learning style:

Leadership style to use:

Plan:

Resources:

Accountability metrics:

12. DEVELOPMENT FIRST

In 1995 David Peterson and Mary Dee Hicks wrote *Development F.I.R.S.T.* It gives simple yet powerful steps for implementing a development plan that will help you or your direct report make sure your big ideas have staying power so that they do not disappear like last year's well-intentioned New Year's resolution. Include these topics in your conversations with your direct reports or have them bring these answers to your one-on-ones. For your own development, write out your answers to further illuminate the process.

Each step follows the F.I.R.S.T. acronym:

1. FOCUS ON PRIORITIES: What are the most important issues or competencies to focus on in your development plan? Remember, one or two key areas are enough. It's a good idea to work with them for a month or two until you have them mastered.

- Where are you now and where do you want to go?

- What are you actually going to do differently?

- How will these things benefit you and the organization?

2. IMPLEMENT SOMETHING EVERY DAY: Peterson and Hicks suggest spending five minutes a day on development. These micro-initiatives can lead to macro impacts. They suggest finding situations that have *high stakes* and visibility, *novelty* to stretch your comfort zone, *challenges* where you have to do more than in the past, and *interaction* where you have to work through others over whom you don't have position power.

- Can you take a risk each day?

- What is one small step toward your goal?

- How can you employ your strengths?

- What resources or training will help you take these steps?

- What do you need to face?

3. REFLECT ON YOUR EXPERIENCE: This involves spending time really thinking about what has and hasn't worked in the past.

- What have you learned from your successes and mistakes?
- Write down what has been the highlight of each day.
- Write down what you feel most proud of each day.
- What patterns do you see with this daily reflection?
- What have you learned from your hardships?

4. SEEK FEEDBACK AND SUPPORT: The more people you involve in your development plan, the more able you will be to hit your targets. Can you get feedback to make sure you are on the right track? They can provide: 1) feedback, 2) direction, 3) new strategies, 4) support, 5) motivation, and 6) accountability.

- Who are the best people to get feedback from?
- Who are the best people to get support from? (They may be different.)
- Can you tell them exactly what you need and how they can support you?
- What kind of feedback will not be useful to you? Let them know that also.
- How can you support and foster mentoring relationships with them?

5. TRANSFER LEARNING INTO NEXT STEPS: When you have successes, how do you best codify them so you can see the patterns, efforts, and support that allowed you to move forward? Often in seminars or training I will ask participants how they had a success, and their first answer is: "I don't know, I just did it." I want their second, third, and fourth answers to what steps, training, and support made this possible, so they can replicate it.

- Write down your success steps.
- Ask others to list what they saw you do that was helpful.
- To highlight the "how," teach someone else what you did.
- Teach your learning to your team so they can benefit from it.

- Ask others to help hold you accountable for your new behaviors by giving you feedback when you fall back into old habits.
- What are some ways to celebrate your successes?
- What are your next goals to which you can generalize this learning?

STAR PERFORMER ACTION PLAN

Review the Star Profile and *Coach's Corner* strategies to assist you in developing others. Now answer the following questions to help you make your Star Performer Action Plan. Remember, micro-initiatives create macro impacts.

Which competencies or practices are you already doing that you want to continue?

1. _____
2. _____
3. _____

What new practices do you want to incorporate?

1. _____
2. _____
3. _____

What resources do you need to make this happen?

1. _____
2. _____
3. _____

Who can support you and hold you accountable?

1. _____
2. _____
3. _____

How might you sabotage your efforts and best intentions?

   1. _____

   2. _____

   3. _____

What will be your first steps in this plan?

   1. _____

   2. _____

   3. _____

Share this plan with your support people. Good luck!

CHAPTER FIVE

COMMUNICATION AND EMPATHY
TOOLS AND STRATEGIES

The single biggest problem in communication is the illusion that it has taken place. —George Bernard Shaw (Nobel Prize–winning playwright)

Τhis section provides the tools and strategies to help you become a Star Performer in the areas of Communication and Empathy. Communication and Empathy are the foundation of all social or relationship skills. A definition of Communication is illustrated with a research example followed by a Star Profile of John Davies, founder of Davies Public Relations, a top communication and public relations firm. Davies shares *11 Secrets & Current Practices* that help him shine as a Star Performer in Communication. He also describes some of the pitfalls he encounters in his business.

The *Coach's Corner* presents a definition of Empathy, the research that supports how important it is for peak performance, and 12 proven strategies used by executives and leaders for the development of these skills. It also includes a Star Performer Action Plan, which will help you transform general ideas and concepts into tangible applications for guaranteed performance as a Star Performer.

WHAT IS THE COMMUNICATION COMPETENCY?

The Communication competency includes listening with an open mind, sending convincing and clear messages, and cultivating an empathetic give-and-take. A speaker reads the emotional cues expressed by the listener and meets the listener by fine-tuning his message. For communication to be effective, the message has to be received with the intent intact, just as the sender had planned. Difficult situations and delivering bad news are not easy communications, but a Star Performer knows how to express information diplomatically and directly by creating a free flow and exchange that goes back and forth, until there is mutual understanding of each person's perspective.[1]

EMOTIONAL INTELLIGENCE RESEARCH EXAMPLES

The biggest single complaint of Americans in the job force is poor communication with their managers. Two-thirds of those interviewed believe this problem actually prevents them from doing their best work. Another study of 130 executives and managers shows that people prefer working with and relating to others who know how to successfully handle and communicate their emotions and requests.[2]

What makes a good communicator? There are five basic skills that determine whether a co-worker is an effective communicator: listening skills, such as asking good questions; being open-minded; understanding the other; not interrupting; and asking for suggestions.[3]

ARE YOU A STAR PERFORMER IN COMMUNICATION OR JUST AVERAGE?

Stars exhibit both average and Star behaviors consistently. Where are you?

AVERAGE

- Engages the audience
- Clarifies or emphasizes the message

STAR

- Effective in give-and-take
- Fine-tunes delivery[4]

STAR PROFILE: JOHN DAVIES, CEO AND FOUNDER, DAVIES PUBLIC RELATIONS

WHY JOHN DAVIES IS A STAR PERFORMER IN COMMUNICATION

In 1985 John Davies founded Davies Public Relations, one of the most successful strategic communications firms in California. The company has won over 250 awards for excellence in advertising, design, and communications and is the third-largest public relations firm in the state and the top 50 in the nation.

For 20 years, Davies ran numerous political campaigns and had an 85% win ratio. His focus has always been on studying human behavior and effective communications strategies to influence decision-making processes, no matter the venue. Whether it is helping a politician refine his or her remarks and presentation or designing a public relations campaign over heated political and environmental issues, John Davies is one of the best. His seminars and coaching have consistently received the highest ratings from audiences all over the country.

DAVIES WAS ASKED:

- How did he learn these communication competencies?
- What does he do to be such an effective communicator?
- What are his daily practices?
- What are the pitfalls he needs to be aware of?

EARLY LEARNING EXPERIENCES

John wasn't always a Star in Communication. As a matter of fact, he was unable to speak intelligibly until the age of 10 or 11 due to a speech impediment now called verbal aproxia, a condition that kept him from feeling how his tongue moved around in his mouth. Davies simply couldn't be understood, so he developed an avoidant pattern, specifically to make sure he didn't have to speak in public. "People treated me as stupid, and then I seemed to believe maybe I was stupid," he told me. "I couldn't spell or read well and was in a special remedial reading class." Young Davies decided he wanted to learn how to speak like others, but after hundreds of hours studying people's communication skills he came to realize that most people were actually poor communicators! This insight informed his future decisions about the importance of clear expression.

Davies said that after two years of speech therapy he "got his voice" and claims he hasn't stopped talking since! "Once I got my voice I experimented, and at one point became the class clown. But I flunked eighth grade and had to stay back a year. I felt like a loser again, but staying back turned out to be a gift. Since I was older than everyone else, I naturally had more physical and emotional maturity. And so, I decided I had to get my act together and stop being a loser."

Sports helped build his confidence. He played football, ran track and cross-country, and wrestled. During sixth grade his gym teacher, Don Edick, had kind words for him just as he was beginning to feel his oats. He shared with Davies that he was a late bloomer and would be good in sports someday because he was fast. "You are just like my son; you are smart but no one has figured it out including you, and you are a really fast runner!" Edick's comments were a moment that Davies remembered as he faced Round Two of his communication challenges.

Another defining moment for Davies was being part of the wrestling team, with a coach who happened to teach the advanced English courses and recruited his students for the team. So Davies ended up on a team that featured an unusually high percentage of the smartest kids in the school. He realized he could actually keep up with them and began to embrace more of his own strengths. At the age of 17 or so, he became involved in the student government and ran for president. Naturally, he had to make a speech. He pulled it off but lost by one vote. Why? He admitted he didn't vote for himself! But Davies became the vice president and this turned out to be a critical learning period as he immersed himself in the political arena.

Davies was one of the student officers who dealt with state issues through the Principals' Association. He realized then that the school principals were hesitant to take a stand on important issues because of political ramifications. This was frustrating for Davies because he wanted to get things done. Important ideas that foretold his future began to crystallize in his mind as he came to understand that, in order to succeed, a person needed to learn how to craft a message and deliver powerful communications.

11 SECRETS & CURRENT PRACTICES OF JOHN DAVIES—STAR PERFORMER

In interviewing Davies, *11 Secrets & Current Practices* emerged that help make him a Star. Think about these practices and how to apply them to your own business or setting. Pick one or two to try out.

1. TOUCH THE HEART

Davies agrees that engaging the audience, clarifying or emphasizing a message, effective give-and-take, and fine-tuning your delivery are crucial elements in successful communication. He also strongly believes that Stars "touch people's hearts" with their words. Effective communication is really more emotional than logical. Davies is always searching for the passage into the heart. Many of the strategies below synergize to arouse other people's emotions.

2. UNDERSTAND WHAT PEOPLE WANT

Davies is deeply concerned about what his clients want.

In an initial meeting, instead of talking about his capabilities and interests as many firms do, he focuses on asking pertinent questions of his client, to better understand their needs, goals, and vision of success. Davies wants to assess whether or not there is a good fit, to make sure he can add real value. He calls himself in this role "The Server of the Question."

3. FIND YOUR PASSION

Davies defines passion as "Being your best without any compromise or change." He firmly believes, "The anatomy of powerful communication is about passion. Passion needs to ooze out of every pore of your body." Davies knows that when a person is passionate, his message is convincing, persuasive, and genuine. In his speech training for politicians, Davies teaches candidates to get in touch with their passion on a physical level. Once they know what it feels like in their body, they can access and retrieve it more easily. They also work to discover what they are most passionate about, beyond speaking points, and delve into other juicy areas of their lives such as their personal relationships, a sport they love, places they've traveled to, and art. To further spark their passion he asks, "When are you most happy?" Getting in touch with the answer to this question provides a wellspring of core energy, which the candidate can develop and use as fuel to feed the feeling tone behind his or her speeches.

Davies also asks more pertinent questions such as:

- Why should I vote for you?
- How is my life going to be better because of you?

If a candidate cannot find his passion, Davies often suggests he not run. Period.

Davies thought John Kerry was neither passionate nor believable in the 2004 campaign. Kerry appeared to be in conflict during his speeches, and Davies believes he looked like he wasn't 100% behind what he said.

It is no surprise that people wondered, "Will he protect us?" In fact, Davies has video clips of Kerry speaking, nodding yes and then saying NO. Other tapes show Kerry often changing his blink rate— getting more rapid with issues that he did not believe—leaving the audience with a bad impression.

Bush, on the other hand, who is not as polished nor as good a speaker as Kerry, appeared confident and passionate and therefore believable.

Davies shares his perceptions of these two candidates, knowing that a person's perception is his or her reality. He coined the term *perceptioneering,* which he uses as his tag line, to describe one of the things his company does.

4. FIND YOUR UNIQUENESS

Davies is always interested in accessing people's strengths and unique abilities. His goal is to use those capabilities in the most effective manner. When Davies is working with clients, he pays close attention to the skills and capabilities that set them apart from others. His focus is to discover their unique talent and skill set, and then he and his team craft these findings into the most effective and compelling message and marketing campaign.

In his own company Davies uses people's unique abilities to synergize talents. He believes that each person contributes in his or her own way to the success of a project, and he looks for a multitalented combination rather than insisting that everyone be the same.

Davies has a demanding and rigorous hiring process that includes using the Kolbe Assessment (to look at preferred instincts in action), other assessments, and multiple interviews. He is always looking for a full complement of abilities across his company. The new hires see from the interview process that Davies Public Relations is unique in its approach, values, and climate. They report that the "challenge and the people" are the key reasons to join the team.

5. READ PEOPLE

In a recent training of community leaders, Davies discussed how touching or scratching one's nose while speaking is an indication of lying (think Pinocchio). He illustrated his point by showing a video of George Bush Sr. telling his audience, "We are winning the war against drugs," while unconsciously rubbing his nose close to 10 times, almost on cue! Davies is aware of how people reveal themselves in countless non-verbal ways when we closely tune in to their message.

In his own company, Davies is able to read which employees need "touches" or personal contact from him or Brandon Edwards, a principal in the firm and the COO. Edwards states, "I don't pick up these cues, but John sees them or senses them, and we are able to connect with people in a 'just in time' process that lets them see we know them and value them."

When Davies is unable to read his audience or their reaction, he conducts a focus group or gives a survey. He knows it is crucial to establish what the audience is feeling and thinking. Davies emphasizes that to be a strategic communicator you must be clear about the target you are trying to hit.

COACHING EXAMPLE

As an Executive Coach, I worked with an executive who had great difficulty reading his audience's reactions to his talks. He was unable to tell if people were receptive, bored, or irritated. On some unconscious level he was able to read that something was going on, but unable to discern what it was or what to do differently. Instead of finding out, he would just talk more and more. The audience felt talked at versus engaged. Because of his inability to read his audience and change his strategy, his efforts to communicate were backfiring on him.

This executive's career began to derail, as he was simply trying too hard. All he had to do was stop, ask some questions, and find out what they needed. The cues were there, but a micro-initiative in a different direction would have a major impact on his effectiveness and his career.

6. ACKNOWLEDGE/DO NOT OFFEND

Davies believes it is important to acknowledge what other people say. Acknowledging also lets the listener know that he or she is being heard and that his or her ideas count. Davies is generous in giving clients credit for coming up with ideas and strategies, rather than having to toot his own horn. He also refuses to threaten or offend people at a meeting and is extremely concerned that everyone feels safe when with him. He makes a point, though, of switching what he is saying or how he is saying it if he is working with a "Contrarian." This is a person who will disagree and take the opposite opinion just for the sake of discussion.

7. SUMMARIZE AND INTEGRATE

Davies wants his clients to feel that he totally understands their concerns and where they want to go. He does this by summarizing what he hears them say and feeding it back to them. This is an effective way to establish successful give-and-take in a conversation. He will then integrate new information and strategies to help move them forward. Stephen Covey's Fifth Habit says it all: "Seek first to understand, before you are understood."

8. BE PREPARED

Davies believes preparation is the key to being a Star Communicator. That means:

- Review the client goals.
- Research all the relevant issues.
- Know all sides of the story.
- Prepare for rebuttals to client and community responses.
- Review presentations.
- Prep staff for what they need to do to support you and the client.
- Make sure all the details are covered before a client meeting or presentation.

Davies has trained his staff to be well-prepared and proactive. He also expects them to provide all the back research and support he needs before working with clients.

9. TRAINING AND PERSONAL GROWTH

Davies is dedicated to taking time out every year to have several offsite retreats with his staff. These sessions help align the company in the "Davies Way" and give everyone a chance to master the urgency, complexity, and change that takes place at work. He also realizes that his team needs "practice time" away from the demands of their clients to provide the service and quality that bears his name. Although some of these retreats cost up to $20,000 in lost billing, Davies is confident that the investment in his people and the Davies brand results in the excellence and integrity he requires.

One recent training was designed to practice teamwork and give new leaders time to interact with their team by doing business simulations in a non-client setting. Davies, Edwards, and the facilitators gave the team feedback on their results. On one activity, the teams assembled a series of nuts and bolts from memory after brief exposure to a model. They then compared their product to the model for errors. Each team did it numerous times and decreased their time and errors to near perfection. The teams were competitive, enthusiastic, and committed. The conversation after the exercise was about what the teams learned about their leadership, teamwork, project management, communication, and how to improve these in work projects.

Davies is also personally committed to learning and has been a part of the "Strategic Coach" for over five years. This organization holds quarterly meetings that focus on business and personal innovation and success. As part of the process, Davies feels that writing down his personal and business goals every year and reviewing them four times a year is very beneficial. He reports, "When I review them I discover that most are already accomplished and some I believe get done simply by writing them down."

10. QUALITY IN ALL

Davies takes a great deal of time mentoring his staff on the "Davies Way" to guarantee that all of the products they create reflect the highest quality. There are hundreds of details to be attended to that require meticulous care, such as writing a quality cover letter for a campaign; working with graphic artists and printers; stuffing envelopes; putting on labels; meeting deadlines; communicating clearly and timely with clients; and dealing effectively with vendors, mishaps, and changes.

Davies wants his staff to be proactive, accountable, and responsible for serving the clients in a superb manner. Not only is Davies's name on everything that leaves the office, but so is his touch.

11. FINDING THE "NEEDLE IN THE HAYSTACK"

Davies believes it is crucial to: "Find a way for us and our clients to be successful by uncovering and creating a perception and a message that work. We then uncover the best and most visible means to deliver those so-called needles to our clients."

The needles are the output, gems, and strategies that accumulate from doing all of the strategies, 1-10 on the previous pages. The campaigns are built around these elements. They include:

- The question that has not been asked
- The hidden reason for or against a cause
- Identifying the main leverage point(s) to influence people
- The unique abilities of the client
- The passion that needs stoking and stroking

Davies's team comes up with numerous approaches for a client and then refines them over and over again. Aside from John Davies, his staff is made up of experts in communication, public relations, media, political campaigns, and crisis communication. In crafting the message, the team looks for stories, metaphors, graphics, and images that make a passionate appeal, one that touches people's hearts and will leave a lasting impression.

Davies's toolbox contains all of the most compelling practices including influence and persuasion theories, change strategies, psychology, sociology, media, leadership, non-verbal communication, crisis communication, and relationship building.

This section is about communication, but you can see that Davies is also a Star in many of the other EI competencies, such as Accurate Self-Assessment, Confidence, Trustworthiness, Achievement Orientation, Initiative, Conscientiousness, Adaptability, Service Orientation, Empathy, Conflict Management, Teamwork and Collaboration, and Influence.

WHAT PITFALLS DOES DAVIES NEED TO BE AWARE OF IN COMMUNICATION?

Davies knows that communication is a highly interpretative process. In his business, people are very emotional and highly committed to the projects at hand. When asked about his potential pitfalls or blind spots, he mentioned the following four, which are applicable to all of us.

- "Being blinded by your passion and losing your discriminatory process." Passion can be overused, and it is possible to be seen as a bully instead of exuberant.

- "Timing of when to speak." It is sometimes tricky to know when to speak and when not to speak. People want to be heard, and managing your need to be heard with that of the client's need is critical.

- "Being condescending or threatening. Managing your emotions is critical, and it is important to be aware of any subtle tones or irritation in your voice, because it can affect or even subvert the entire message being communicated."

- "Trying to get credit for things and not giving appropriate credit." In the "idea world" it is crucial to acknowledge the source of good ideas and to only take credit for something if it is true. If you are in doubt about how the idea was actually created, it is best to give others credit.

ACTIONS: REVIEW DAVIES'S CURRENT PRACTICES

Looking at Davies's current practices, what practices can you incorporate to become a Star Performer in Communication?

Which ones do you want to add to your Star Performer Action Plan?

1. _____
2. _____
3. _____

THE COACH'S CORNER: 12 STRATEGIES FOR ENHANCING COMMUNICATION AND EMPATHY

Below are 12 proven strategies that you can use to improve your communication and empathy. Every leader has to communicate to get his or her points across. Stars have a set of tools that they use judiciously to be effective. Below are key strategies I teach to executives to incorporate into their daily routines. As you read through the list, be aware of what you are already doing and what actions or micro-initiatives you could do more of.

Communication is important to all of us, but leaders especially need to be understood and to have empathy for others. Below are eight of the basic premises that make this such a challenging endeavor:

1. You are always communicating, even if you are not saying anything.

2. Everything you say counts. There are no second attempts, editing, or deleting of what you say.

3. When your words leave your mouth, you have no control over how they are going to be interpreted.

Everything you say counts. There are no second attempts, editing, or deleting of what you say.

4. Listeners are constantly constructing or "storymaking." That means they are always interpreting what you say.

5. Your words are transformed or reorganized to fit into the listener's personal story or preconceived idea of you and/or similar situations.

6. There will be more than one story. Each listener will create his or her own.

7. The story that is created from your communication determines the meaning, not what you actually say.

8. It is the story, not what you say, that will be remembered, passed on, and communicated to others.[5]

...the likely outcome of your communication is that you will be misunderstood, and therefore you need to be very clear, deliberate, and focused in your communication.

Given these premises, the likely outcome of your communication is that you will be *misunderstood,* and therefore you need to be very clear, deliberate, and focused in your communication. Below are strategies and tools to help you win the empathy and communication battle to reach your targets. These strategies deal with listening, empathy, delivery, and other skills to use with your team or groups.

Read through the following strategies and think about how these behaviors will help you or your direct reports become Star Performers. Pick one or two to try out.

1. EMPATHY SKILLS

Empathy is one of the 20 EI competencies. It is presented here as part of Communication because the skills to enhance empathy are many of the same ones for improving communication. Empathy is one of the building blocks for many of the other competencies including Communication, Trustworthiness, Self-Awareness, Building Bonds, Conflict Resolution, Service Orientation, Leadership, Change Catalyst, and Influence.

WHAT IS THE EMPATHY COMPETENCY?

Empathy is the ability to 1) understand other people and 2) accurately hear the unspoken or partly expressed thoughts, feelings, and concerns of others. It implies taking an active interest in other people's concerns.

EMOTIONAL INTELLIGENCE RESEARCH EXAMPLES

Empathy requires self-awareness, as our sensitivity to others' feelings derives from our ability to be aware and sensitive to our own feelings.

Physicians who are better at recognizing emotions of patients are more successful at treating them than their less sensitive counterparts.[6] Spencer and Spencer found the ability to read others' needs appears to come naturally to the most successful managers of product teams. Empathy was found to be effective for sales in small and large retailers.[7] Empathy was also found to reduce stereotyping that can cause anxiety and poorer performance by the stereotyped individual.[8]

ARE YOU A STAR PERFORMER IN EMPATHY OR JUST AVERAGE?

Stars exhibit both average and Star behaviors consistently. What about you?

AVERAGE

- Listens
- Reads non-verbals
- Is open to diversity

STAR

- Actively listens
- Sees and is sensitive to others' perspectives
- Understands others[9]

HOW TO LISTEN

A. EXPRESSED AND UNEXPRESSED FEELINGS

The Star "sees others' perspectives and understands them." This includes the content of what they are saying and the feelings they are having. The content of what someone is saying is the easier of the two. For someone to really feel heard, knowing how he or she feels allows a deeper sense of being understood. This is challenging because often people don't know how they feel, so besides being invisible to you their feelings are also unknown to them.

What can help with this process is a modification of what is called the Johari Window, first conceived in 1955 by Joseph Luft and Harry Ingram. It is a visualization or graphic chart that helps to give voice to people's feelings, including those that are known and expressed as well as those that are unknown and unexpressed. What to do depends on the expression of feelings and whether or not they are known.

FLUSHING OUT FEELINGS

EXPRESSED	UNEXPRESSED
	2 **Known to self,** **and known to others**
1 **Known to self** **and expressed**	**3** **Not known to self,** **but known to others**
	4 **Not known to self and** **not known to others**

QUADRANT 1: FEELINGS ARE KNOWN TO SELF AND EXPRESSED

- **Listen for the "blinking words":** The blinking words are the feelings; they have the emotional content. You want your ear to be sensitized to them as though they are flashing brightly. Consider: "I am so *frustrated* with the project, I don't know what to do next." "Frustrated" is the blinking word. You can hear how it stands out in the sentence. Here are two possible responses:
  - ▲ "What are you thinking about doing next?"
  - ▲ Or, "Tell me what is making you so frustrated." This one is much better.

QUADRANT 2: FEELINGS ARE KNOWN TO SELF AND OTHERS BUT ARE UNEXPRESSED

- **Observe body language:** Do you pick up any gestures or poses that may illuminate what is going on for this person? Slumped body, low voice, flat affect, irritated when talking?
- **Ask questions:** Try to understand what is happening for the other person by inquiring. "You seem down today. What is going on?" "You seem tense today. Can I help you with anything?"
- **Put yourself in the other person's shoes:** If you were in the same situation, what might you be feeling? "If I were in your situation, I would be feeling overwhelmed. How is this for you?"

QUADRANT 3: FEELINGS ARE NOT KNOWN TO SELF, BUT ARE KNOWN TO OTHERS AND UNEXPRESSED

- **This is known as a "blind spot":** Ask the person if he or she wants some feedback and use the SSBIR Feedback model on pages 252-254. It is ideal if you make the issue part of his or her development plan.

- **Be sensitive. Do not pry:** Remember, you can make a mental note of what is going on for the person and bring it up at another, more appropriate time. "I noticed the other day in the meeting that you were unusually quiet. What was going on for you?"

- **Observe body language:** Do you pick up anything that may get at what is going on for this person? Slumped body, low voice, flat affect, irritated when talking?

- **Ask questions:** Try to understand what is happening for the other person by inquiring. "You seem down today. What is going on?" "You seem tense today. Can I help you with anything?"

- **Put yourself in the other person's shoes:** If you were in the same situation, what might you be feeling? "If I were in your situation, I would be feeling overwhelmed. How is this for you?"

QUADRANT 4: FEELINGS ARE NOT KNOWN BY SELF OR OTHERS

For the obvious reasons, these will not be addressed.

B. LISTENING AT LEVEL 3

When I was a doctoral student, I helped Dr. Byron Norton train master level students in their counseling skills using the Carkuff Model. The students would listen to a counselee and then paraphrase what they just heard, without asking questions or giving advice. This kind of listening is a lot more difficult than it sounds. The natural tendency is to want to give advice and help the person. In this context, helping is not just listening. You can really help once the person truly feels heard. In order to get an "A" in the class, students were required to make sure at least 75% of their responses were at what is called "Level 3." It takes a lot of concentration and skill, but the people talking really feel understood.

THE FOUR LEVELS OF LISTENING

Level 1: Paraphrase content

Level 2: Paraphrase feelings

Level 3: Paraphrase feelings and content

Level 4: Paraphrase feelings, content, and meaning

Leaders benefit greatly by training in Level 3 and Level 4 listening. Here is an example:

Susan is Vice President of Marketing for a California Internet health products company that just acquired a smaller company that manufactures unique items to add to her company's line. She will be picking up three new direct reports from the acquired company. In addition, Susan has a family of three kids and a husband, who also works.

Susan has been asked to assess the new company's marketing staff back at their home offices in North Carolina.

She has a brief talk with her boss, Helen.

Susan: "I am not looking forward to this trip. I am on total over-whelm and feel pulled in so many different directions between my staff, the new people, and my family. I'm sunk because I feel like I can't please all of them and I'm really upset because my son's game is Friday and I have to be on a plane that day."

HELEN CAN COME BACK WITH ANY OF THE FOLLOWING FOUR LEVELS OF LISTENING AND RESPONSE:

LEVEL 1: PARAPHRASE CONTENT

"You have a lot on your plate. Can you take another flight?"

LEVEL 2: PARAPHRASE FEELINGS

"You seem very stressed and upset."

LEVEL 3: PARAPHRASE FEELINGS AND CONTENT

"You seem very overwhelmed and stressed with trying to please your team, the new staff, plus your family. You also seem disappointed that you will miss your son's game."

LEVEL 4: PARAPHRASE FEELINGS, CONTENT, AND MEANING

"You seem very overwhelmed and stressed with trying to please your team, the new staff, plus your family. You are afraid that someone will be upset and let down. It is hard for you to not be all things to all people."

For you to be a Star Performer in Empathy, the majority of your responses should be coming from Level 3, highlighting the content and the other person's dominant feelings. Level 4 is even better because it goes deeper and incorporates patterns and themes that you know about the person.

QUESTIONS AND ACTION APPLICATIONS:

- Practice Level 3 responses with your family and children.
- Then practice Level 3 responses with your team or staff.
- Teach your staff the Level 3 responses and provide a practice session.
- Use Level 3 responses with your clients or customers.
- Do you feel you are getting more adept at reading into others' unexpressed emotions?
- Evaluate your empathy skills weekly and ask a trusted colleague or direct report if he or she feels you are demonstrating a good understanding of the person.

2. LISTENING AND RAPPORT-BUILDING SKILLS

Stephen Covey says, "Most people do not listen with the intent to understand; they listen with the intent to reply."

This is one reason many people and leaders are poor listeners. Empathy is the foundation of listening, and this section presents listening strategies and tips to help you become a Star in Communication and Empathy.

THINKING INSTEAD OF LISTENING: The average person can speak at about 150 words per minute but can think a lot faster, between 450 and 600 words a minute. There is obviously plenty of room to multi-think with your mind busy chattering away while so-called listening. For example, while you are sitting at a meeting, this abundance of nonstop thinking may be going through your mind: "What am I going to have for lunch? Why is this person taking so long to get to the point? Should I buy that new car or wait till the end of the year? I wonder who is going to fill the marketing role. What can I do to get out of here earlier to make my son's game?"

See if any of the following barriers to effective listening happen for you or your team. Check the ones that you or your team exhibit and start changing them today.

SEVEN BARRIERS TO LISTENING

Put a check next to the ones you use the most.

☐ **1. REHEARSING A RESPONSE:** All of your thoughts are on putting together a response to the questions that might come up. Or you are practicing how you are going to say your piece.

☐ **2. FALSE REASSURANCES:** You nod your head or say "Yeah," while looking for that tiny opening when you can jump in and speak.

☐ **3. CLICHÉS:** You offer all kinds of clichés, such as "I'm with you" or "I totally understand," when you really aren't or don't.

☐ **4. MISDIRECTED QUESTIONS:** You ask questions that divert or interrupt the person speaking and fail to really explore what the person is saying.

☐ **5. NOT FOCUSING:** You pay attention to something or someone just outside of the conversation, such as the person who just walked by the window or the sounds of conversation in the next room.

☐ **6. DAYDREAMING:** Your mind is elsewhere—on your next vacation, your next meal, or playing tennis on the weekend.

☐ **7. SELECTIVE LISTENING:** You only catch a few words and pretend to listen.

LISTENING AND RAPPORT-BUILDING TIPS

1. PSYCHOLOGICAL BREATH OF THE RELATIONSHIP

Listening is to a relationship like breath is to the body. Without air we cannot survive. Think about a time you were holding your breath while under water. One minute can feel like an eternity. Remember how you forced yourself up to the surface and were gasping for air. If you are a leader and are not listening well to your people, they can suffocate in their feelings of insignificance. For you to establish a vital and thriving relationship, they must know you are listening to them.

2. INCREASE THE "EMOTIONAL BANK ACCOUNT"

This metaphor was first introduced in Stephen Covey's *The 7 Habits of Highly Effective People.* Each interaction with your people adds to the so-called mutual "emotional bank account" you have with them. By listening, acknowledging, asking for their ideas, supporting, and providing resources for them, you contribute to their account, maybe $50 at a time. You want the account to have $800-$1,000 or more and keep growing. There will be times when you want them to stay late or do something that you know they don't want to do. Because you have built this emotional bank account, you now have the funds to withdraw, say, $150 or $200 and not go bankrupt. Your people will be willing to be there for you because of the strength of your relationship or emotional bank account. (The Debilitating Boss, on the other hand, is constantly withdrawing money and has bankrupt accounts.)

3. PEOPLE TEND TO LIKE PEOPLE WHO ARE LIKE THEM

It is smart to have something besides work in common with each of your direct reports. For your team to feel connected with you, part of your conversations should be around what you have in common with them. For one person it may be family, for someone else it might be a favorite sports team, cars, music, or travel. Find at least one area of shared interest or passion outside of the workplace to cultivate real rapport.

4. ATTENDING BEHAVIOR

I worked with an executive who listened intensely but always exhibited a frown on his face. He also failed to physically acknowledge who he was talking with by nodding his head or even raising his eyebrows. When I was coaching him, I quickly noticed this intense behavior, felt uncomfortable with his response to me, and talked to him about it. It turned out that he was neither unhappy nor critical. Unfortunately, when this executive paid deep attention to another person he just frowned. He never realized that he appeared so off-putting. He was grateful for the blunt feedback and made it his primary coaching goal to become more aware of his attending behavior and change his expression when dealing with others.

For many years before the executive succeeded in changing his attending behavior, most of his direct reports had misinterpreted his expression. They dreaded having a meeting with him because, under his cold glare and frown, they thought:

- "He doesn't like me."

- "He thinks I'm an idiot and not making any sense."

- "He is mad at me for something I did."

By making one simple micro-initiative, this executive allowed his people to feel listened to and understood by him instead of judged or criticized.

TO DEMONSTRATE GOOD LISTENING, YOU NEED TO:

- Not talk. (This is not so obvious for some people.)
- Nod your head occasionally.
- Softly look at the person, gazing more at the top part of his or her face. Do not stare.
- Move away from the computer screen and face whomever you are listening to.
- Open your body posture. Avoid crossed arms. Don't keep looking at your watch.

5. GIVE BRIEF VERBAL ACKNOWLEDGEMENTS

Brief verbal acknowledgements let people know you are listening. These are not the clichés from the barriers listed on pages 233-234. Say "ah-hah," "yeah," "mmmm," "wow," "interesting," "really," "O.K.," "that's nice" periodically during the conversation. This is very subtle and another example of micro-initiatives.

Pace your responses. If you keep interjecting, "That's nice…," it will make whomever you are speaking to think you want him or her to stop or that you are bored.

6. MATCHING AND MIRRORING

You can use many kinds of assessments, from the Myers-Briggs Typing Indicator to the Kolbe, DISC, or Sensory Preference VAK style (see pages 248-250) to discover how your people operate and gather information. You can then match or mirror back their particular orientation to understanding and processing data and make a strong connection.

The effort you make to identify and use this information with your team, direct reports, managers, and peers will help propel you into the top 10% of Star Performers.

QUESTIONS AND ACTION APPLICATIONS:

- Which barriers to listening do you do the most?

- Practice adding to the emotional bank account with all direct reports and key stakeholders.

- Get feedback from a trusted co-worker on the effectiveness of your attending behavior.

- Establish commonalities or interests outside of work that you can talk with your people about that can help build the relationship.

- Identify the specific language to use with each of your people that matches their way of taking in information.

3. WHITE SPACE ISSUES

"If you are not sick and tired of saying the same thing over and over again, you are not saying it enough."

The word *intelligence* comes from a Latin derivation meaning "entering through the lines." People are always using their intelligence to enter or read into the lines of what you are saying or not saying. They fill in the white spaces between your words almost automatically, because it gives them a sense of understanding, control, or security. In the caveman days, gossip served a similar function. It was information that gave tribes the sense of understanding the meaning of things. They could "connect the dots," which helped their survival.

Today, gossip or "making stories" serves a similar purpose. Whether you like it or not, people will always put a personal spin on everything you say, and they do it almost instantaneously. Are their interpretations positive, accurate, or constructive? Probably not! Following is an illustration of what usually happens when you speak and others "listen."

AN EXECUTIVE SAYS ABOUT A POSSIBLE ACQUISITION:

"We are looking into all kinds of possibilities that will help us maintain our viability and profitability."

HOW PEOPLE FILL IN THE WHITE SPACE:

"I didn't think we were in such trouble. This may be worse than I thought. I wonder if I should start looking elsewhere."

"If we are looking to purchase another company, that means there will be layoffs and my job could be in jeopardy."

"Oh no, with this going on in the executive office, they will never have time to focus on my project. This is going to hurt my career advancement."

If you don't fill in the white space, your people will, and you will be reacting to all the misinterpretation.

HERE IS HOW YOU CAN FILL IN THE WHITE SPACE WITH WHAT IS POSITIVE, ACCURATE, AND CONSTRUCTIVE:

AN EXECUTIVE SAYS ABOUT A POSSIBLE ACQUISITION:

"We are looking into all kinds of possibilities that will help us maintain our viability and profitability. Right now there are a few exciting opportunities. Now, because of due diligence, I can't tell you exactly what. But what I can tell you is our process. We have a small team of seasoned executives who are looking at all the facts. This will be a well-thought-out and informed decision. Our criteria in the decision are that we:

"First, don't interrupt our day-to-day business and focus.

"Second, that we keep all the talent here.

"Third, we want this to be growth for you and the company. We want you to be a part of any changes that go on.

"We plan to have a monthly lunch meeting to answer your questions and keep you informed. Contact me or my office if you have questions."

In this scenario, the leader tried to fill in the white space to the best of his or her ability, answering many of the questions people may have. If you can respond to the "unasked questions," you build credibility and security. People won't have to "create their own stories" as much.

WHITE SPACE

The following visual will help you see and remember the process.

The bold line indicates what you said:

" � ▬▬▬▬▬▬▬▬▬▬▬▬▬▬▬▬▬▬▬▬▬▬▬▬▬▬▬▬▬ "

The minus or hyphen signs indicate what gets filled in quickly by others. Remember, they are entering through the lines to grasp what it seems you have said. Again, it is usually inaccurate and judgmental, and rarely gives you the benefit of the doubt.

– –

– –

– –

" ▬▬▬▬▬▬▬▬▬▬▬▬▬▬▬▬▬▬▬▬▬▬▬▬▬▬▬▬▬ "

+++

+++

+++

Positive signs indicate what you say when you proactively fill in the white space with accurate and positive data, talking about opportunities.

" ▬▬▬▬▬▬▬▬▬▬▬▬▬▬▬▬▬▬▬▬▬▬▬▬▬▬▬▬▬ "

White space is always going to get filled in by others. You can plan ahead and inform your people of what you know and prevent too many misunderstandings.

QUESTIONS AND ACTION APPLICATIONS:

- Explain to your staff how filling in white space is natural and how you want them to become conscious of how they are doing it.

- Ask, "What are the ways you can become more aware of how you and others fill in the white space?"

- Challenge yourself and others on some of their assumptions as you and they fill in the white space.

- Constantly ask for feedback about your communications. Ask, "What did you hear?" Then re-clarify.

- Ask your team to let you know if they are not hearing enough from you and are beginning to fill in white space negatively.

- Evaluate whether their interpretations are Positive, Accurate, and Constructive. This is called a PAC interpretation. If what you read or hear is not accurate and constructive, make sure you clarify.

- Remember, white space is going to get filled in by others anyway. You can be preventative and informing by telling your people what you know.

- Use the term *white space* so it remains a viable image and concept for your team.

4. INTENTION/INTERPRETATION GAP

Everything you say has *inferred intention* and *direction* to it. Even if you didn't mean to, the receiver hears a message and intended action to your words. For example:

Mary is an executive with a high-tech company. She talks fast, is extremely busy, is always multitasking, and is driven to get results. She has a meeting with her staff to motivate them to finish a project, so they can enjoy a long weekend. She begins:

"I'm working my tail off to get this project done. I'm sure you don't want me breathing down your neck to see how well you are doing. We missed our last deadline, and I won't let this happen again. Mike here has put together a nice template for all of us to follow."

This is what her people hear:

- "Does she think she is the only one here who is working hard? Doesn't she see what everyone else is doing?"

- "Yeah, breathing down my neck is just what I want from her. Oh no."

- "Does she think I blew the last deadline? I know she looked right at me when she said that."

- "Look at all the work I do, and Mike gets all the credit. She doesn't know I exist."

- "She thinks I am the weak link here and that I don't know what I'm doing. She hasn't talked to me in a month. I'm just as good as Mike."

Mary didn't put much time into thinking about what she wanted to say to the group. As a consequence, she easily gets misinterpreted by what *she didn't say* as much as by what *she did say*. Her intention to motivate the group backfired. She would have been more successful if she would have: 1) taken 3-4 minutes preparing what to say and how to say it, 2) initially asked them how they were doing with the project, and 3) delivered what she had prepared to say.

It is natural to have a gap between what your intention is as the speaker and what the interpretation of what you said is as the listener. Many leaders live by faulty assumptions that can cause many problems such as: "Because I said it, everyone has received it." The listeners assume that *you really thought about this* and there is something *specific* you are saying. In

> *The listeners assume that you **really thought about this** and there is something **specific** you are saying.*

other words, they are inferring that you have clarity in your communication.

RECEIVER'S INFERENCES INCLUDE:

- You spent time thinking about this situation.
- You know exactly what you want.
- There is a clear purpose in all of your communications.
- You know what they can do or not do to add value.
- You have all the answers.

These inferences are based on what you say, your behavior, and your non-verbals. As leaders, we know that many of these assumptions are false, but these are the expectations of your followers as they are listening to you, *at least initially*. If these expectations are not met, then the opposite of these inferences are made and then validated and revalidated.

For example:

- You don't know what you are doing.
- You don't have the answers.
- You don't think anyone has any value.
- You are not clear about where you, the team, or the organization are going.
- You are not a leader who is credible and respected.

INTENTION/INTERPRETATION GAP

Everything you say has inferred intention and direction to it.

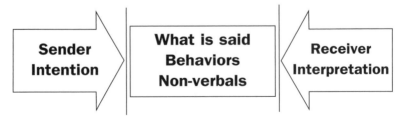

To abate this gap, it is important for both the sender and receiver to be proactive in their parts of the communication. The key questions to ask are:

- Was the communication delivered in a clear, intentional manner?
- Did the communication get received as intended?

To assist in this process, it is necessary to take specific steps. The Intention/Interpretation Quotient (iiQ) was developed as a tool to delineate the steps and evaluate the process. The goal is to use this as a measurement when directions are given by a leader to his or her team or after a problem-solving discussion. The U.S. Army has found that flawed execution comes from flawed assumptions. The iiQ helps elucidate these assumptions.

INTENTION/INTERPRETATION QUOTIENT (iiQ)

Each of the following questions is worth up to 10 points. Mark a number between 1 and 10, where 10 is highest, to show the effectiveness of a particular communication and listening session. Add up the Intention and Interpretation points to come up with an overall iiQ.

Intention: Did the speaker and speakers...	1-10 pts
1. Make their intentions and expectations known?	
2. Communicate to match their listener's style?	
3. Express their assumptions?	
4. Check to see if they were understood?	
5. Have clear directions?	
Total Intention Points	
Interpretation: Did the listener and listeners...	1-10 pts
1. Hear all the communication?	
2. Ask clarifying questions?	
3. Express their assumptions?	

4. Add to and build on the conversation?	
5. Challenge in an effective manner?	
Total Interpretation Points	

Intention Quotient =

Interpretation Quotient =

Overall iiQ =

There are a number of ways to decrease the gap between intention and interpretation.

QUESTIONS AND ACTION APPLICATIONS:

- Introduce the Intention/Interpretation Quotient and use it. Have one person assess your meetings, and rotate that responsibility.

- Where is the gap between intention and interpretation? Which side has the biggest score?

- What gap patterns exist in your team?

- Discuss the scores and ways to lessen the gap.

- As a leader, take time to truly prepare what and how you are going to communicate your points.

- Get feedback from your team about your effectiveness in delivering messages.

5. POWER OF LANGUAGE: METAPHORS, STORIES, AND WORDS

How a leader uses language is critical to effective communication. The choice of metaphors, stories, words, and visual pictures separates the Star communicator from the average. As Mark Twain said, "The difference between the right word and almost the right word is the difference between lightning and a lightning bug."

People remember a metaphor or story more than any other form of communication. Tune in to utilizing these two communication strategies and you will successfully hit the communication target with your direct reports.

A. METAPHORS

A metaphor is defined as a mental bridge that links the unknown with the known, describing one thing in terms of another.[10] When someone says, "X is like Y" a metaphor usually follows. For example:

"My boss's feedback feels **like** a two-by-four against my head."

"The culture here is **like** everyone is breathing in lattes."

"Great leaders and managers treat their direct reports **like** chess players rather than checkers."

"Star communicators fine-tune their delivery **like** an archer spending extra seconds aiming to ensure he hits the bull's-eye."

It is important to train your ears to recognize people's metaphors and then incorporate these metaphors into your responses. Using your followers' metaphors will help them know they have been heard and honored. People have a special relationship with their metaphors, just like they do with their name. We know communication can be enhanced when we use a person's name. The same is true for metaphors because they are your windows into how people perceive their world.[11]

Metaphorical communication is ambiguous and open to interpretation. Because people crave stability and want to avoid imbalance, they will listen closer, think harder, and become more experientially involved.[12]

REMEMBER:

"A single word can possess multiple meanings, yet as the common saying goes, one picture can be worth a thousand words. And if one picture can be worth a thousand words, then one experience can be worth a thousand pictures, and then one metaphor can be worth a thousand experiences.

"But in the end, a metaphor only possesses value when:

- It is able to interpret the experiences…
- In a manner that provides the picture…
- That produces words…
- That have meaning…
- For that particular person."[13]

Luckner and Nadler's *Processing the Experience* presents a guide for using metaphorical language, metaphor-making questions, and metaphor themes that leaders can use to enhance their communication. The themes for creating metaphors include:

Journey theme – "Our train is just leaving the station and we are not sure what the next stop will be with this product."

Systems theme – "You won't be able to race at the same unbearable speed without taking time to change your oil or the spark plugs. What will help you recharge?"

Healing theme – "This loss of our key employee is a big wound for us. It will take time to close up and develop new skin and move forward as we have."

Cyclic and Natural Phenomena theme – "The best way for us to be prepared for this storm of new interest in our products is to be prepared. What will we need in our first-aid kits to get through this next month?"

B. STORIES

A story is the development and elaboration of a metaphor into more of a discourse. It is also rich with visual pictures and innuendo that asks the listener to engage by filling in the blanks with his or her imagination. The individual must search through a number of stored or imagined experiences in order to find personal meaning. The searching stimulates mental associations, which make the communication more memorable and meaningful. The creative process involved in searching through and reorganizing new experiences helps individuals become active collaborators in processing and generalizing their learning.[14]

In 1974 I was working on my Master's thesis. It involved creating a curriculum of facilitative activities to do with Outward Bound courses to enhance awareness and personal relevance that could transfer back easily to home and work environments. The curriculum involved applying Emotional Intelligence competencies to the Outward Bound experience some 16 years before the term *Emotional Intelligence* was coined.

The research design involved four experimental groups and four control groups. I was anxious and apprehensive about my ability to do the courses, implement the curriculum, and gather the research. A few days before I left for the summer project, I bumped into my faculty advisor, Dr. George Brown, the founder and program chair of the Confluent Education program. I bombarded him with my worries and fears for about 10 minutes. When I finally took a breath he said, "Let me see your hand." I stretched out my hand, and he put his fist on top and declared, "You have my seal of approval. I know you will do great and whatever you don't know you will be able to figure out." He then smiled and walked away.

I felt totally bewildered. What had just happened? Over the next day or two I realized that Dr. Brown had expressed his faith in my ability to find my own answers and implement them. This brief interaction was a significant learning for me. His faith in me translated to more faith in myself to stay with what is ambiguous and uncertain until I figure it out.

This story illustrates how the simple sharing of an experience opens up poignant questions and invites personal responses from your listeners.

- Who are the people that have faith in you?
- Who is in your corner?
- Whom do you need to express your faith in?

This story also elucidates George Brown's ability to use Emotional Intelligence—his empathy, trustworthiness, service orientation, leadership, influence, and communication—in a micro-initiative that yielded macro impacts for me.

C. WORDS: HOW YOU TAKE IN AND RELATE TO THE WORLD

Another excellent configuration for understanding different people's communication styles comes from Neuro-Linguistic Programming (NLP), an application used in numerous settings, including sales, education, psychotherapy, and trainings of all sorts. NLP originated when researchers studied Star communicators in the 1970s and teased out powerfully effective strategies that they were using and defined them according to their sensory preferences. People take in and digest information about their world in three ways: Visual (V), Auditory (A), and Kinesthetic (K). Look, listen, and watch your team members and learn how to discern whether they are V, A, or K. Then, to have the most impact, feed them your information tailored specifically to their preference.

3 SENSORY PREFERENCE STYLES FOR TAKING IN AND REPRESENTING THE WORLD CALLED THE V.A.K.

V=VISUAL STYLE: Revolves around vision and sight.

Talks fast, uses visual phrases such as "I can *see* clearly…" "Let me paint you the picture…" "See what I'm saying…" "In view of…" "It looks like…" and "It is still cloudy to me..."

A=AUDITORY STYLE: Revolves around hearing.

Talks methodically and carefully selects words. Uses phrases such as "To tell the truth…" "clear as a bell," "that clicks with me," "I *hear* what you are saying," "what an earful," "it sounds good," and "loud and clear."

K=KINESTHETIC STYLE: Revolves around tactileness and motion.

May talk slowly, sometimes painfully so. Uses phrases such as "catch my drift," "sharp as a tack," "get in touch," "come to grips," "get a handle on it," "hang in there," and "cool and calm."

QUESTIONS AND ACTION APPLICATIONS:

- When preparing to talk to your team, think of stories or metaphors from your own experience that give your talk more vividness and highlight your points.
- Really listen hard to the words and metaphors of your people and mirror them back to them when communicating.
- What are your preferences for taking in information and communicating? Are you a V? An A? A K?
- Write down the ways each of your people takes in informa-tion from the V.A.K. above. When speaking to each person,

make sure you start with his or her preference before falling back to your own.

- When you speak before a group, make sure you dip into all three sensory preference styles so that you successfully reach the entire audience. See it. Hear it. Feel it.

6. CLARITY: CONNECTING THE DOTS
TO A BETTER FUTURE

"Clarity is king" should be the motto for every leader. In each of your communications, you should be connecting the dots for your team members. Given the communication challenges and the Intention/Interpretation Gap, leaders need to over-communicate and employ a variety of methods to get the job done.

More clarity = More security = Better work =
More job satisfaction

In *The One Thing You Need to Know,* Marcus Buckingham focuses on the key initiatives of a leader as it relates to creating a better future. He says:

"Their job is to rally people to a better future…They are instigators. Driven by the compulsion for a better future, their challenge is to do everything in their power to get other people to join together to make this future come true. They (need to) find a way to make many people…excited by and confident in this better future. If, through their words, actions, images, pictures, and scores, they can tap into those things we all share, they will succeed as leaders."

Connecting the dots is a way to keep employees informed. People want to feel significant, get involved in something greater than themselves, and contribute as vital members of the team. If you don't connect the individual to key purposes and goals, he or she will feel disconnected and unmotivated. Make sure you ask the following questions to clarify your future:

1. Who do we serve?
   - Customers, employees, or shareholders?
   - Is there a specific type of customer you are going after?
2. What is our core strength?
   - What is our unique strength that others don't have?
   - How do you keep it in focus?
3. What is our core score?
   - What metrics are useful to track and keep improving?
   - How do you continually share the scores and keep everyone current?[15]

Connecting the Dots: What to Communicate About Frequently

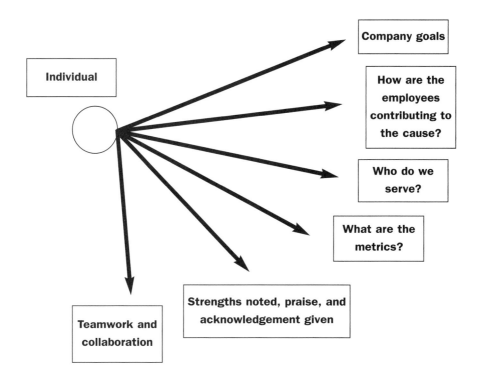

QUESTIONS AND ACTION APPLICATIONS:

- Decide what methods you can utilize and how often you can connect the dots for your team and organization.

- How can you get each of your leaders and team members to pass the communications about connecting the dots into the organization?

- How do you get people who don't have clarity to speak up so they can get the answers?

- Design a "clarity meter" and ask your people on a 1-10 scale, 10 being the highest, to rate your clarity with them. Inquire what could be better, regardless of the scores they give you.

- Use a "brief back," like the army does. This is where, after you have said something, you ask your people to give you the "brief back" or to summarize back to you briefly what they heard or will do.

7. GIVING FEEDBACK: SSBIR

Like delegation and coaching, giving feedback is another skill that can greatly enhance performance when both delivered and received well.

SOMETIMES IT IS DIFFICULT TO GIVE FEEDBACK. WHY? ASK YOURSELF:

- Does the individual want to hear the feedback?
- How honest can I be?
- Will I hurt the person's feelings?
- What if he or she gets defensive?
- Will there be retribution?
- What will the person do with the feedback?
- What if he or she doesn't hear it and the same things keep happening?

- Will this hinder our relationship?
- Is this worth my risk?

THE PROCESS

The following model is adapted from the Center for Creative Leadership. This model can help in giving effective feedback. The goal of the feedback is for the person to both receive and use it. First the summary steps are listed with sentence stubs of what you say; then each step is explained in more detail.

GIVING FEEDBACK

Set the Stage: Intention/readiness to listen

- "I'd like to talk to you about something. Will this time work?"
- "My intention is to help you develop."
- "Can I give you some feedback?"

State the Situation: What happened and where?

- "In the meeting today..."
- "When you spoke to..."
- "In the report you wrote..."

State the Behavior: What did you see or hear, without interpretations?

- "When you came late to the meeting..."
- "When you said..."
- "Three people said..."
- "I saw two errors..."
- "When the report was late..."

State the Impact: On multiple stakeholders and time frames

- "The customer was disappointed..."
- "Others on the team were angry..."

- "This is a poor reflection on you, because…"
- "The organization wondered if…"
- "We lost money and time…"
- "I was disappointed and embarrassed…"
- "My boss asked me what was happening and was concerned..."

Resolution: How would you like to see the situation resolved?

- "What thoughts do you have on how this can be resolved?"
- "How can we prevent this from happening again?"
- "Next time I'd like to see this happen…"
- "Instead can you do…?"

FEEDBACK TOOL EXPLANATION

STEP ONE: SET THE STAGE

This step gives listeners an opportunity to get ready to hear the feedback. Or, they may say that now is not a good time. If they are ready, they will be less reactive. This is usually just one sentence. If the timing doesn't work for them, ask them to specify when it will work.

STEP TWO: STATE THE SITUATION

The second step anchors what you are specifically talking about. It is the "what," "where," or "when."

STEP THREE: STATE THE BEHAVIOR WITHOUT INTERPRETATIONS

This third step is very challenging. It helps to write out what you will say before you give the feedback. You want to have it stated as a videotape would capture it. You do not want them to say, "No, I didn't," in response; instead, the behavior should be irrefutable.

Here are some BAD examples of how to state behavior:

- "Your attitude has gotten worse."

  They could say – "No it hasn't."

- "Your work is sloppy."

  They could say – "No it isn't."

- "I don't think you are putting your all into it."

  They could say – "Yes I am."

Here are some good examples for stating behavior:

- "In the meeting today you raised your voice and were pointing fingers at people."

- "The customer reports that you were acting rude and were slow in responding to her."

- "You told me that you would let me know if you were going to be late with the project and you never mentioned it."

The recipients could still try to deny these, but their ground would be less stable as you are reporting facts rather than interpretations.

STEP FOUR: STATING THE IMPACT

This is the most important step. Ideally you should have 3-4 impacts. The more impacts the better. This is your leverage to demonstrate all the people or situations, time, and money that have been impacted.

- "The customer was disappointed…"

- "Others on the team were angry…"

- "This is a poor reflection on you, because…"

- "Waiting for you to arrive has cost us hundreds of dollars in wasted time."

- "We won't see the impact of this mistake immediately, but six months from now when we go to renew the order, the customer may not want to do business with us again."

STEP FIVE: RESOLUTION

This last step starts with a quiz.

- "What thoughts do you have on how this can be resolved?"
- "How can we prevent this from happening again?"

If you receive feedback and do not change for the better, you will be perceived more negatively than if you had not received the feedback.

If they have accepted the feedback, they will be able to give you some ideas of how to prevent these behaviors in the future. If they have *NOT* accepted the feedback, you will have to be more assertive and tell them what you want to see them do instead.

If you receive feedback and do not change for the better, you will be perceived more negatively than if you had not received the feedback.

In using this model, take a few moments to write down your notes before giving feedback. This micro-initiative will increase your chances of them hearing the feedback and having them be less defensive.

WHEN TO GIVE FEEDBACK

1. FREQUENTLY: This gives you the best chance to reinforce positive behavior and influence changes in acceptable behavior. It makes it easier to focus on a specific behavior. So that your people don't only think feedback is negative, surprise them as much as you can with positive feedback.

2. TIMELY: Speak to employees when the experience is fresh. Don't give feedback only on exceptionally positive or negative things. Remember successive approximation or to give feedback when they are approaching the goal, not only when they have reached the goal.

3. OPPORTUNITY FOR DEVELOPMENT: Make employees aware of potential opportunities and provide steps to achieve their goals.

4. TO SOLVE PERFORMANCE PROBLEMS: Regular and frequent feedback puts money in the emotional bank account between people. It also makes it easier to be direct on a performance problem. When trust and respect have been built, it is easier to make a withdrawal from the account.

SUMMARY TIPS FOR GIVING FEEDBACK

- If it is important, make an appointment to give the feedback.
- Be sensitive to the power imbalance (i.e., doing it in your office versus a neutral ground).
- Keep it simple.
- Leverage their strengths.
- Prepare the feedback to fit the learning style.
- Offer suggestions and support.
- Get their feedback about the feedback.

QUESTIONS AND ACTION APPLICATIONS:

- How would you rate how well you give feedback?
- Practice the SSBIR model and ask for feedback on how well you communicated.
- Teach the feedback model to your team and practice giving feedback using real-life scenarios. Discuss which statements seemed to best hit the mark.
- Make feedback a process that you are getting feedback on and continually try to improve it.

8. ASSUMPTION LADDER: ARRIVING AND DELIVERING COMMUNICATION

Communication is the mechanism to deliver your thoughts to others. These next strategies are all about our thinking process and how to communicate our thoughts. We will start off with defining mental models—how did you *arrive* at them and how can you *deliver* them to others to be most effective.

A. WHAT IS A MENTAL MODEL?

Deepak Chopra stated that we have as many as 60,000 thoughts a day. Ninety-five percent of those thoughts are the same ones we had yesterday.[16] Why is that? The same thoughts keep recycling, and that is one reason we use only 5-10% of our brainpower. These same or similar thoughts form patterns or clusters of our beliefs, yet leave out a plethora of other possible views. Senge defines "mental models" as "deeply ingrained assumptions, generalizations, or even pictures or images that influence how we understand the world and how we take action."

...we have as many as 60,000 thoughts a day. Ninety-five percent of those thoughts are the same ones we had yesterday.

The term *mental model* has been used by psychologists since the 1940s. Cognitive psychologists, cognitive scientists, and more recently managers use the term. In his book *The Fifth Discipline,* Senge popularized the term as one of his five disciplines. In the *Fifth Discipline Fieldbook*, "mental model" is defined as "both the semi-permanent tacit 'maps' of the world which people hold in their long-term memory, and the short-term perceptions which people build up as part of their everyday reasoning process."[17]

B. WHY IS UNDERSTANDING OUR MENTAL MODELS IMPORTANT?

The mental models we carry around are usually *invisible* to us and others yet are very powerful in their influence over our actions and responses to anything that occurs in our world. Often these mental models hold us prisoners to the "same old story" when openness to new learning is necessary to grow and advance in our careers. To continually learn and grow we must *think* and *act* differently, and our invisible mental models hold us back like a prisoner's ball and chain.

As a leader, it is important to make explicit your thinking. We have the tendency to take shortcuts when we think and speak.

People don't have the benefit of seeing our thinking process, what we focused in on, what we discounted, or what building blocks we crafted to support our thoughts and decisions. So isn't it natural that people may have a difficult time following our ideas or suggestions? We reach a destination, but no one knows what roads we took, where we stopped along the way, or how long it took us. We leave out important parts of how we arrived at these ideas. Thus, our buy-in from others can be minimized.

People don't have the benefit of seeing our thinking process, what we focused in on, what we discounted, or what building blocks we crafted to support our thoughts and decisions.

C. HOW DO WE USE THE LADDER?

The Assumption Ladder is a modification of Chris Argyris's Ladder of Inference, introduced in Senge's *The Fifth Discipline*. I have been using it in organizations for over 10 years with great success. When I return a year later and do follow-up assessments on the changes that took place, the Assumption Ladder is usually the tool that gets rave reviews. It has staying power because it is visual, makes sense to people, brings self-awareness to their thinking process, and helps in communicating their ideas.

The goal is to walk people up the ladder. It allows you to lay out your thinking process and mental models. You want to invite people up the ladder, as well, to see if they agree with your data, selection of data, assumptions about the data, conclusions, and then the actions you suggest. If they know how you arrived, they may be more willing to go along with you. Or they may disagree, but it is more constructive to disagree with your selection of data and your assumptions than to argue with you about your conclusions.

In summary, the ladder gives you the steps or rungs to describe how you arrived at your decision and to deliver it for maximizing buy-in.

Assumption Ladder

The goal is to make your thinking visible to others as you walk up the ladder

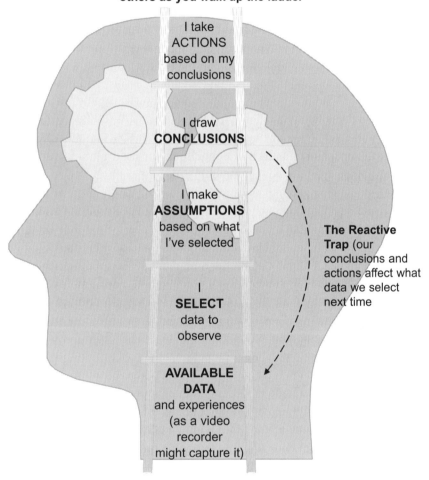

I take
ACTIONS
based on my
conclusions

I draw
CONCLUSIONS

I make
ASSUMPTIONS
based on what
I've selected

I
SELECT
data to
observe

**AVAILABLE
DATA**
and experiences
(as a video
recorder
might capture it)

**The Reactive
Trap** (our
conclusions and
actions affect what
data we select
next time

Adapted from Luckner, J.L. and Nadler, R.S. *Processing the Experience.* Dubuque, Iowa: Kendall/Hunt Publishing Company, 1997.

Assumption Ladder
Applications

**Below are some examples of sentences and sentence stubs
that will help you walk up or down the ladder.**

As a Listener:

I hear your actions.
What are they based on?
How did you arrive at these plans?

Tell me what conclusion you are drawing...
Could it be possible that...

Tell me what your assumptions are...
I'm curious, tell me more...
Is that the only way to look at it?

What piece are you looking at?
I see you're focusing on...
What is standing out to you from the data?

Give me all the facts...
What are all the findings?

As a Speaker:

Therefore, this is my plan...
These are steps I am taking...

It's obvious to me...
Therefore, I feel...
As a result...
To summarize // Here we go again...

So, I'm assuming...
Here's what I attribute...
The next step for me is...

I am focusing on this piece...
Here's what I see happening...
Here's what I'm selecting...
This stands out to me...

Here are all the facts...
Here are all the findings...

ACTIONS

CONCLUSIONS

ASSUMPTIONS

SELECTED DATA

AVAILABLE DATA

Pay attention to intentions / Make your thinking visible

Adapted from Luckner, J.L. and Nadler, R.S. *Processing the Experience.*
Dubuque, Iowa: Kendall/Hunt Publishing Company, 1997.

SOME POINTERS:

- Once a decision or conclusion is made it becomes a force that looks for self-validation, and it is hard to entertain new data or ideas.

- The ladder slows down the thinking process, and with more people commenting on the data and their assumptions you can get more creative and sound decisions. Your team can help ensure quality decisions.

- If two people are at the top of their ladders, you get debate and disagreement. If both people are low on the ladder, you will get more of a dialogue before people are fixed to their positions and defending them.

- The Assumption Ladder Applications tool gives you sentence stubs to walk up and down the ladder. It is especially helpful when a direct report or client is at the top of the ladder and you want to find out how he or she arrived there. It gives you an opportunity to insert a new selection of data, which opens up thinking and other viable possibilities.

- The ladder is a universal EI tool. It helps with:

  Self-Awareness, Accurate Self-Assessment, Empathy, Service Orientation, Communication, Influence, Leadership, Conflict Management, Change Catalyst, Teamwork and Collaboration, and Developing Others.

LADDER CARRIER:

It is a good idea to introduce the ladder as a tool to enhance communication and understanding of others' viewpoints. To utilize the ladder to its fullest, you, the leader, a facilitator, or another leader should bring the ladder into your conversations. This person can be the "ladder carrier" and use terms that will help the team visualize the ladder.

- "You are up on the ladder on this one."

- "Can you make your thinking more visible?"
- "What are your assumptions in this decision?"

DO'S AND DON'TS WHEN USING THE LADDER

DO	DON'T
Get people to hold your ladder as you go up	Use the ladder as a weapon
Open up for multiple viewpoints	Try to knock others off their ladder
Invite others to challenge you	Get defensive
Practice walking up and down the ladder	Expect this to be easy
Listen and inquire versus just advocating	Advocate without inquiry

QUESTIONS AND ACTION APPLICATIONS:

- Introduce mental models and the ladder to your team.
- Pick a facilitator to help integrate the ladder by inquiring which rung people are on and encouraging them to walk up the ladder.
- Get copies of the ladder for everyone to use and get a poster of the ladder for your conference room.
- Use the ladder if there is a disagreement and see if the data and selection of data are the same. If so, go to the varying assumptions and locate where the disagreement lies.

9. BALANCING INQUIRY AND ADVOCACY

In *The Fifth Discipline*, Senge introduces the concept of balancing inquiry and advocacy. This is where you ask more about the other person's viewpoints instead of only advocating your own. This concept is borrowed from "action science," a field of inquiry developed by Chris Argyris and Donald Schon. Their goal is to explore the reasoning and attitudes that underlie human interaction. It uncovers a person's "mental models," those tacit assumptions and stories we carry in our mind about people, places, things, and every aspect of our world. These mental models are mental maps, usually untested and unexamined.

Balancing inquiry and advocacy is another tool to help unearth and get a tangible handle on what people's mental models are. Without imposing discipline on teams engaged in a discussion, what we generally hear are the propositions, ideas, or recommendations that people are advocating. Often this stuff is expressed with a great deal of passion, and so instead of inquiring about the recommendations and specific assumptions made, there is often passionate disagreement as well, without any resolution or clarity.

What is needed is to balance the natural emotional process of advocating with the unnatural, more rational process of inquiry. It is a good idea to question people about how they arrived at their decision and then dig into their assumptions to understand more. The best way to proceed is to improve the team's inquiry process. Ask the following questions:

- Tell me, how did you make this decision or recommendation?
- What things were you considering with this idea?
- What assumptions underlie this recommendation?
- Is there a time this solution wouldn't work?
- What would you need to make this successful?
- How long do you think this process would take?
- What potential risks have you considered?

QUESTIONS AND ACTION APPLICATIONS:

- In one of your meetings, introduce the concept of balancing inquiry and advocacy.
- Have people use inquiry with the existing ideas on the table before going on to the next idea.

- Work on and practice your inquiry skills.
- Evaluate the team meeting's effectiveness. (See Team Meetings in Chapter 3, page 120.)

10. THE LEFT-HAND COLUMN

This is another strategy, introduced by Senge in *The Fifth Discipline,* to illuminate our mental models. On a single piece of paper, draw one line down the middle. On the right-hand side, title the column "WHAT WAS SAID." Fill in the column with the actual dialogue of what was said in a recent conversation with a co-worker. On the top of the left-hand column, write "WHAT WAS THOUGHT, BUT NOT EXPRESSED" and fill in this column with thoughts you had that were not spoken. The reason the left-hand column is not expressed is usually because of *trust issues* or skill issues on *how to say* what is difficult to another. So this becomes the first step in identifying what is in the left-hand column. The team can brainstorm examples of how to best express the left-hand column.

LEFT-HAND COLUMN	RIGHT-HAND COLUMN
What was thought, but not expressed	What was said

QUESTIONS AND ACTION APPLICATIONS:

- Work with your team and choose one conversation that may have caused some conflict. Have people write the actual right-column conversation and then the left-hand column of what was thought but not said. This can be done anonymously. Then you can exchange or read people's left-hand column. Discuss how the left-hand column can be expressed in a constructive manner. Use discretion depending on the level of conflict and how blunt people are with their left-hand column.

- If trust is the issue and you are not sure if people want to hear about your left-hand column, talk about trust in your team and ways to enhance it.

- One exercise that helps is to have people complete the following statement and share with a partner or in the group. The answer to this statement is usually in the left-hand column. "For me to trust, you should…"

- Fill in 5-10 responses, the later responses force you to dig deep into what you need for trust.

11. DIALOGUE VS. DISCUSSION

Dialogue is a way of thinking and reflecting together to come up with better ideas, more creativity, and innovation. It focuses on learning from one another and building shared meaning, making sure to include everyone's perspective in the mix.[18] Dialogue means the "flow of meaning" between people and "to gather together." With shared meaning come shared actions. Dialogue is about evoking insight, which is a way of reordering knowledge, usually around the taken-for-granted assumptions that people bring to the table. Better decisions and execution result when decisions start with a dialogue. Thinking together will produce better results than thinking alone will.

IN MOST ORGANIZATIONS, DIALOGUES DO NOT HAPPEN BECAUSE OF:

- time constraints
- hierarchies
- strong opinions and trying to be the smartest person in the room
- poor listening
- competition and defensiveness
- political agendas
- "un-discussable" topics

A discussion is a conversation that is focused on getting closure, usually with only one or a limited perspective. Discussion comes from the same word root as *concussion* or *percussion*. It evokes an image of something being beaten or shaken, and the result is something that is not whole, but rather is shattered or broken. Only pieces or fragments are left. A discussion is what generally takes place in most organizations because they are driving to find one answer, and usually driving too fast and expecting an answer too quickly. We know how to drive to one solution, but what we don't know as well is how to stay with the ambiguity and entertain multiple solutions to get the best answer. That's where dialogue comes in. There is a time for discussion, but not at the exclusion of dialogue (which is usually the result).

> *We know how to drive to one solution, but what we don't know as well is how to stay with the ambiguity and entertain multiple solutions to get the best answer.*

Here is a continuum that illustrates the process from debate and discussion to dialogue.[19]

DISCUSSION-DIALOGUE CONTINUUM

DEBATE AND DISCUSSION	DIALOGUE
Breaking issues into pieces and fragments	Seeing the whole among parts
Finding distinctions and exceptions	Finding connection and patterns
Taking stands and justifying	Inquiring into assumptions
Telling and selling	Learning and seeking understanding
Finding one answer	Creating shared meaning through multiple descriptions

Adapted from Ellinor and Gerard, 1998.

QUESTIONS AND ACTION APPLICATIONS:

- Talk with your team about the differences between a dialogue and a discussion.
- Establish when you should have a dialogue versus a discussion.
- Clearly identify when you are in the dialogue process versus the discussion process.

12. DIALOGUE ROLES

In order to make quality decisions, it is useful to identify and clarify the following four dialogue roles. Ideally, each role should have a voice. This ensures that you are engaged in a lively dialogue rather than a discussion.

Dialogue roles raise the awareness of the team so that decisions are not just coming from the loudest or most confident person. In some meetings, people feel that their responsibility is only to "move" new ideas and thus fail to integrate them with other responses or determine how to implement them effectively.

THE 4 KEY DIALOGUE ROLES ARE:

MOVER – Moves a new idea forward to the group.

OPPOSER – Opposes or disagrees with the moved idea.

SUPPORTER – Supports either the moved or opposed idea and may add onto another idea.

INTEGRATOR – Pulls together the differing ideas, looks for "both/and" solutions, summarizes and refocuses the group, and keeps the end in mind. The integrator role is the one the facilitator usually takes, but anyone on your team can take it on.

QUESTIONS AND ACTION APPLICATIONS:

- Ask: Which roles are most prevalent in your team meetings? Which roles are under-utilized? Why?

- Assess what % of time people advocate their ideas versus inquiring or asking questions. Ask the group to call out their best guess. What can your team do to inquire more?

- An observer can track how many mover, opposer, supporter, and integrator statements along with questions were made during a meeting. At the end of the meeting, share what is called the "Dialogue Metric" to see if you can increase the questions and also determine which role is underrepresented.

STAR PERFORMER ACTION PLAN

Review the Star Profile and *Coach's Corner* strategies to assist you in mastering Communication and Empathy. Now answer the following questions to help you make your Star Performer Action Plan.

Which competencies or practices are you already doing that you want to continue?

1. _____
2. _____
3. _____

What new practices do you want to incorporate?

1. _____
2. _____
3. _____

What resources do you need to make this happen?

1. _____
2. _____
3. _____

Who can support you and hold you accountable?

    1. _____

    2. _____

    3. _____

How might you sabotage your efforts and best intentions?

    1. _____

    2. _____

    3. _____

What will be your first steps in this plan?

    1. _____

    2. _____

    3. _____

Share this plan with your support people. Good luck!

CHAPTER SIX

THE GAME PLAN

THE COACH'S CORNER

Great leadership starts with you—by choosing a few actions that you can initiate today. Keeping Score helps you pull together some of the activities and goals you've highlighted along the way and gets you on track to get them done! Like a coach, your ability to have a game plan, follow it, and stay committed will move you into the top 10%. The average performer may make a plan, but won't stay committed to it.

You have read how the Stars who were interviewed had habits or rituals of specific actions that made them Stars. Henrik Fisker's confidence included his decisiveness and capturing the moment of empowering his people. Paulette Jones's teamwork and collaboration was highlighted by her strategic use of meetings. Mark French's prowess in the development of others centered on his recruitment of Stars, using one-on-ones, and giving feedback. John Davies's communication expertise focused on finding the client's passion and unique talents and communicating in a way that touched people's hearts.

Throughout the book I have described powerful micro-initiatives, seemingly small and doable tasks that create macro impact. With the Scorecard, you will select a few of these micro-initiatives to ingrain as daily practices. Knowing your score is important reinforcement. Many leaders see these initiatives as their "second checklist" to do *after* their primary job responsibilities are over. If that remains the case, these critical actions to improve yourself and others get done haphazardly and infrequently. You will remain good, but you will not become great.

GOAL: The goal of this book is to give you and the people you lead specific skills and actions to raise your Emotional Intelligence, thus creating more Stars in your organization.

BENEFITS: Why take the time to improve your Emotional Intelligence and do a few things more frequently?

- Leaders high in Emotional Intelligence are more productive.[1]
- Great leaders also have a positive impact on profitability, turnover, employee commitment, customer satisfaction and retention.[2]
- The more great leaders an organization develops, the more it will become an outstanding organization.[3]
- Emotions are contagious. As a top leader, you influence the whole climate of your team as much as 50-70%.[4]
- Gallup has found that if U.S. workers were 5% more engaged, it would boost national productivity by $79 billion a year.
- As a leader, you pass on your leadership legacy. As we have seen, new leaders emulate the practices of their best bosses.
- The best way to retain your good people is to have positive and productive relationships with them.
- People who are positive have been shown to live longer.[5]
- The Department of Labor has found that job satisfaction is a better predictor of longevity than smoking or exercise habits.[6]

Consequence for Not Raising Emotional Intelligence

- The reasons for losing customers and clients are 70% EQ-related.[7]
- 50% of time wasted in business is due to lack of trust.[8]
- Key executive derailers include lack of impulse control and the inability to work on teams.[9]

- The cost to replace a manager or sales position is 250% of his or her compensation package.[10]

STRATEGY: REVIEW YOUR STAR PERFORMER ACTION PLANS

Hopefully, you have already implemented a few of these activities and have seen significant and positive changes in your leadership skills as well as a new focus, dedication, and collaborative spirit on the part of your team.

Now it's time to review your Star Performer Action Plans and take your concepts about change and improvement onto the playing field. Spend some quality time studying your plans from each chapter. Then pick no more than two activities/goals that you think will benefit you the most right now. Remember the 80-20 rule: 20% of your effort can lead to 80% of your results.

As an alternative, your team can choose some of the strategies to do as a team, where everyone is working on implementing tools such as giving feedback, using the delegation tool, or implementing the leadership checklist and teambuilding. Then as a team you can assess your result, talk about your learnings, and adjust the process.

Your focus should be on what you can realistically accomplish over the next month. Use SMART goals, which stands for Specific, Measurable, Actionable, Realistic, and Time dependent. When you have mastered these goals, take on new activities, tools, or goals from another chapter until those are mastered. Mastering a skill or tool here means that you are doing it 80% of the time; it is a habit for you. So your scores on the Scorecard should be consistently 8-10.

THE PLAYS

Below are the plays listed in the book to choose from for your Star Performer Action Plan. Check the boxes for the ones you want to practice.

Self-Confidence

Star Profile: Henrik Fisker, CEO, Fisker Coachbuild, LLC

10 Secrets & Current Practices of a Star Performer

1. Take Private Time (p. 73) ☐
2. Get Third Opinions (p. 73) ☐
3. Evaluate Capacities (p. 73) ☐
4. Shoot from the Hip (p. 73) ☐
5. Go with That Gut Feeling (p. 74) ☐
6. Take Initiative (p. 74) ☐
7. Identify Your Strengths and Weaknesses (p. 74) ☐
8. Take Responsibility for Your Mistakes (p. 75) ☐
9. Reinforce People (p. 75) ☐
10. Be Willing to Make Decisions That Are Exceptions
    to the Rule (p. 75) ☐

The Coach's Corner: 10 Strategies for Confidence

1. Being on Your Case vs. Being on Your Side (p. 77) ☐
2. Reflections on Thinking (p. 82) ☐
3. Busting Perfection: Creating Realistic Expectations (p. 84) ☐
4. Success Rules: Who Is Running You? (p. 89) ☐
5. Success Log (p. 91) ☐
6. Current Success Log (p. 92) ☐
7. The Five Pivotal People in Your Life (p. 93) ☐
8. Visualization (p. 93) ☐
9. Decisiveness (p. 94) ☐
10. Thin-Slicing (p. 95) ☐

Teamwork and Collaboration

Star Profile: Paulette Jones, Director of Technical and Strategic
    Business Development, NMB Technologies Corporation

10 Secrets & Current Practices of a Star Performer in
    Teamwork and Collaboration

1. Start the Day with "An Attitude of Gratitude" (p. 102) ☐

2. Focused Greeting of People (p. 103) ☐

3. Communication (p. 103) ☐

4. Red Flag Meetings (p. 103) ☐

5. Revenue Gap Meetings (p. 104) ☐

6. BAT Teams (Business Acquisition Teams) (p. 104) ☐

7. Team Meetings (p. 105) ☐

8. Continual Process Review (p. 105) ☐

9. Valuing Staff (p. 105) ☐

10. Humor (p. 105) ☐

**The Coach's Corner: 24 Strategies for Teamwork
and Collaboration**

1. Shared Vision (p. 108) ☐

2. Trust Among Members (p. 108) ☐

3. Expectations and Guidelines (p. 109) ☐

4. Communication Skills and Conflict Resolution (p. 109) ☐

5. Systems Thinking (p. 110) ☐

6. Personal Leadership (p. 111) ☐

7. Appreciation of Differences (p. 111) ☐

8. Accountability and Consequences (p. 112) ☐

9. Ongoing Learning and Recognition (p. 113) ☐

10. Mentor Others (p. 113) ☐

11. Meeting Mastery and Meeting Menace (p. 114) ☐

12. Snapshot Management: "The One Hand Rule" (p. 116) ☐

13. Meeting Menace Checklist (p. 118) ☐

14. Team Meetings (p. 120) ☐

15. Guidelines for Running a Great Meeting (p. 122) ☐

16. How to Establish Roles Within a Team Meeting (p. 122) ☐

17. "Stand-Ups"—Short Team Meetings (p. 123) ☐

18. The Meeting Checklist (p. 124) ☐

19. "Nails" Teambuilding Activity (p. 131) ☐

20. "Performance and Accountability" Teambuilding
    Activity (p. 135) ☐

21. "Expectations" Activity (p. 138)   ☐
22. Team Assessment (p. 140)   ☐
23. 100 Leadership Check-In Questions (p. 142)   ☐
24. Teamwork Ingredients Survey (p. 148)   ☐

Developing Others

Star Profile: Mark French, University of California
at Santa Barbara Basketball Team

13 Secrets & Current Practices of a Star Performer
in Developing Others

1. Leader's Point of View (POV): Basketball
   as a Metaphor for Life (p. 159)   ☐
2. Practice (p. 160)   ☐
3. Bonding and Team Meetings (p. 161)   ☐
4. Recruiting Stars (p. 161)   ☐
5. Building Effective Relationships (p. 163)   ☐
6. Self-Assessments and Goal Setting (p. 164)   ☐
7. One-on-Ones (p. 164)   ☐
8. Supportive Learning (p. 165)   ☐
9. Timely Feedback (p. 166)   ☐
10. Focus on Strengths (p. 167)   ☐
11. Take Personal Responsibility (p. 167)   ☐
12. Performance Review (p. 168)   ☐
13. Briefings Before and After the Game (p. 170)   ☐

The Coach's Corner: 12 Strategies for Developing Others

1. Hiring Stars (p. 172)   ☐
2. Behavioral Questions List (p. 173)   ☐
3. One-on-One Meetings (p. 186)   ☐
4. Soaring with Strengths (p. 190)   ☐
5. Input + 1 (p. 191)   ☐
6. Circle of Influence (p. 192)   ☐
7. Performance = Potential – Interferences or P=P–I (p. 196)   ☐

8. Delegation (p. 196) ☐

9. Coaching for Performance (p. 199) ☐

10. Scaling Questions (p. 202) ☐

11. Motivation Skills Matrix (p. 203) ☐

12. Development First (p. 208) ☐

Communication and Empathy

Star Profile: John Davies, CEO and Founder,
Davies Public Relations

11 Secrets & Current Practices of a Star Performer
in Communication and Empathy

1. Touch the Heart (p. 217) ☐

2. Understand What People Want (p. 217) ☐

3. Find Your Passion (p. 218) ☐

4. Find Your Uniqueness (p. 219) ☐

5. Read People (p. 219) ☐

6. Acknowledge/Do Not Offend (p. 220) ☐

7. Summarize and Integrate (p. 221) ☐

8. Be Prepared (p. 221) ☐

9. Training and Personal Growth (p. 222) ☐

10. Quality in All (p. 222) ☐

11. Finding the "Needle in the Haystack" (p. 223) ☐

The Coach's Corner: 12 Strategies for Communication and Empathy

1. Empathy Skills (p. 226) ☐

2. Listening and Rapport-Building Skills (p. 232) ☐

3. White Space Issues (p. 237) ☐

4. Intention/Interpretation Gap (p. 240) ☐

5. Power of Language: Metaphors, Stories, and Words (p. 244) ☐

6. Clarity: Connecting the Dots to a Better Future (p. 250) ☐

7. Giving Feedback: SSBIR (p. 252) ☐

8. Assumption Ladder: Arriving and Delivering
Communication (p. 257) ☐

9. Balancing Inquiry and Advocacy (p. 263) ☐

10. The Left-Hand Column (p. 265) ☐

11. Dialogue vs. Discussion (p. 266) ☐

12. Dialogue Roles (p. 268) ☐

In order to make the best decisions, ask yourself the following questions and fill in your answers.

1. What are the one or two things you can do now that will bring you and your team the greatest benefit(s)?

2. Who are your support people that will keep you accountable?

3. What do you see as your biggest obstacle to this goal?

4. How will you get over this?

5. What will keep you motivated? What rewards will help?

6. What are your first steps?

7. When will you start?

KEEPING SCORE:
YOUR LEADERSHIP SCORECARD

Once you have chosen your specific goals and actions, keep a weekly scorecard to help you monitor your progress and stay on track. Here is an example from a new manager who wanted to implement two key activities from the Teamwork and Collaboration and Developing Others chapters. They are:

1. Team meetings

2. One-on-one meetings

His Scorecard for one week looked like this:

WEEK OF: JULY 7-11

GOAL OR ACTION	FREQUENCY	SUPPORT	SELF-RATING: 1-10
1. Hold team meeting	2 X month	Mgr, team	7
2. One-on-one w/ direct reports	1 X month	Mgr, team	5

Actions: 1. Get more input for the agenda

2. Schedule one-on-one a month ahead

At the end of the week he reviewed his actions and determined how well he had done and what he could do to improve. For his first goal he had two team meetings, one for training issues and the other for basic team information. He felt good about them, even though his team didn't do much talking. He decided that next time he would prepare the agenda ahead of time and get more of their involvement.

He didn't feel as good about the second goal, because he had one-on-ones with only two of his four people, while he had wanted to see all of them in the month. He decided to schedule himself a month ahead of time to ensure that he made enough time for everyone. Your support is important; the more people you involve in your actions, the more successful you will be.

As you evaluate yourself, be fair and just and not only "on your case." If you get in the 8-10 range for a month, you are doing great and probably have achieved your goals. If not, reread the appropriate section in the book and repeat another month before choosing more activities. Also, think of getting your supervisor to give you some mentoring or think about getting an Executive Coach to help you.

THE LEADERSHIP SCORECARD

Here is the LEADERSHIP SCORECARD. It is set up as a weekly template you can copy and put in a three-ring notebook or collect in a file. It's best done by hand instead of on the computer. At the end of the week, evaluate how well you did and mark your scores. Congratulate yourself and document if there are other ways to enhance your efforts.

Begin reviewing your Star Performer Action Plans today and kick off a new season of great leadership. These micro-initiatives, done consistently, will propel you into the top 10% and enhance your team's effectiveness.

On the following page is an example of a scorecard to use.

MONTH: _____

YEAR: _____

WEEK OF:

GOAL OR ACTION	FREQUENCY	SUPPORT	SELF-RATING: 1-10

Actions to enhance:

Being a leader is about your commitment to your growth and serving others. You are under the spotlight 24/7 and have more influence over others than you could ever imagine. Your disciplined actions can influence your team and organization to have many winning seasons. You hold the keys—use them wisely. Good luck.

RESOURCES

The following are resources to develop your Emotional Intelligence, including 360-degree feedback, research, tools, and training.

Authentic Happiness

The main site for the field of positive psychology and the work of Martin Seligman. The site has articles you can download and a series of free assessments.

www.authentichappiness.org

Center for Breakthrough Thinking

Provides trainings, products, and services in "Breakthrough Thinking, Question Forward and Smart Questions."

www.breakthroughthinking.com

info@breakthroughthinking.com

Center for Social and Emotional Education

Developing leaders in Social and Emotional Education; has training institutes and speakers.

212 707-8799

www.csee.net

sel@csee.net

Collaborative Growth

Provides EQ certification for organizations and trainers. Sponsor of the EQ Symposium.

303 271-0021

www.cgrowth.com

Contact@cgrowth.com

Competency and Emotional Intelligence

A journal that comes out four times a year based in England.
44 (0)20 8662-2000
www.competencyandei.com

EI Consortium
Consortium for Research on Emotional Intelligence in Organizations, housed at Rutgers University

Organization created by Daniel Goleman and Cary Cherniss and others for advancement, research, and practice related to Emotional Intelligence in organizations. The site has research articles and downloadable PDFs.
www.eiconsortium.org

EI World

A center for research and development of Emotional Intelligence based in England. Offers three EI assessments, Baron EQi, Baron EQ 360™, and the MSCEIT™, plus articles, products, and services.
www.eiworld.org

EQ Alliance

An association of EI practitioners and allies to raise awareness of EI tools and best practices.
www.nexusEQ.com/assoc

EQ Directory

A directory of Emotional Intelligence resources.
650 685-9880
www.eq.org

EQ Map

Certifies professionals in the EQ Map. Also stress management experts with 20 years of experience leading business from stress toward resiliency.
800 252-3774
www.essisystems.com

EQ Network
EQ Europe Education

Network for trainers, teachers, and counselors who are interested in Emotional Quality and Human Respect.

www.eqee.org

network@eqee.org

EQ University

Offers online assessment, training, and development. Certifies people in Baron EQi™ and the Baron EQ 360™.

877 700-3305

www.equniversity.com

Gallup Organization

Provides market research and consulting services around the world. Publisher of the Gallup Poll, a widely recognized barometer of American opinion. Gallup Consulting has great research articles and practices on leadership development, employee engagement, climate, and strength-based strategies.

www.gallup.com

Hay Group

Certifies professionals in the ECI360™, the Goleman and Boyatzis EI model, presented in this book. They also have added assessments for professional trainers, the Inventory of Leadership Styles™ (ILS), and Organizational Climate Survey™ (OCS). Research articles are available on the site.

877 267-8375

http://ei.haygroup.com

Institute of HeartMath

Does research, education, and training on bringing the heart and brain into synchronization, which helps communication and performance.

831 338-8500

www.heartmath.org

Multi-Health Systems, Inc.

Distributes the Baron EQi™, Baron EQ 360™, and the MSCEIT™, along with other clinical, educational, forensic, and organizational products and resources.

> 800 456-3003
>
> www.mhs.com

6 Seconds

Brings EI into schools, organizations, and communities. The website has articles, a newsletter, and an EQ store.

> 650 685-9885
>
> www.6seconds.org

The Success Principles

Jack Canfield, co-creator of Chicken Soup for the Soul®, *which has sold over 80 million books, is also the co-author of* The Success Principles. *The authors have created books, training, and e-coaching on the 64 principles of success.*

> 800 237-8326
>
> www.thesuccessprinciples.com

Talent Smart

Developed its own 360-degree EI assessment, along with products and other assessments.

> 888 818-SMART
>
> www.talentsmart.com

True North Leadership, Inc.

Developed a 7-day EI training and a 2-day EI training based on Leaders' Playbook *for corporations and organizations. 360-degree feedback using the ECI and executive coaching. The website has EI tools, curriculums, and free downloads.*

> 805 683-1066
>
> www.truenorthleadership.com

NOTES

INTRODUCTION

1. D. Goleman, *Working with Emotional Intelligence* (New York: Bantam Books, 1998).

2. R.E. Kelley, *How to Be a Star at Work* (New York: Times Books, 1998).

3. C. Cherniss and D. Goleman, *The Emotionally Intelligent Workplace: How to Select for, Measure, and Improve Emotional Intelligence in Individuals, Groups, and Organizations* (San Francisco: Jossey-Bass, 2001).

4. D. Goleman, *Working with Emotional Intelligence* (New York: Bantam Books, 1998), 5.

5. Ibid., 3.

6. C. Cherniss and D. Goleman, *The Emotionally Intelligent Workplace: How to Select for, Measure, and Improve Emotional Intelligence in Individuals, Groups, and Organizations* (San Francisco: Jossey-Bass, 2001), 21.

7. D. Goleman, *Working with Emotional Intelligence* (New York: Bantam Books, 1998).

8. D.C. McClelland, "Identifying competencies with behavioral-event interviews," *Psychological Science* 9, no. 5 (1999): 331–9.

9. R. Boyatzis and A. McKee, *Resonant Leadership, Renewing Yourself and Connecting with Others Through Mindfulness, Hope and Compassion* (Boston, MA: Harvard Business School Press, 2005).

CHAPTER ONE

1. C. Hymowitz, "Chiefs with Skill of a COO Gain Favor as Celebrity CEOs Fade," *Wall Street Journal* (April 7, 2005).
2. M. Gimein, "You Bought. They Sold," *Fortune* (September 2, 2002).
3. *Santa Barbara News-Press* (November 23, 2005).
4. J. Alexander, "From the President," *Leadership in Action* 22, no. 4 (September/October, 2002).
5. G. Colvin, "Catch a Rising Star," *Fortune* (February 6, 2006), 50.
6. Ibid., 48.
7. Ibid.
8. Ibid., 50.
9. Ibid.
10. Ibid.
11. R.E. Kelley, *How to Be a Star at Work* (New York: Times Books, 1998).
12. C. Cherniss and D. Goleman, *The Emotionally Intelligent Workplace: How to Select for, Measure, and Improve Emotional Intelligence in Individuals, Groups, and Organizations* (San Francisco: Jossey-Bass, 2001).
13. Hay Group, *Inventory of Leadership Styles and Organizational Climate:* Survey Certification material (Boston, MA: 2003).
14. C. Cherniss and D. Goleman, *The Emotionally Intelligent Workplace: How to Select for, Measure, and Improve Emotional Intelligence in Individuals, Groups, and Organizations* (San Francisco: Jossey-Bass, 2001).
15. J. Zenger and J. Folkman, *The Extraordinary Leader* (New York: McGraw-Hill, 2002).
16. D. Goleman, *Working with Emotional Intelligence* (New York: Bantam Books, 1998).

17. D. Goleman, R. Boyatzis, and A. McKee, *Primal Leadership: Realizing the Power of Emotional Intelligence* (Boston, MA: Harvard Business School Press, 2002).

18. *Fortune,* "Most Powerful Women" (October 2003).

19. *Wall Street Journal* (February 10, 2005).

20. *Fortune,* "Most Powerful Women" (October 2003).

21. *Wall Street Journal* (February 10, 2005).

22. L. Kehoe, "Carly Fiorina," *Financial Times* (2002).

23. *Wall Street Journal* (February 10, 2005).

24. A. Fisher, "Most Admired Companies" *Fortune* (March 6, 2006).

25. J.A. Byrne, "The Fast Company Interview: Jeff Immelt," *Fast Company* (July 2005).

26. Ibid.

27. Ibid.

28. *BusinessWeek* online, "The Education of Jeff Immelt" (April 9, 2002).

29. Ibid.

30. J.A. Byrne, "The Fast Company Interview: Jeff Immelt," *Fast Company* (July 2005).

31. Ibid.

32. Ibid.

33. Ibid.

34. A. Ignatius, "In Search of the Real Google," *Time* (February 20, 2006).

35. D.A. Vise and M. Malseed, *The Google Story* (New York: Bantam Dell).

36. CBS News, *60 Minutes* "Defining Google," (Jan 2, 2005).

37. D.A. Vise and M. Malseed, *The Google Story* (New York: Bantam Dell), 20.

38. Ibid., 16.

39. Ibid.

40. Woopidoo.com, Business Quotes (November 2005).

41. Google.com, Corporate Information (November 2005).

42. D. Wharton and G. Klein, *Conquest: Pete Carroll and the Trojans' Climb to the Top of the College Football Mountain* (Chicago: Triumph Books).

43. H. Halladay, "Lemonade from Lemons in the Rose Bowl," Leadernotes.com (January 6, 2006).

44. D. Wharton and G. Klein, *Conquest: Pete Carroll and the Trojans' Climb to the Top of the College Football Mountain* (Chicago: Triumph Books), 42.

45. Ibid.

46. Ibid., 43.

47. Ibid., 47–8.

48. P. Sellers, "eBay's Secret," *Fortune* (2004).

49. Ibid.

50. Ibid.

51. Ibid.

52. *Santa Barbara News-Press* (June 15, 2002).

53. J. Conason, "The Third Term," *Esquire* (December 2005).

54. CBS News, *60 Minutes* (June 20, 2004).

55. D. Polman, "Dean's Victory Marks Historic Shift in Party," *Santa Barbara News-Press* (February 13, 2005).

56. "Howard Dean," *Time* (January 12, 2004).

57. Ibid.

58. Ibid.

59. Ibid.

60. C. Marinucci, "Chevron Redubs Ship Named for Bush Aide," *San Francisco Chronicle* (May 5, 2001).

61. D. Plotz, "Condoleezza Rice: George W. Bush Celebrity Adviser," *Slate* (May 12, 2000).

62. CNN, "Smart, Savvy, Strong-Willed Rice Charts Her Own Course" (2001).

63. Answers.com, Who2 Personalities, GuruNet Corporation (2005).

64. D. Goleman, *Working with Emotional Intelligence* (New York: Bantam Books, 1998).

65. Ibid.
66. Ibid.
67. D.O. Clifton and P. Nelson, *Soar with Your Strengths* (New York: Delacorte Press, 1992).
68. J. Zenger and J. Folkman, *The Extraordinary Leader* (New York: McGraw-Hill, 2002).
69. D.O. Clifton and P. Nelson, *Soar with Your Strengths* (New York: Delacorte Press, 1992).
70. M. Buckingham, *One Thing You Need to Know* (New York: Free Press, 2005).
71. J. Zenger and J. Folkman, *The Extraordinary Leader* (New York: McGraw-Hill, 2002).
72. C. Flora, "Mirror Mirror: Seeing Yourself as Others See You," *Psychology Today* (June 2005).
73. C. Cherniss and D. Goleman, *The Emotionally Intelligent Workplace: How to Select for, Measure, and Improve Emotional Intelligence in Individuals, Groups, and Organizations* (San Francisco: Jossey-Bass, 2001).
74. www.keepem.com (2005).
75. J. Krueger and E. Killhan, "Why Dilbert is Right," *Gallup Management Journal* (March 9, 2006).
76. *Gallup Management Journal*, "Positivity Increases Productivity" (July 8, 2004).
77. Hay Group, *Inventory of Leadership Styles and Organizational Climate:* Survey Certification material (Boston, MA: 2003).
78. J. Zenger and J. Folkman, *The Extraordinary Leader* (New York: McGraw-Hill, 2002).
79. Ibid., 5.
80. Ibid., 187–8.
81. M. Buckingham, *One Thing You Need to Know* (New York: Free Press, 2005).

CHAPTER TWO

1. D. Goleman, *Working with Emotional Intelligence* (New York: Bantam Books, 1998).
2. R.E. Boyatzis, *The Competent Manager: A Model for Effective Performance* (New York: Wiley, 1982).
3. D. Goleman, *Working with Emotional Intelligence* (New York: Bantam Books, 1998).
4. C.K. Holahan and R.R. Sears, *Self-Confidence in High-IQ People and Career Success in the Gifted in Later Maturity* (Stanford: Stanford University Press, 1995).
5. A. Howard and D.W. Bray, *Managerial Lives in Transition* (New York: Guilford Press, 1988).
6. Hay Group, Certification material (Boston, MA: 2001).
7. D. Goleman, *Working with Emotional Intelligence* (New York: Bantam Books, 1998), 51.
8. W. Bennis, *Managing People Is Like Herding Cats* (Provo, UT: Executive Excellence Publishing, 1997).
9. D. Stauffer, "How Good Data Leads to Bad Decisions," *Harvard Management Update* 7, no. 12 (2002).
10. L.E. Anderson and W.K. Balzer, "The Effects of Timing of Leaders' Opinion on Problem-solving Groups," *Group and Organizational Studies* 16 (1991).
11. D. Stauffer, "How Good Data Leads to Bad Decisions," *Harvard Management Update* 7, no. 12 (2002).
12. D. Goleman, *Working with Emotional Intelligence* (New York: Bantam Books, 1998).
13. Ibid.

CHAPTER THREE

1. Goleman, D. *Working with Emotional Intelligence* (New York: Bantam Books, 1998).
2. Goleman, D. *Working with Emotional Intelligence* (New York: Bantam Books, 1998).
3. Hay Group Certification Material (Boston, MA: 2001).

4. J. Kotter, *Leading Change* (Boston, MA: Harvard Business School Press, 1996).

5. P. Senge, *The Fifth Discipline: The Art and Practice of the Learning Organization* (New York: Doubleday, 1990).

6. Ibid., xix, xxi.

7. J.M. Kouzes and B. Posner, *Leadership Challenge* (San Francisco: Jossey-Bass, 1987).

CHAPTER FOUR

1. D. Goleman, *Working with Emotional Intelligence* (New York: Bantam Books, 1998).

2. Ibid.

3. Ibid.

4. C. Cherniss and D. Goleman, *The Emotionally Intelligent Workplace: How to Select for, Measure, and Improve Emotional Intelligence in Individuals, Groups, and Organizations* (San Francisco: Jossey-Bass, 2001).

5. Hay Group, Certification material (Boston, MA: 2001).

6. D. Smith and G. Bell, *The Carolina Way: Leadership Lessons from a Life of Coaching* (New York: Penguin Press, 2004).

7. Ibid.

8. M.A. Dalton and G.P. Hollenbeck, *How to Design an Effective System for Developing Managers and Executives* (NC: Center for Creative Leadership, 1996).

9. D.C. McClelland, "Identifying competencies with behavioral-event interviews," *Psychological Science* 9, no. 5 (1999): 331–9.

10. P. Falcone, *96 Great Interview Questions to Ask Before You Hire* (New York: American Management Association, 1997).

11. D. Grote, "Driving True Development," *Training* (July 2005).

12. Ibid.

13. D.O. Clifton and P. Nelson, *Soar with Your Strengths* (New York: Delacorte Press, 1992).

CHAPTER FIVE

1. D. Goleman, *Working with Emotional Intelligence* (New York: Bantam Books, 1998).
2. Ibid.
3. Ibid.
4. Hay Group Certification Material (Boston, MA: 2001).
5. J.L. Luckner and R.S. Nadler, *Processing the Experience* (Dubuque, IA: Kendall/Hunt Publishing, 1997).
6. H. Friedman and R. DiMatteo, *Interpersonal Issues in Healthcare* (New York: Academic Press, 1982).
7. B.K. Pilling and S. Eroglu, "An Empirical Examination of the Impact of Salesperson Empathy and Professionalism and Mercantile Salability on Retail Buyers' Evaluations," *Journal of Personal Selling and Sales Management* 14, no. 1 (1994): 55–8.
8. C.M. Steele, "A Threat in the Air: How Stereotypes Shape Intellectual Identity and Performance," *American Psychologist* 52 (1997): 613–29.
9. Hay Group Certification Material (Boston, MA: 2001).
10. G. Combs and J. Freedman, *Symbol, Story and Ceremony: Using Metaphor in Individual and Family Therapy* (New York: W.W. Norton and Company, 1990).
11. Ibid.
12. J.L. Luckner and R.S. Nadler, *Processing the Experience* (Dubuque, IA: Kendall/Hunt Publishing, 1997).
13. M.A. Gass, *Book of Metaphors: A Descriptive Presentation of Metaphors for Adventure Activities, Volume II* (Dubuque, IA: Kendall/Hunt Publishing, 1995), XV.
14. G. Combs and J. Freedman, *Symbol, Story and Ceremony: Using Metaphor in Individual and Family Therapy* (New York: W.W. Norton and Company, 1990).
15. M. Buckingham, "Great Managers Understand Their People," *Working Knowledge* (Cambridge, MA: Harvard Business School, April 11, 2005).

16. A. Robbins, Interview with Deepak Chopra in *Powertalk: Strategies for Lifelong Success* (1996).
17. P. Senge, C. Roberts, R. Ross, B. Smith, and A. Kleiner, *The Fifth Discipline Fieldbook: Strategies and Tools for Building a Learning Organization* (New York: Doubleday, 1994).
18. L. Ellinor and G. Gerard, *Dialogue: Rediscovering the Transforming Power of Conversation* (New York: John Wiley and Sons, Inc., 1998).
19. P. Senge, C. Roberts, R. Ross, B. Smith, and A. Kleiner, *The Fifth Discipline Fieldbook: Strategies and Tools for Building a Learning Organization* (New York: Doubleday, 1994).

CHAPTER SIX

1. C. Cherniss and D. Goleman, *The Emotionally Intelligent Workplace: How to Select for, Measure, and Improve Emotional Intelligence in Individuals, Groups, and Organizations* (San Francisco: Jossey-Bass, 2001).
2. J. Zenger and J. Folkman, *The Extraordinary Leader* (New York: McGraw-Hill, 2002).
3. Ibid.
4. Hay Group, *Inventory of Leadership Styles and Organizational Climate:* Survey Certification material (Boston, MA: 2003).
5. T. Rath and D.O. Clifton, *How Full Is Your Bucket?* (New York: Gallup Press, 2004).
6. Department of Labor, 1988.
7. Six Seconds website, 6seconds.org, 2004.
8. Ibid.
9. J.B. Leslie and E. Van Velsor, "A Look at Derailment Today: North America and Europe," Center for Creative Leadership (Greensboro, NC: 1996).
10. Center of Creative Leadership, ccl.org, 2003.

REFERENCES

Alexander, J. "From the President," *Leadership in Action*, Volume 22, Number 4, September/October, 2002.

Anders, G. "How Traits That Helped the Executive Climb the Corporate Ladder Came to Be Fatal Flaws," *Wall Street Journal*, February 10, 2005.

Anderson, L.E. and Balzer, W.K. "The Effects of Timing of Leaders' Opinion on Problem-solving Groups," *Group and Organizational Studies*, 16, 1991.

Answers.com. Who2 Personalities, GuruNet Corporation, 2005.

Auerbach, J. *Personal Executive Coaching: Complete Guide for Mental Health Professionals*. Ventura, CA: Executive Coach College Press, 2001.

Bennis, W. *Managing People Is Like Herding Cats*. Provo, Utah: Executive Excellence Publishing, 1997.

Boyatzis, R.E. *The Competent Manager: A Model for Effective Performance*. New York: Wiley, 1982.

Boyatzis, R.E. and McKee, A. *Resonant Leadership: Renewing Yourself and Connecting with Others Through Mindfulness, Hope and Compassion*. Boston, MA: Harvard Business Press, 2005.

Buckingham, M. *One Thing You Need to Know*. New York: Free Press, 2005.

Buckingham, M. "Great Managers Understand Their People," *Working Knowledge*, Cambridge, MA: Harvard Business School, April 11, 2005.

Byram, Smith, and Paese. *Grow Your Own Leaders*. Upper Saddle River, NJ: Financial Times Prentice Hall, 2002.

Byrne, J.A. "The Fast Company Interview: Jeff Immelt," *Fast Company,* July 2005.

Carkuff, R., *The Art of Helping.* (8th edition). Amherst, MA: Human Resource Development Press, 2000.

CBSNEWS.com. "Clinton Cheated 'Because I Could,'" June 17, 2004.

CBS News, 60 Minutes, *Defining Google*, January 2, 2005.

Center of Creative Leadership, ccl.org, 2003.

Cherniss, C. and Goleman, D. *The Emotionally Intelligent Workplace: How to Select for, Measure, and Improve Emotional Intelligence in Individuals, Groups, and Organizations.* San Francisco: Jossey-Bass, 2001.

Clifton, D.O. and Nelson. *Soar with Your Strengths.* New York: Delacorte Press, 1992.

Colvin, G. "Catch a Rising Star," *Fortune,* February 6, 2006.

Combs, G. and Freedman, J. *Symbol, Story and Ceremony: Using Metaphor in Individual and Family Therapy.* New York: W.W. Norton and Company, 1990.

Conason, J. "The Third Term," *Esquire,* December 2005.

Covey, S. *The 7 Habits of Highly Effective People.* New York: Simon and Schuster, 1989.

CNN. "Smart, Savvy, Strong-Willed Rice Charts Her Own Course," 2001.

Csikszentmihalyi, M. *Good Business: Leadership, Flow and Making of Meaning.* New York: Penguin Group, 2003.

Dalton, M.A. and Hollenbeck, G.P. *How to Design an Effective System for Developing Managers and Executives.* NC: Center for Creative Leadership, 1996.

Department of Labor, "Study on Job Satisfaction and Productivity," 1988.

Dunning, D., Heath, C. and Suls, J.M. "Picture Imperfect," *Scientific American Mind,* Volume 16, Number 4, 2005.

Ellinor, L. and Gerard, G. *Dialogue: Rediscovering the Transforming Power of Conversation.* New York: John Wiley and Sons, Inc., 1998.

Falcone. P. *96 Great Interview Questions to Ask Before You Hire.* New York: American Management Association, 1997.

Flora, C. "Mirror Mirror: Seeing Yourself as Others See You," *Psychology Today*, June 2005.

Fortune, "Most Powerful Women," October 2003.

Friedman, H. and DiMatteo, R. *Interpersonal Issues in Healthcare.* New York: Academic Press, 1982.

Gallup Management Journal, "Positivity Increases Productivity," July 8, 2004.

Gallup Poll. *Approval Rating and Country Satisfaction.* September 12-18th, 2005.

Gallwey, T. *The Inner Game of Work*, New York: Random House, 2000.

Gass, M.A. *Book of Metaphors: A Descriptive Presentation of Metaphors for Adventure Activities. Volume II.* Dubuque, IA: Kendall/Hunt Publishing, 1995.

Gimein, M. "You Bought. They Sold." *Fortune,* September 2, 2002.

Goleman, D. *Emotional Intelligence.* New York: Bantam Books, 1995.

Goleman, D. *Working with Emotional Intelligence.* New York: Bantam Books, 1998.

Goleman, D., Boyatzis, R. and McKee, A. *Primal Leadership: The Hidden Driver of Great Performance.* Harvard Business Review, December 2001.

Goleman, D., Boyatzis, R. and McKee, A. *Primal Leadership: Realizing the Power of Emotional Intelligence.* Boston, MA: Harvard Business School Press, 2002.

Google.com, Corporate Information, November, 2005.

Grote, D. "Driving True Development," *Training,* July 2005.

Hay Group. Certification Material. Boston, MA: 2001.

Hay Group. *Inventory of Leadership Styles and Organizational Climate.* Survey Certification material. Boston, MA: 2003.

Halladay, H. "Lemonade from Lemons in the Rose Bowl," Leadernotes.com, January 6, 2006.

Hersey, P., Blanchard, K.H., and Johnson, D.E. *Managing Organizational Behavior.* Upper Saddle River, NJ: Prentice Hall, 1996.

Holahan, C.K. and Sears, R.R. "Self-Confidence in High-IQ People and Career Success in the Gifted in Later Maturity," Stanford: Stanford University Press, 1995.

Howard, A. and Bray, D.W. *Managerial Lives in Transition.* New York: Guilford Press, 1988.

Hymowitz, C. "Chiefs with Skill of a COO Gain Favor as Celebrity CEOs Fade," *Wall Street Journal*, April 7, 2005.

Ignatius, A. "In Search of the Real Google," *Time,* February 20, 2006.

Kaplan, R.E. *Beyond Ambition: How Driven Managers Can Lead Better and Live Better.* San Francisco: Jossey-Bass, 1991.

Kaye, B. and Jordan-Evans, S. *Retention and Engagement Drivers Report.* Career Systems International, 2004.

Kaye, B. and Jordan-Evans, S. *Love It Don't Leave It.* San Francisco: Berrett-Koehler, 2003.

Kehoe, L. "Carly Fiorina," *Financial Times,* 2002.

Kellerman, B. *Bad Leadership: What It Is, How It Happens, Why It Matters.* Boston, MA: Harvard Business School Press, 2004.

Kelley, R.E. *How to Be a Star at Work.* New York: Times Books, 1998.

Kotter, J. *Leading Change.* Boston, MA: Harvard Business School Press, 1996.

Kouzes, J.M. and Posner, B. *Leadership Challenge.* San Francisco: Jossey-Bass, 1987.

Krueger, J. and Killhan, E. "Why Dilbert is Right," *Gallup Management Journal*, March 9, 2006.

Leslie, J.B. and Van Velsor, E. "A Look at Derailment Today: North America and Europe," Center for Creative Leadership, Greensboro, NC: 1996.

Liedtke, M. "Oracle CEO to Settle Suit by Donating $100 Million," *Santa Barbara News-Press*, November 23, 2005.

Lipman-Blumen, J. *The Allure of Toxic Leaders.* New York: Oxford University Press, 2005.

Luckner, J.L. and Nadler, R.S. *Processing the Experience.* Dubuque, Iowa: Kendall/Hunt Publishing, 1997.

Marinucci, C. "Chevron Redubs Ship Named for Bush Aide," *San Francisco Chronicle,* May 5, 2001.

Maslow, A. *Toward a Psychology of Being.* Princeton, NJ: Van Nostrand, 1968.

McCaffrey, S. "Clintons Earn Big Bucks, But Have Big Bills," *Santa Barbara News-Press*, June 15, 2002.

McClelland, D.C. "Identifying competencies with behavioral-event interviews," *Psychological Science*, Volume 9, Number 5, 331–39, 1999.

Nadler, G. and Chandon, W.J. *Smart Questions.* San Francisco: Jossey-Bass, 2004.

Nadler, R.S. "Teamwork Is an Unnatural Act," *PIHRA Scope*, Vol. XLXI, No.6, June 1998.

Peterson, D. and Hicks, M.D. *Development First.* Minneapolis, MN: Personnel Decisions International, 1995.

Pike, R.E. *Creative Training Techniques*, Amherst, MA: HRD Press, 2003.

Pilling, B.K. and Eroglu, S. "An Empirical Examination of the Impact of Salesperson Empathy and Professionalism and Mercantile Salability on Retail Buyers' Evaluations," *Journal of Personal Selling and Sales Management*, 14 (1), 55-8, 1994.

Plotz, D. "Condoleezza Rice: George W. Bush Celebrity Adviser," *Slate*, May 12, 2000.

Polman, D. "Dean's Victory Marks Historic Shift in Party," *Santa Barbara News-Press*, February 13, 2005.

Rath, T. and Clifton, D.O. *How Full Is Your Bucket?* New York: Gallup Press, 2004.

Robbins, A. Interview with Deepak Chopra in *Powertalk: Strategies for Lifelong Success*, 1996.

Salovey, P. and Mayer, J. *Emotional Intelligence, Imagination, Cognition and Personality.* 9(3), 185-211, 1990.

Santa Barbara News-Press, June 15, 2002.

Scholtes, P. *The Team Handbook.* Madison, WI: Joiner Associates, Inc., 1988.

Seligman, M.E.P. *Authentic Happiness.* New York: Free Press, 2002.

Sellers, P. "eBay's Secret," *Fortune*, October 18, 2004.

Senge, P. *The Fifth Discipline: The Art and Practice of the Learning Organization.* New York: Doubleday, 1990.

Senge, P., Roberts C., Ross R., Smith B., and Kleiner, A. *The Fifth Discipline Fieldbook: Strategies and Tools for Building a Learning Organization.* New York: Doubleday, 1994.

Six Seconds website, 2004. *www.6seconds.org*

Smith, D. and Bell, G. *The Carolina Way: Leadership Lessons from a Life of Coaching*, New York: Penguin Press, 2004.

Spencer, L.M. and Spencer, S.M. *Competence at Work: Models for Superior Performance.* New York: Wiley, 1993.

Stauffer, D. "How Good Data Leads to Bad Decisions," *Harvard Management Update*, Volume 7, Number 12, 2002.

Steele, C.M. "A Threat in the Air: How Stereotypes Shape Intellectual Identity and Performance," *American Psychologist*, Vol. 52, 613–29, 1997.

Sullivan, D. *Pure Genius.* Niles, IL: Nightengale-Conant, 2002.

Time, "Howard Dean," January 12, 2004.

Vise, D.A. and Malseed, M. *The Google Story*, New York: Bantam Dell.

Wall Street Journal, February 10, 2005.

Wharton, D. and Klein, G. *Conquest: Pete Carroll and the Trojans' Climb to the Top of the College Football Mountain.* Chicago: Triumph Books.

Woopidoo.com, Business Quotes, November 2005.

Zenger, J. and Folkman, J. *The Extraordinary Leader.* New York: McGraw-Hill, 2002.

Zenger, J., Sandholtz, K., and Folkman, J. *Leadership Under the Microscope.* Oren, UT: Extraordinary Performance Group, Inc., 2004.

ABOUT THE AUTHOR

Dr. Relly Nadler, educated as a clinical psychologist, has become a world-class executive coach and team trainer. He is the president and CEO of True North Leadership, Inc., an Executive and Organizational Development firm. Dr. Nadler brings his expertise in Emotional Intelligence to all his keynotes, consulting, coaching, and training. He also founded the Leader's Emotional Intelligence Development (LEID) Institute, an executive boot camp for high achievers.

A licensed psychologist and Master Executive Coach, Dr. Nadler has been working for more than 30 years with top executives and their teams to become "Star Performers." He is the author of two best-selling leadership and team performance books, and is a sought-after speaker and consultant on leadership, Emotional Intelligence, teambuilding, executive coaching, and experiential learning. His latest books are *Leaders' Playbook*, *Leaders' Playbook Field Guide,* and *Leadership Keys and Field Guide*. They are the first in a series of EI curriculums and toolkits for leaders and their direct reports to move into the top 10% of performance.

Dr. Nadler has coached CEOs, presidents, and their staffs, developed and delivered innovative leadership programs for such organizations as Anheuser-Busch, BMW, EDS, MCI, and Danone Water Products, and created and facilitated team trainings for DreamWorks Animation, Comerica Bank, America Honda, and General Motors Defense. He is recognized around the world for his expertise in linking experiential learning and Emotional Intelligence to business objectives.

Dr. Nadler has worked for and consulted to Outward Bound Schools in North Carolina, Canada, Colorado, and Japan. He is the co-author of *Processing the Experience*, a "classic" in the field of Experiential Education. His concept of "Edgework" explains the power and steps of pushing past your comfort zone to new achievements, a core aspect of Outward Bound programs and being a successful leader and person.

Dr. Nadler received his B.A. from the University of Hartford and his M.A. in Confluent Education at the University of California, Santa Barbara. He received his Psy.D. in Counseling Psychology from the University of Northern Colorado. Dr. Nadler is on the faculty of The College of Executive Coaching, a post-graduate institute, training professionals in personal and executive coaching, and is certified in the use of Daniel Goleman's and the Hay Group's Emotional Competence Inventory.

Currently, Dr. Nadler's work is identifying, developing, and teaching tools for organizations, teams, and individuals to increase Emotional Intelligence and become "Star Performers."

INDEX

A

Abdul-Jabbar, Kareem, 44–45
Accountability, 112, 131, 135–137, 198
Achievement orientation
  assessment, 56
  behavioral question list for, 176
  Carly Fiorina and, 22
  Condoleeza Rice and, 42–43
  Howard Dean and, 39, 40–41
  interaction with bosses and, 61
  Jeffrey Immelt and, 25
  John Davies and, 224
  Meg Whitman and, 35
  Pete Carroll and, 32–33
  Rudy Giuliani and, 18–19
  Sergey Brin and, 28–29
  strength utilization and, 66
Acknowledgement, 113, 220–221,
  236, 251. see also Recognition
Action plans
  communication skills and, 269–270
  development of others
    and, 210–211
  review of, 273
  self-confidence, 96–98
  Star Performer, 67–68
  teamwork and collaboration,
    150–151
Actions, 260, 261
Active listening. see Listening skills
Adaptability
  assessment, 56, 63
  behavioral question list for, 175
  Bill Clinton and, 38
  Condoleeza Rice and, 42–43
  Howard Dean and, 40–41
  Jeffrey Immelt and, 24, 25
  Meg Whitman and, 35

Adaptability *(cont.)*
  Pete Carroll and, 32–33
  Rudy Giuliani and, 19
Adelphia, 10, 45
Adversity, 189–190
Advocacy, 263–265
AIDS, 37
Albright, Madeleine, 42
Amygdala, 45–47
Andrea's story, 78–79
Appreciation, staff, 105
Assessment, self. see Action plans;
  Self-assessment
Assessment, team, 140–141
Assumption ladder, 257–263, 260, 261
Aston Martin, 71
AT&T, 21
Attending behaviors, 235–236
Attention, 47, 234
Auditory style of learning, 249
Authentic Happiness, 48
Awareness, social. see Social
  awareness

B

Baby Boomers, 13–14
Ballmer, Steven, 24
Bank account, emotional, 234
Baseball, 99
Basketball, 44–45, 156–157
BAT teams, 104
Behavior, 253, 254–255
Behavioral question list, 173–183
*Blink: The Power of Thinking
  Without Thinking*, 95
BMW, 71, 72

Body language. *see* Non-verbal
      communication
Bond building
      assessment, 57
      behavioral question list for, 174–175
      Bill Clinton and, 38
      Condoleeza Rice and, 42–43
      development of others and, 161
      Howard Dean and, 39
      interaction with bosses and, 61
      Pete Carroll and, 32–33
      Sergey Brin and, 28–29
      strength utilization and, 66
Bonus plan review, 187
Boomers, Baby, 13–14
Bosses, 58–59, 61–62
Bottom line, 60
Boyatzis, Richard, 4, 50
Brain anatomy, 45–47
Briefings, 170–171
Brin, Sergey, 26–29
Brookings Institution, 36
Buckingham, Marcus, 49, 154, 250
Bush, George H. W., 41
Bush, George W., 41, 218–219
Business Acquisition teams, 104
Butterfield, Gregg, 185

C

Carter, Jimmy, 37
CCL. *see* Center for Creative
      Leadership (CCL)
Center for Creative Leadership
      (CCL), 189
Change
      assessment, 57
      behavioral question list for, 181
      Bill Clinton and, 36, 38
      Carly Fiorina and, 21
      Howard Dean and, 39, 40–41
      Jeffrey Immelt and, 26
      Meg Whitman and, 34–35
      Pete Carroll and, 32–33
      Rudy Giuliani and, 19

Change *(cont.)*
      Sergey Brin and, 28–29
      strength utilization and, 66
      training and, 129
Chaos management, 128
Cherniss, Cary, 14
Chrysler, 94–95
Clarity, 250–252, 251
Clifton, Donald O., 48
Climate, corporate, 60
Clinton, Bill, 36–38
Clinton, Hillary, 20
Coaching, 5, 114–125, 189,
      204–205, 206–207
Collaboration. *see also* Teamwork
      assessment, 57
      clarity and, 251
      competency, 99
      Henrik Fisker and, 73
      as important EI trait, 14, 15–16
      John Davies and, 224
      mastery of, 107–113
      playbook for, 274–276
      Star Performers and, 100–101
      strategies for, 106–107
Columns, 265–266
Commonalities, 235
Communication skills
      assessment, 57
      assumption ladder and, 257–263
      basic skills required, 214
      behavioral question list
            for, 178–179
      Bill Clinton and, 38
      Carly Fiorina and, 21–22
      clarity as, 250–252, 251
      competency, 213–214
      dialogue roles and, 268–269
      dialogue vs. discussion, 266–268
      empathy and, 226–232. *see also*
            Empathy
      feedback and, 252–257
      Howard Dean and, 40–41
      as important EI trait, 14

Communication skills *(cont.)*
  inquiry and advocacy, balance
    of, 263–265
  intention/interpretation gap,
    240–244, 242, 243–244
  John Davies and, 215–225
  language and, 244–250
  listening skills. *see* Listening
    skills
  Paulette Jones and, 103
  Pete Carroll and, 32–33
  playbook for, 277–278
  Rudy Giuliani and, 19
  Sergey Brin and, 29
  strategies for, 225–226
  strength utilization and, 65
  teamwork and, 109–110
  white space issues and,
    237–240, 239
Community service, development
  of others and, 189
Companions, competency, 64–65
Compassion, 4, 217
Competency companions, 64–65
Competition, 266
Comprehension, 46
Concern, circle of, 193–194
Conclusions, 260, 261
Confidence. *see* Self-confidence
Conflict management
  assessment, 57
  behavioral question list for, 182
  Condoleeza Rice and, 43
  interaction with bosses and, 61
  Jeffrey Immelt and, 26
  John Davies and, 224
  strength utilization and, 65
  teamwork and, 109–110
Conscientiousness
  assessment, 56
  behavioral question list
    for, 182–183
  Condoleeza Rice and, 42–43
  Meg Whitman and, 35

Conscientiousness *(cont.)*
  Rudy Giuliani and, 19
  Sergey Brin and, 28–29
Consensus exercise, 133–134
Consequences, 112
Consultation, Emotional
    Intelligence and, 5
Cooperation, teamwork and, 101
Corporate fraud, 9–10
Course corrections, 187
Covey, Stephen, 105, 158, 165, 187,
    192, 196–197, 221, 232, 234
*Creative Training Techniques
    Handbook,* 130
Csikszentmihalyi, Mihaly, 49
Cultural considerations,
    assessment, 63
Customer service, 251. *see also*
    Service orientation
Cycle time, 127–128

D

Data, assimilation of, 260, 261
Davies, John, 215–225, 271
Davies Public Relations, 215
Daydreaming, 234
Dean, Howard, 38–41
Debate, 267
Decision-making, 46, 94–95, 95–96
Defensiveness, 63, 266
Degree of Difference (D.O.D.),
    50–54
Delegation, development of others
    and, 196–199
Dell, 33
Dementors, 189
Derailers. *see* Obstacles, personal
Development of others
  behavioral question list
    for, 179–180
  competency, 153
  delegation and, 196–199
  examples of, 154–155
  F.I.R.S.T., 208–210

Development of others *(cont.)*
  hiring emotionally intelligent
    employees, 172–183
  as important EI trait, 14–15
  influence, circle of, 192–196
  Input+1, 191–192
  Interview Rating Scale, 183–186,
    184–185
  Mark French and, 156–171
  motivation skills matrix,
    203–207, 203
  one-on-one meetings and, 186–190
  overview of, 171–172
  performance and, 196, 199–201
  playbook for, 276–277
  scaling questions and, 202–203
  strength utilization and, 190–191
Dialogue, 266–268, 267, 268–269
Difference, degree of, 50–54
Differences, appreciation of, 111–112
Directive style of leadership,
    204, 206
DISC, 236
Discretionary effort, 61
Discussion, 266–268, 267
Disequilibrium, 127
Disney, 34
Diversity, 111–112, 129
D.O.D., 50–54
DreamWorks Animation, 12

E

eBay, 33–35
Ebbers, Bernard, 10
ECI. *see* Emotional Competence
    Inventory (ECI)
Education, continuing, 113
Efficacy, 70. *see also* Self-confidence
Effort, discretionary, 61
Eisner, Michael, 9
Ellison, Larry, 10
Emotional bank account, 234
Emotional Competence Inventory
    (ECI), 3

Emotional Intelligence, 2
Emotional Intelligence
  benefits of improving, 272
  consequences for not raising,
    272–273
  defined, 2–3
  dynamic nature of, 12
  four areas of, 14–16
  generational considerations
    and, 13–14
  sentence completions, 145–146
Emotional Quotient Inventory
    (EQi), 50
Empathy. *see also* Communication
    skills
  assessment, 57
  behavioral question list for, 174
  Bill Clinton and, 36, 38
  Carly Fiorina and, 22
  developing skills for, 226–232
  Howard Dean and, 41
  as important EI trait, 15–16
  Jeffrey Immelt and, 26
  John Davies and, 224
  leaders and, 4
  Meg Whitman and, 35
  Pete Carroll and, 32–33
  playbook for, 277–278
  Rudy Giuliani and, 19
  strength utilization and, 66
Employees, 59–60
Empowering style of leadership, 205
Encouragement, teamwork and, 101
Enron, 10, 45
EQi, 50
Equality, 127
Evaluation. *see also* Feedback
  bonus plan review and, 187
  of others, 73, 77–81
  performance reviews and, 168–169
  post-game, 170–171
  process review, 105
  self. *see* Self-assessment
Executive functioning, 46, 47

Expectations, 85–86, 88, 101, 109, 138–139
Experiential teambuilding exercises, 125–134
Expression of feelings, 228–230
The Extraordinary Leader, 47

F

Facilitation, meeting, 120–125
Fast Company, 24
Fatal flaws. *see* Obstacles, personal
Feedback, 51, 166–167, 209, 252–257
The Fifth Discipline, 258, 259, 263, 265
Financial skills, Carly Fiorina and, 21
Financial Times, 21
Fiorina, Carly, 9, 20–23
F.I.R.S.T., 208–210
Fisker, Henrik, 69, 71–76, 271
Fisker Coachbuild, LLC, 71
Flexibility, Henrik Fisker and, 75
Florist Transworld Delivery. *see* FTD
Focus, circle of, 193–194
Folkman, Joseph, 47, 51, 64–65
Football, 30–33
Forbes Magazine, 27, 41
Ford, 71
Fortune, 10–11, 20–21, 33
Franklin, Benjamin, 54
Frank's story, 114–116
Fraud, corporate, 9–10
French, Mark, 156–171, 192, 271
FTD, 34
Fun, importance of, 129

G

Gatorade, 94
GE. *see* General Electric
General Electric, 10–11, 23
General Motors, 185
Generalizations, 83, 90
Generation X, 13–14

Generational considerations, 13–14
Giuliani, Rudy, 17–20
Gladwell, Malcolm, 95
Global Crossings, 10
Global Initiative, 36–37
GM. *see* General Motors
Goal setting, 164, 189, 251
Goleman, Daniel, 2, 14, 45, 50
Good Business, 49
Google, Inc., 26–27
Gossip, 237–240
Gratification, delayed, 45–46
Gratitude, 102–103
Great leadership, 4. *see also* Star Performers
Greenberg, Hank, 9
Greetings, 103
Growth, 189, 222
Guidelines, teamwork and, 109

H

Hardships. *see* Adversity
Hasbro, 34
Hay Group, 50, 60
Hess, Stephen, 36
Hewlett-Packard, 20
Hierarchies, 266
Hiring emotionally intelligent employees, 172, 173–183, 183–186
Holyfield, Evander, 46
How to Be a Star at Work, 14, 100
Humor, 105

I

Iacocca, Lee, 94–95
Ice breakers, 131
Illness, Rudy Giuliani and, 20
Immelt, Jeffrey, 10, 23–26
Impact, 198–199, 253–254, 255
Implementation, 208
Impulse control, 19, 40, 46–47, 61, 63
Inferred intention. *see* Intention

Influence
    assessment, 57
    behavioral question list for, 177
    Bill Clinton and, 36, 38
    Carly Fiorina and, 21–22
    circle of, 193–194
    Condoleeza Rice and, 43
    development of others and,
        192–196
    Howard Dean and, 39, 40–41
    Jeffrey Immelt and, 26
    John Davies and, 224
    Meg Whitman and, 35
    people of, 93
    Pete Carroll and, 32–33
Ingeni Design Company, 71
Initiative
    assessment, 56
    behavioral question list for, 173
    Bill Clinton and, 38
    Carly Fiorina and, 22
    Condoleeza Rice and, 42–43
    degree of difference (D.O.D.)
        and, 50–54
    Henrik Fisker and, 74
    Howard Dean and, 39, 40–41
    as important EI trait, 14
    interaction with bosses and, 62
    Jeffrey Immelt and, 25–26
    Meg Whitman and, 35
    Pete Carroll and, 32–33
    Rudy Giuliani and, 18–19
    Sergey Brin and, 28–29
    strength utilization and, 66
Input, team, 101
Input+1, 191–192
Inquiry, 263–265
Instinct. see Intuition
Integration, 221
Integrators, 268
Integrity, assessment, 63
Intelligence, 2–3, 11–12, 237
Intention, 240–244, 242, 243–244
Interference, 129, 196

Interpretation, 240–244, 242, 243–244
Interrupting, 214
Interview Rating Scale, 183–186,
        184–185
Interviewing. see Hiring emotionally
        intelligent employees
Intuition, 73–74, 95–96
IQ, 2–3, 11–12

J

Jaguar, 71
Jones, Paulette, 99, 101–106, 271

K

Kehoe, Louise, 21
Kelley, Robert, 14, 100
Kerry, John, 218–219
Keyboards, 101
Kinesthetic imprint, 128
Kinesthetic style of learning, 249
Kolbe, 236
Korbel, Josef, 42
Kozlowski, Dennis, 10, 44

L

Land Rover, 71
Language, 128, 244–250
Leader, defined, 1
Leadership. see also Coaching;
        Mentoring
    100 check-in questions, 142–148
    assessment, 57, 63, 145
    behavioral question list for,
        181–182
    Bill Clinton and, 38
    bosses, debilitating and, 58–59
    Carly Fiorina and, 21–23
    Condoleeza Rice and, 42–43
    degree of difference (D.O.D.),
        50–54
    development of others and,
        15–16. see also Development
        of others

Leadership *(cont.)*
  Emotional Intelligence and, 5
  excellence in, 47–50
  Great, 4
  Howard Dean and, 39–41, 40–41
  importance of, 60–61
  Jeffrey Immelt and, 25–26
  Meg Whitman and, 35–36
  perfectionism and, 87
  personal, 111
  Pete Carroll and, 32–33
  profiles of. *see* Profiles, Star
  Rudy Giuliani and, 18–19
  scorecard for, 279–281, 279, 281
  Sergey Brin and, 27–29
  state of, 9–11
  strength utilization and, 66
  styles of, 204–205, 207
Learning. *see also* Training
  meta, 128
  neurological function in, 46
  ongoing, 113
  styles of, 155, 207, 248–250
  supportive, 165–166
  transfer of, 209–210
Left-hand column, 265–266
Lincoln, 71
Listening skills, 214, 226, 228–232,
  232–237, 260, 261
Logs, success, 91–92
Lucent Technologies, 21
Luckner, John, 191–192

M

Management. *see* Leadership;
  Relationship management;
  Self-management
Management by Objectives
  (MBOs), 187
Marshmallow study, 46–47
Matching, 236
Mayer, John, 2
Mazda, 71
MBOs. *see* Management by
  Objectives (MBOs)

McKee, Annie, 4
Meetings
  checklists for, 118–119, 124–125
  facilitation of, 120–125
  mastery of, 114–119
  one-on-one, 164–165, 186–190
  types of, 103–105
Memory, 47
Mental models, 258–259
Mentoring, 113, 189
Mercury, 71
Meta learning, 128
Metaphor, 133, 245–246
Metrics, clarity and, 251
Microsoft, 24, 33
Mirroring, 236
Mission, assessment, 146–147
Models, mental, 258–259
Moskovits, Martin, 13
Motivation, 155, 203–207, 203
Movers, 268
Myers-Briggs Typing Indicator, 236

N

Nails, 130, 131–132
National Basketball Association
  (NBA), 44–45
National Security Advisor, 41
NBA, 44–45
Neff, Tom, 10
Negativity, 83
Nelson, Paula, 48
Networking, 14, 73
Neurological functioning, 45–47
Non-verbal communication, 227,
  229–230, 242
Norton, Byron, 230

O

Observations, selection of, 260, 261
Obstacles, personal
  assessment, 62–64
  Bill Clinton and, 38

Obstacles, personal *(cont.)*
   Carly Fiorina and, 22
   Condoleeza Rice and, 43
   course corrections and, 187
   gratification, delayed, and, 45–46
   Henrik Fisker and, 76
   Howard Dean and, 41
   identification of, 6, 74–75
   John Davies and, 224
   leadership development and, 48
   Mark French and, 171
   one-on-one meetings and, 189
   Paulette Jones and, 106
   Rudy Giuliani and, 19
   self-control and, 45–46
   self-management and, 49–50
Offensiveness, 220–221
One Hand Rule, 116–119
The One Thing You Need to Know, 49, 154, 250
Open-mindedness, 214
Opinions, 266
Opposers, 268
Oracle, 10
Organizational awareness
   assessment, 57
   behavioral question list for, 179
   Bill Clinton and, 38
   Condoleeza Rice and, 43
   Jeffrey Immelt and, 26
   Meg Whitman and, 35
   Rudy Giuliani and, 19
Organizational climate, 129

P

Page, Larry, 26–27
Paraphrasing, 231–232
Passion, 144, 218–219
PayPal, 34
People, reading, 219–220
People of personal influence, 93
Perceptioneering, 219
Perfectionism, 63, 84–88, 85

Performance
   development of others and, 196, 199–201
   exercises, 131, 135–137
   issues with, 52
   metrics, 187
   perfectionism and, 87
   reviews, 168–169
Pike, Bob, 130
Pitt, Harvey, 44
Planning, 46
Playbook, defined, 1
Politics
   Bill Clinton and, 36–38
   Bush/Kerry campaign, 218–219
   Condoleeza Rice and, 41–43
   George H. W. Bush and, 41
   George W. Bush and, 41, 218–219
   Hillary Clinton and, 20
   Howard Dean and, 38–41
   office, 266
   Rudy Giuliani and, 17–20
Positive Psychology, 48
Potential, development of others and, 196
Practice, importance of, 160–161
Praise. *see* Acknowledgement
Prefrontal lobes of the brain, 46–47
Preparation, 221
Pressure. *see* Stress
Priorities, focus on, 208
Problem solving, 164–165, 200–201, 257
Proctor and Gamble, 24, 34
Productivity, 48, 59
Profiles, Star
   Bill Clinton, 36–38
   Carly Fiorina, 20–23
   Condoleeza Rice, 41–43
   Howard Dean, 38–41
   introduction to, 16–17
   Jeffrey Immelt, 23–26
   Meg Whitman, 33–36
   Paulette Jones, 101–106

Profiles, Star *(cont.)*
  Pete Carroll, 30–33
  Rudy Giuliani, 17–20
  Sergey Brin, 26–29
Projective technique, 127
Psychology, Positive, 48
Public Accounting Oversight
  Board, 44
Pure Genius, 85–86

Q

Quaker Oats, 94
Quality, 222–223
Questioning, self, 82–83

R

Reactive Trap, 260
Reasoning, 46
Recognition, 189. *see also*
  Acknowledgement
Recruiting, 161–163
Red flags, 103–104
Reflection, 209
Reinforcement, 129
Relationship management. *see also*
  Development of others
  assessment, 57
  building effective relationships
    and, 163–164
  experiential teambuilding
    exercises, 125–134
  as important EI trait, 14–16
  leadership and, 47, 51–52
  one-on-one meetings and, 164–165
Relationship-building
  assessment, 144
Renewal habits, sentence
  completions, 147–148
Resolution, 254, 256
Resonant Leadership, 4
Resources, delegation and, 198

Responsibility
  Henrik Fisker and, 75
  job responsibilities, 187
  leadership and, 47
  Mark French and, 167–168
Revenue gap, 104
Review. *see* Evaluation
Rice, Condoleeza, 41–43
Risk, 20, 63, 128, 143–144
Roles, 122–124, 268–269
Rumors, 237–240

S

Salovey, Peter, 2
Scaling questions, 202–203
Scorecard, leadership, 279–281,
  279, 281
Secretary of State, 41
Selection of observations, 260, 261
Selective listening, 234
Self-care, 73
Self-assessment
  Andrea's story, 78–79
  behavioral question list
    for, 180–181
  Bill Clinton and, 37–38
  development of others and, 164
  importance of, 6–8, 54
  John Davies and, 224
  perfectionism and, 84–88
  Pete Carroll and, 32–33
  question redirection and, 79–81
  reflections on thinking
    and, 82–83
  Rudy Giuliani and, 18, 19
  Star Profile Assessment, 54–58
Self-awareness
  assessment, 56
  behavioral question list for, 180
  Bill Clinton and, 37–38
  as important EI trait, 14–16
  Rudy Giuliani and, 18, 19
  sentence completions, 147

Self-confidence
  assessment of, 56
  behavioral question list for, 175
  Carly Fiorina and, 22
  competency, 69
  decisiveness and, 94–95
  evaluation and, 77–81
  Henrik Fisker and, 71–76
  Howard Dean and, 39, 40–41
  as important EI trait, 15–16
  interaction with bosses and, 61
  Jeffrey Immelt and, 24–25
  John Davies and, 224
  Meg Whitman and, 35
  people of influence and, 93
  perfectionism and, 84–88
  Pete Carroll and, 32–33
  playbook for, 274
  reflections on thinking and, 82–83
  Sergey Brin and, 28–29
  Star Performers and, 70
  strength utilization and, 66
  success log and, 91–92
  success rules and, 89–91
  thin-slicing and, 95–96
  visualization and, 93–94
Self-control
  assessment, 56
  behavioral question list
    for, 173–174
  Bill Clinton and, 37–38
  Condoleeza Rice and, 43
  Howard Dean and, 41
  impulses and. *see* Impulse control
  lack of, 45–46
Self-defeating behaviors. *see*
  Obstacles, personal
Self-efficacy, 70. *see also*
  Self-confidence
Self-management, 14–16, 52, 56,
  147–148
Self-promotion, assessment, 63
Seligman, Martin, 48
Semel, Terry, 34

Senge, Peter, 258, 259, 263, 265
Sensory Preference VAK style, 236
Sensory preferences, 248–250
September 11, 2001, 17, 23
Service orientation
  assessment, 57
  behavioral question list for, 176
  Bill Clinton and, 36, 38
  Carly Fiorina and, 22
  Condoleeza Rice and, 43
  Howard Dean and, 39, 40–41
  Jeffrey Immelt and, 26
  Meg Whitman and, 34–35
  Sergey Brin and, 28–29
  strength utilization and, 66
The 7 Habits of Highly Effective
  People, 105, 158, 165, 192,
  221, 234
Signature strengths, 48–49
Similarities, 235
Smithburg, William, 94
Snapple, 94
Snapshot Management, 116–119
Soar with Strengths, 48
Social awareness, 14–16, 57
Socratic approach to problem
  solving, 164–165
Spirit, teamwork and, 101
Sports, 216. *see also* Baseball;
  Basketball; Football
SSBIR, 252–257
Stability, 22
Staff, appreciation, 105
Stage, setting of, 253, 254
Star Performers
  action plan for, 67–68, 96–98,
    150–151, 210–211, 269–270
  defined, 3–4
  derailment and, 44–45
  EQ and, 2–3
  Henrik Fisker, 71–76
  John Davies and, 215–225
  Mark French, 156–171
  New Rules for Success, 13

Star Performers *(cont.)*
   Paulette Jones, 101–106
   profiles of. *see* Profiles, Star
Stengel, Casey, 99
Story-making, 128, 226, 246–248
Strengths
   awareness of, 49–50
   clarity and, 251
   defined, 47
   development of others and, 155,
      190–192
   focusing on, 167
   identification, 48–49, 74–75
   one-on-one meetings and, 189
   strategic use of, 64–66, 65, 66
Stress, 59, 86, 129, 192
Stride Rite, 34
Success, 2, 89–91, 91–92, 223–224.
   see also Star Performers
Sullivan, Dan, 49, 85
Support, 209
Supporters, 268
Systems thinking, 111

T

Taboo topics, 266
Teamwork. *see also* Bond building;
   Collaboration
   100 leadership check-in
      questions, 142–148
   assessment, 57
   behavioral question list for,
      177–178
   Bill Clinton and, 36, 38
   clarity and, 251
   competency, 99
   experiential teambuilding
      exercises, 125–134, 135–137,
      138–139, 140–141
   as important EI trait, 14, 15–16
   ingredients survey, 148–150
   interaction with bosses and, 61
   John Davies and, 224

Teamwork *(cont.)*
   leadership and, 60
   mastery of, 107–113
   Paulette Jones and, 101–106
   playbook for, 274–276
   Sergey Brin and, 28–29
   Star Performers and, 100–101
   strategies for, 106–107
   strength utilization and, 65
Testing, 46–47
Thinking, systems, 111
Thin-slicing, 95–96
Tichy, Noel, 11
Time, private, 73
Time constraints, 266
Training. *see also* Learning
   *Creative Training Techniques
      Handbook,* 130
   development of others and, 190
   Emotional Intelligence and, 5
   experiential teambuilding
      exercises, 125–134
   failure of, 129
   importance of, 222
Triggers, 49–50, 155
Trojans, USC, 30–33
Trust, 108–109, 144–145. *see also*
   Trustworthiness
Trustworthiness
   assessment, 56
   behavioral question list for, 178
   Bill Clinton and, 38
   Henrik Fisker and, 73–74
   Jeffrey Immelt and, 24, 26
   John Davies and, 224
   Meg Whitman and, 35
   people, reading and, 219–220
   Pete Carroll and, 32–33
   Rudy Giuliani and, 19
   Sergey Brin and, 28–29
   strength utilization and, 65
Tyco International, 10, 44
Tyson, Mike, 46

U

Understanding
    Bill Clinton and, 38
    Carly Fiorina and, 23
    as communication skill, 214, 217
    Howard Dean and, 41
    Pete Carroll and, 32–33
    Rudy Giuliani and, 18
Uniqueness, 219
University of California women's
    basketball team, 156–157
University of Southern California
    Trojans, 30–33
USC Trojans, 30–33

V

Values, assessment, 146–147
Vision, 21, 108, 144, 189
Visual style of learning, 248
Visualization, 93–94
Volvo, 71

W

Wall Street Journal, 21
Weaknesses. *see* Obstacles,
    personal
Webster, William, 44
White space issues, 237–240, 239
Whitman, Meg, 33–36
Win-Win Agreement, 187, 196–197
Workers. *see* Employees
*Working with Emotional
    Intelligence,* 3
WorldCom, 10, 45

X

X Generation, 13–14

Y

Yahoo!, 34

Z

Zenger, John H., 47, 51, 64–65

HOW TO ENGAGE THE AUTHOR

TO BRING EMOTIONAL INTELLIGENCE COMPETENCIES INTO YOUR ORGANIZATION

Contact:

True North Leadership, Inc.

1170 Camino Meleno

Santa Barbara, CA 93111

805 683-1066   FAX 805 692-6738

Rnadler@truenorthleadership.com

RELLY NADLER IS AVAILABLE FOR CONSULTING, COACHING AND TRAINING

- Keynotes and Presentations
- Multi day Leadership Development training for your teams, based on Emotional Intelligence
- Executive coaching – senior leaders and emerging leaders 360 degree feedback
- Teambuilding training for Executive teams and departments
- "Relly tele" – telecourses to help in utilizing the tools
- Organizational consulting
- Organizational assessments
- Succession planning

Visit our website for more information on these services, for free EI tools and to sign up for our mailing list: **www. truenorthleadership.com**

 For more information about the book and bulk orders, contact *Psyccess Press*, a division of True North Leadership, Inc., at the above address.

PRODUCTS

Bring the Leaders' Playbook *curriculum to your teams!*

LEADERS' PLAYBOOK FIELD GUIDE

This is designed for managers, leaders, and coaches. It is a complete *turn-key curriculum* for a team leader or coach. It includes:

CD AND NOTEBOOK

1. Powerpoint presentations with notes include:
   - EI introduction with political and CEO profiles
   - Mental models and Assumption Ladder presentation
   - Communication Tools: Feedback, delegation and coaching tools
2. PDFs of the key tools and checklists to distribute to your teams
   - EI Star Profile™
   - Derailer Detector™
   - Meeting Menace Checklist™
   - Team meetings
   - Guidelines for running a great meeting
   - How to establish roles within a team meeting
   - The Meeting Checklist™
   - Teamwork Ingredients Survey™
   - 100 Leadership Check-In Questions
   - Hiring Checklist™
   - Motivation Skills Matrix™
   - Feedback Tool™
   - Delegation Tool™

- Coaching for Performance Tool™
- Assumption Ladder™

3. Curriculum agendas for implementing the tools

4. More teambuilding activities – not in the *Playbook*

Site licenses and affiliate programs available.

Go to our website for more information on the products and prices, for free EI tools, and to sign up for our mailing list: **www. truenorthleadership.com**

LEADERSHIP KEYS

These are 11 cue cards of some of the most powerful *Leaders' Playbook* tools and more.

Ideal for your team members to have readily available for immediate use and application. Great for coaches to give to their clients. Affiliate programs available.

Leadership Keys includes:

- A manual for understanding the tools and how to explain them to your team
- Exercises to practice the tools
- Four sets of the Leadership Keys
- CD with 10 tools and audio explanation

TRUE NORTH LEADERSHIP, INC.

Relly Nadler, Psy.D.

1170 Camino Meleno

Santa Barbara, CA 93111

805 683-1066   FAX 805 692-6738

Rnadler@truenorthleadership.com

www.truenorthleadership.com

WWW.TRUENORTHLEADERSHIP.COM